Innovation and Industry Evolution

Innovation and Industry Evolution

David B. Audretsch

The MIT Press
Cambridge, Massachusetts
London, England

This book was set in Palatino by Asco Trade Typesetting Ltd., Hong Kong and was printed and bound in the United States of America.

Library of Congress Cataloging-in-Publication Data

Audretsch, David B.
  Innovation and industry evolution / David B. Audretsch.
      p.   cm.
  Includes bibliographical references and index.
  ISBN 0-262-01146-8 (alk. paper)
  1. New business enterprises. 2. Technological innovations-Economic aspects.
3. Economic development. I. Title.
HD62.5.A93   1995
338'.064—dc20   94-33655
                                                                      CIP

For Alexander

Contents

Tables

Figures

Acknowledgments

I would like to thank a number of people for their support and assistance in writing this book. I am grateful to the Wissenschaftszentrum Berlin für Sozialforschung (WZB), and particularly Professor Dr. Horst Albach for supporting my research project on *Technological Change and Industrial Restructuring*, which has resulted in this book. Not only were substantial financial resources required to purchase a number of different and expensive data bases, but processing the data involved considerable expertise from computer and research assistants. I am especially grateful to Manfred Fleischer, whose staid support and countless efforts over the years have helped me to avoid, or at least minimize, the impediments that typically bog down a large and complicated research project. Special thanks also goes to my secretary, Christiane Loycke de Roux, whose contribution extends far beyond typing the many drafts of this manuscript. Her patience, goodwill, and editorial assistance in undertaking the numerous revisions are greatly appreciated.

F. M. Scherer and three other referees for The MIT Press had numerous insights and invaluable observations on an earlier draft of this manuscript. I also thank my colleagues here in Berlin who provided numerous comments and suggestions on various parts of the manuscript: Professor Dr. Horst Albach, David Soskice, Michael Burda, Joachim Schwalbach, and Jim Jin. In addition, Maryann P. Feldman, Paul Geroski, Steven Klepper, Frank Lichtenberg, José Mata, Manfred Neumann, Harris Schlesinger, Paula Stephan, and Roy Thurik commented on specific chapters. I would also like to thank participants at seminars at Georgia State University, the University of Alabama, Free University of Berlin, Humboldt University, Keio University of Tokyo, the Wissenschaftszentrum Berlin für Sozialforschung, the National Bank of Portugal, as well as the 1991, 1992, and 1993 conferences of the European Association for Research in

Industrial Economics (EARIE) in Italy, Stuttgart, and Tel Aviv, and the tenth annual Corsica summer school on industrial economics in 1992 for their useful comments.

I also would like to thank the *Review of Economics and Statistics* for granting permission to include parts of my articles in chapter 4. Chapter 5 is the result of joint work with Zoltan Acs, parts of chapter 4 are the result of joint research with Talat Mahmood, and chapter 6 is the result of joint work with Hideki Yamawaki.

1   Introduction

When Soviet Premier Nikita Khrushchev banged his shoe on the negotiating table of the United Nations, challenging President John F. Kennedy, "We will bury you," the West was alarmed. At the heart of Khrushchev's challenge was not necessarily a military threat, but rather an economic one. After all, the Soviets had beaten the Americans in the space race with the launching of *Sputnik* just several years earlier; and perhaps even more disconcerting was the growth in Soviet productivity, which appeared to greatly exceed that in the West during the 1950s.[1]

Thus by the 1960s there was little doubt among politicians, intellectuals, and economists about the credibility of the threat from the East. Even as late as 1966, the Joint Economic Committee of the United States Congress warned of a "planned average annual increase in industrial output of 8.0–8.4 percent during 1966–70" in the Soviet Union (Noren, 1966, p. 301). After all, the nations of Eastern Europe, and the Soviet Union in particular, had a "luxury" inherent in their systems of centralized planning—a concentration of economic assets on a scale beyond anything imaginable in the West. For example, before the Berlin Wall fell, the East German economy consisted of 224 firms—*Kombinate*, or combines—of which around 180 were in manufacturing (Audretsch, 1993). There was essentially one firm, and one firm only, for each major manufacturing industry. This degree of concentration and centralization was the rule and not the exception in Eastern Europe.[2] The intellectual antecedents for this giantism undoubtedly lie in Karl Marx's (1912) admiration for the large-scale technologies of the British Industrial Revolution. This attitude was reflected in Marx's forceful articulation of the view that, in the competitive process, the large-scale

---

1. See Moore (1992, p. 72) for a recent documentation of the "view held widely at the time that Soviet central planning produce persistently high growth rates into the foreseeable future."
2. See Acs and Audretsch (1993).

capitalist always beats out his smaller counterpart. Marx, in fact, had written, "The battle of competition is fought by the cheapening of commodities. The cheapness of commodities depends, *ceteris paribus*, on the productiveness of labour, and this again on the scale of production. Therefore, the large capitals beat the smaller."[3]

The fear in the West was not only that the accumulation of economic assets would lead to unprecedented productivity growth in the Soviet Union and Eastern Europe; of even greater concern was the assumed leaps and bounds in technological progress that would emerge from the huge and concentrated research and development (R & D) programs being assembled. From the vantage point of the late 1950s and early 1960s, the West seemed not only on the verge of losing the space race, but perhaps even more important, the economic growth race.

Although there may have been considerable debate about what to do about the perceived Soviet threat some three decades ago, there was little doubt at that time that the manner in which enterprises and entire industries were organized mattered. And even more striking, when one reviews the literature of the day, there seemed to be near unanimity about the way in which industrial organization mattered. It is no doubt an irony of history that a remarkably similar version of the giantism embedded in Soviet doctrine, fueled by the writings of Marx and ultimately implemented by the iron fist of Stalin, was also prevalent throughout the West. It must not be forgotten that the 1950s and 1960s represented the pinnacle of what Michael Piore and Charles Sabel (1984) have termed the era of mass production. During this era, economies of scale seemed to be the decisive factor in dictating efficiency. Why did the United States dominate world trade in industries such as automobiles and steel? Presumably because the greatest endowment of physical capital was found in the United States, enabling its firms and industries to most fully exploit scale economies and enjoy the highest levels of productivity growth. This was the world so colorfully described by John Kenneth Galbraith (1956) in his theory of countervailing power, in which the power of big business was held in check by big labor—that is, unions—and by big government. This was the era of the "man in the gray flannel suit" and the "organization man,"[4] when virtually every major social and economic institution acted to reinforce the stability and predictability needed for mass production (Piore and Sabel, 1984; and Chandler, 1977).

---

3. Quoted from Rosenberg (1992, p. 197).
4. For a description of these, see Whyte (1960) and Riesman (1950).

Not only was the large corporation thought to have superior productive efficiency, but it was also believed to be the engine of technological change and innovative activity. After all, Schumpeter wrote in 1942 (p. 106), "What we have got to accept is that (the large-scale establishment or unit of control) has come to be the most powerful engine of ... progress and in particular of the long-run expansion of output not only in spite of, but to a considerable extent through, this strategy which looks so restrictive ... In this respect, perfect competition is not only impossible but inferior, and has no title to being set up as a model of ideal efficiency." A few years later Galbraith (1956, p. 86) echoed Schumpeter's sentiment when he lamented, "There is no more pleasant fiction than that technological change is the product of the matchless ingenuity of the small man forced by competition to employ his wits to better his neighbor. Unhappily, it is a fiction."

Thus, regarding East-West relations, optimists such as Galbraith spoke of a convergence between the communist systems of Eastern Europe and the Western style of "managed" capitalism. It seemed that both the East and the West were converging toward economies dominated by a handful of powerful enterprises, constrained only by the countervailing powers of the state and workers.[5] The only "trivial" difference would be the ownership. The pessimists, on the other hand, became alarmed that perhaps the West would, after all, be buried by the East—productivity gains and a surge of economic growth emanating from the overpowering Soviet combines would simply overwhelm the outdated and outscaled firms in the West, burdened with antiquated constraints such as antitrust laws.[6]

In fact, as has been made all too clear by the events throughout the Soviet Union and Eastern Europe in the last five years, neither the pessimists nor the optimists in the West were correct. That is, neither did the two economic systems converge in the manner that economists like Galbraith had predicted, nor was the West buried by an avalanche of

---

5. This view is certainly represented in the influential book written by Jean-Jacques Servan-Schreiber in 1968, *The American Challenge*.

6. Perhaps the ascendency of industrial organization as a field in economics during the 1950s and 1960s came from the recognition not only by scholars but also by policymakers and even the public that industrial organization matters. And it became the task of the industrial organization scholars to sort out the issues involving this perceived trade-off between economic efficiency on the one hand and political and economic decentralization on the other. Oliver Williamson's classic 1968 article, "Economies as an Antitrust Defense: The Welfare Tradeoffs," became something of a final statement demonstrating this seemingly inevitable trade-off between the gains in productive efficiency that could be obtained through increased concentration and gains in terms of competition that could be achieved through decentralizing policies, such as antitrust. But it did not seem possible to have both, certainly not in Oliver Williamson's completely static model.

productivity growth and a wave of innovative activity from the East. What happened? What went wrong? A paradox seems to be that the industrial organization of Eastern Europe, which was structured around the principle of giantism and which placed such a high premium on economic growth, resulted in exactly the opposite—stagnation, in terms of both production and technological change.

Marx had warned that because "One capitalist kills many," ultimately, "Capitalism bears the seeds of its own self-destruction".[7] And Schumpeter (1942, p. 134) gloomily concluded that, "Since capitalist enterprise, by its very achievements, tends to automatize progress, we conclude that it tends to make itself superfluous—to break to pieces under the pressure of its own success. The perfectly bureaucratic giant industrial unit not only ousts the small- or medium-sized firm and 'expropriates' its owners, but in the end it also ousts the entrepreneur and expropriates the bourgeoisie as a class which in the process stands to lose not only its income but also, what is infinitely more important, its function." In fact, in what must be one of the greater ironies of history, the mature capitalist countries of the West have been going through not a process of concentration and centralization during these past two decades as Marx and Schumpeter,[8] in his later years, had predicted, but rather a process of deconcentration and decentralization. Consider the example of the United States. Between 1958 and 1979 the share of sales in the United States accounted for by small firms (with fewer than 500 employees) fell from 52 percent to just 29 percent.[9] Similarly, between 1947 and 1980, real gross national product (GNP) per firm rose by nearly two-thirds, from $150,000 to $250,000 (Brock and Evans, 1989). Curiously, however, within the following six years it dropped sharply by 14 percent, to $210,000.[10] And the amount of employment accounted for by the Fortune 500 rose from 8 million, or 34 percent of total employment in 1954, to 16 million, or 58 percent of total employment by 1979. How-

---

7. Interpreting Marx, Alfred Marshall (1923, pp. 176–177) was moved to write that, "Marx and his followers resolved to be practical, and argued that history showed a steadily hastening growth of large business and of mechanical administration by vast joint-stock companies, and they deduced the fatalistic conclusion that this tendency is irresistible; and must fulfill its destiny by making the whole state into one large joint-stock company in which everyone would be a shareholder."

8. For a careful analysis of Schumpeter's prediction that capitalism could not survive, see Scherer (1992).

9. Quoted from *Business Week*, Bonus Issue, 1993, p. 14.

10. For a careful documentation of how economic activity has shifted away from large firms and toward smaller enterprises in the developed industrial nations, see Acs and Audretsch (1993) and Loveman and Sengenberger (1991).

ever, employment accounted for by the Fortune 500 proceeded to fall to 11.9 million, or 40 percent of total employment by 1991 (Case, 1992).

Such a drop in the average firm size is consistent with the startling findings by David Birch (1981) in his long-term study of U.S. job generation. Despite the prevailing conventional wisdom at that time, Birch (1981, p. 8) reported that, "... whatever else they are doing, large firms are no longer the major providers of jobs for Americans." Rather, Birch claimed to have discovered that most new jobs emanated from small firms.[11] The recent shift in economic activity toward small-scale firms has not escaped the attention of the popular press. For example, *The Economist* reports: "Despite ever-larger and noisier mergers, the biggest change coming over the world of business is that firms are getting smaller. The trend of a century is being reversed. Until the mid-1970s, the size of firms everywhere grew; the numbers of self-employed fell. Ford and General Motors replaced the carriage-maker's atelier; McDonald's, Safeway and W. H. Smith supplanted the corner shop. No longer. Now it is the big firms that are shrinking and small ones that are on the rise. The trend is unmistakable —and businessmen and policy-makers will ignore it at their peril."[12]

The economic failure of the Soviet Union and its Eastern European satellites was to a great extent a failure to participate in the microelectronic revolution, which served as a decentralizing catalyst throughout the West. While the computer and microelectronics brought about the demise of the mass-production paradigm in the West, Eastern Europe simply missed the boat.[13] Of course, computerized technology implied a shift away from a

---

11. The exact methodology, application, and interpretation of the underlying data used to make inferences in the job-creation studies have been called into question (Davis, Haltiwanger, and Schuh, 1993; Armington and Odle, 1982; Storey and Johnson, 1987; FitzRoy, 1989; and Brown, Hamilton, and Medoff, 1990). As Brown, Hamilton, and Medoff (1990) point out, job generation may be a deceptive measure because many of the newly generated jobs subsequently disappear. That is, without consideration of the number of job disappearances, focusing solely on the amount of job generation emanating from small firms is misleading and results in an overstatement of the amount of economic activity actually stemming from small firms.
12. "The Rise and Rise of America's Small Firms," *The Economist*, 21 January 1989, pp. 173–174.
13. Sylos-Labini (1992, p. 63) observed that, "In the last two or three decades, after a number of attempts that failed at decentralizing many activities and of giving more discretionary power to managers, the difficulties rose very rapidly and the Soviet economy entered a period of general crisis. (Concentrating economic, organizational, and scientific efforts on military production, the Soviet Union has succeeded, at least for a period, in not losing ground in this sector with respect to the United States and other Western countries. But even this sector—after the latest developments in electronics, which, especially in the United States, owe much to the contribution of small firms—has shown increasing signs of weakness.)" See also Richard R. Nelson (1992).

concentrated and rigid industrial structure and toward a fluid, decentralized system as the most efficient means of production, which constituted a direct threat to the political principle of centralizing all information and decisionmaking under communism. Perhaps in the end the communist economies could have competed, or as some critics feared, even beaten out the West, as long as the predominant technological paradigm was centralizing in nature. However, the advent of microcomputers and the subsequent revolution that decentralized decisionmaking and production in the West proved simply to be incompatible with the entire communist system.

The Soviet Union and Eastern Europe were not the only victims of the shift away from the mass-production paradigm and to a more fluid and turbulent industrial structure. According to *Business Week*,

In recent years, the giants of industry have suffered a great comeuppance—as much from the little guys as from fierce global competition. IBM continues to reel from the assaults of erstwhile upstarts such as Microsoft, Dell Computer, and Compaq Computer. Big Steel was devastated by such minimills as Nucor, Chaparral Steel, and Worthington Industries. One-time mavericks Wal-Mart Stores and The Limited taught Sears, Roebuck a big lesson. Southwest Airlines has profitably flown through turbulence that has caused the big airlines to rack up $10 billion in losses over the past three years. And a brash pack of startups with such names as Amgen Inc. and Centocor Inc. has put the U.S. ahead in biotechnology—not Bristol-Myers, Squibb, Merck, or Johnson & Johnson.[14]

Continuing a trend that has surpassed at least two presidencies, 120,000 jobs were eliminated in "corporate downsizing" in January 1994.[15] Particularly striking is that in the last quarter of 1993, the gross domestic product grew at a stunning rate of 5.9 percent; and at the same time unemployment in the United States was falling. How can these seemingly incompatible phenomena be reconciled? "Between 1987 and 1992, small companies (with fewer than 500 employees) created the bulk of the 5.8 million new jobs in the United States. Over that same period, large companies (with at least 500 employees) recorded a net loss of 2.3 million jobs."[16] This is consistent with the observation by *Newsweek* that,

---

14. *Business Week*, Bonus Issue, 1993, p. 12.
15. *Business Week* (31 January 1994, pp. 30–31) identified corporate downsizings of 1,300 employees by Arco, 2,000 employees by Gillette, 17,000 employees by GTE, and 10,000 employees by Pacific Telesis alone. As *Business Week* notes, "Funny thing. U.S. economic growth is expanding at a considerable clip. Yet some of the best and brightest among America's big corporations are continuing to restructure ... For the American worker, the thought that even the healthiest of companies are shedding pounds is not a pleasant one. The bad news is that such corporate dieting isn't going to stop anytime soon. But this comes as the U.S. economy is generating substantial new jobs, many of them at leaner, nimbler, smaller companies that have not yet developed a midriff bulge."
16. Ibid., p. 12.

In a surging U.S. economy, while America is adding jobs at the stunning rate of 3 million a year, giant companies are still shedding workers by the tens of thousands. Old-line manufacturers such as Scott Paper, former high fliers like Digital Equipment, stodgy electric companies like General Public Utilities—no one seems immune … The story is similar all across American big business. Quaker Oats, the Chicago-based cereals company has announced a re-engineering program that will eliminate an unspecified number of jobs. Ciba-Geigy wants to reduce its U.S. work force of 4,600 by one tenth. Aetna, one of the largest U.S. insurance groups, is in the midst of cutting 4,000 of its 42,000 jobs after eliminating a similar number over the past two years. That's only a foretaste of huge reductions to come in insurance, where 2.1 Americans earn their livings.[17]

A modern-day Rip Van Winkle would be astonished by the degree to which the industrial landscape has been transformed in a relatively short period of time. A number of corporate giants such as IBM, U.S. Steel, RCA, and Wang have lost their aura of invincibility. Only slightly more than a decade ago Peters and Waterman (1982), in their influential best-selling management book, *In Search of Excellence: Lessons from America's Best Run Companies*, identified IBM as the best-run corporation in America, and presumably in the entire world. IBM was viewed as a model corporation, the best of the best, serving as a beacon for all others. At the same time has come the breathtaking emergence of new firms that hardly existed when Ronald Reagan was first elected president, such as Microsoft, Apple Computer, Intel, Gateway, Dell, and Compaq Computer. In the 1980s it took just five years for one-third of the Fortune 500 to be replaced. And in the 1970s it took the entire decade to replace the Fortune 500. By contrast, in the 1950s and 1960s it took two decades.

Perhaps even more impressive than the handful of new enterprises that grew to penetrate the Fortune 500 are the armies of startups that come into existence each year—and typically disappear into oblivion within a few years. In the 1990s there are around 1.3 million new companies started each year (Audretsch, 1994). That is, the U.S. economy is characterized by a tremendous degree of turbulence. It is an economy in motion, with a massive number of new firms entering each year, but only a subset surviving for any length of time, and an even smaller subset that can ultimately challenge and displace the incumbent large enterprises.

Despite the high degree of fluidity and turbulence in the American economy, very little is actually known about the dynamic process through which industries and firms evolve over time. Perhaps this virtual void of knowledge motivated Edwin Mansfield (1962, p. 1023) some thirty years

---

17. "Famine Amid Plenty: Jobs—Profits Are Back at Big American Firms, But Not Employment," *Newsweek*, 23 May 1994, pp. 40–41.

ago to make a plea for a greater emphasis on the dynamic processes by which markets change over time: "Because there have been so few econometric studies of the birth, growth, and death of firms, we lack even crude answers to the following basic questions regarding the dynamic processes governing an industry's structure. What are the quantitative effects of various factors on the rates of entry and exit? What have been the effects of successful innovations on a firm's growth rate? What determines the amount of mobility within an industry's size structure?"

The purpose of this book is to shed some light on industrial markets in motion. In particular, the process by which new firms enter into industrial markets, either grow and survive or exit from the industry, and possibly displace incumbent corporations is examined. At the center of this evolutionary process is innovation, because the potential for innovative activity serves as the driving force behind much of the evolution of industries. And it is innovative activity that explains why the patterns of industry evolution vary from industry to industry, depending on the underlying knowledge conditions, or what Nelson and Winter (1982) call "technological regimes."

Schumpeter (1942, p. 132) concluded that, due to scale economies in the production of new economic knowledge, large corporations would not only have the innovative advantage over small and new enterprises, but that ultimately the economic landscape would consist only of giant corporations: "Innovation itself is being reduced to routine. Technological progress is increasingly becoming the business of teams of trained specialists who turn out what is required and made it work in predictable ways." Perhaps technological change would become a routinized procedure subject to scale economies in large corporations—if the underlying knowledge were predictable and not shrouded in uncertainty. But there is a long tradition in economics, dating back at least to Frank Knight (1921), and more recently to Kenneth Arrow (1962), that, at least in some instances, the production and identification of new economic knowledge is anything but routinized. A recent series of studies[18] found that although large corporations have the innovative advantage in certain industries, in other markets small firms are more innovative. These results not only contradict Schumpeter's rather gloomy prediction that innovative activity has become routinized and thus exclusively subject to scale economies, but support Winter's (1984) notion of the existence of distinct technological regimes:

---

18. See Acs and Audretsch, 1987; 1988; and 1990 for the United States and Pavitt, Robson, and Townsend, 1987 for Great Britain.

the routinized technological regime and the entrepreneurial technological regime.

The link between innovation and industry evolution could be analyzed from a number of different perspectives and even scholarly disciplines. In this book the link between innovation and industry evolution is analyzed through the lens of industrial organization. There is a long-standing tradition in the field of industrial organization that, just as market structure and firm size are considered to influence innovative activity, technological change is viewed as having, at least in certain instances, an impact on the structure of industries.[19] In 1948, John Blair (p. 121) observed that, "The whole subject of the comparative efficiency of different sizes of business has long raised one of the most perplexing dilemmas in the entire body of economic theory ... But a beginning must be made sometime in tackling this whole size-efficiency problem on an empirical basis. The first step in any such undertaking would logically be that of studying the underlying technological forces of the economy, since it is the technology which largely determines the relationship between the size of plant and efficiency."

Studies in industrial organization typically rely on some measure of the technological opportunity class to distinguish between industries where innovative activity plays a more important role from those where it is less important. Although this distinction is certainly crucial, another dimension becomes at least as important—the quality or nature of that innovative activity. Because, as suggested by one of the most prevalent theories of technological change in economics, the knowledge production function (Griliches, 1979), knowledge-generating inputs are needed to produce innovative output. And as Nelson and Winter (1982) emphasized, the nature of those knowledge-generating inputs is determined by the underlying technological regime or information conditions, and differs from industry to industry. What will be emphasized is the manner in which the underlying knowledge conditions, or the technological regime, shapes the observed evolution of industries. In those industries where potentially new economic knowledge is relatively diffuse and asymmetric, there tends to be a high number of diverse experiments—in the form of new and young enterprises—which essentially represent a wide diversity in beliefs about what should be produced and how it should be produced. Of course, not all of those experiments, or beliefs, will prove successful. The selection mechanism in the market serves to eliminate those experiments that are not

---

19. See most recently Phillips (1994).

viable—that is, to essentially separate the wheat from the chaff. Thus the extent to which new firms are entering markets, subsequently growing and possibly even displacing incumbent corporations, or exiting will tend to be shaped by the underlying knowledge conditions generating innovative activity along with the selection mechanism in the market.[20]

To examine industries in motion, or the manner in which individual firms evolve in industries over time, a data base is required that enables the systematic identification of the startup of new firms and then their subsequent performance over time—that is, a longitudinal data base consisting of a panel of firms. In chapter 2 the data base used to identify the startup of new manufacturing firms and track their subsequent performance over time, the United States Small Business Data Base, is introduced. This data base consists of more than 20 million records between 1976 and 1986 and can only be applied and interpreted with a number of important considerations in mind.

The five chapters that follow provide snapshots of the process of industries in motion from various angles. Chapter 3 examines why new-firm startup activity varies so greatly across industries. There is a now blossoming tradition of examining entry behavior in industrial economics, but what distinguishes this chapter is the focus on the underlying technological regimes in shaping variations in the role of startup activity. Rather than asking the question, "Why do firms enter an industry?", the relevant question in chapter 3 is, "Why do economic agents start new firms?" And the answer given is, "To best appropriate the expected value of new economic knowledge." Asymmetries in new economic knowledge combined with high costs of transacting that knowledge lead to divergences in beliefs about potential innovations (or even more plainly, how best to run a firm). If the expected value of new economic knowledge diverges greatly enough across economic agents, and in particular between the decision-making hierarchies of incumbent organizations, agents will have a greater incentive to start new firms. Because these knowledge conditions—that is, the degree to which asymmetries and high transactions costs exists—vary from industry to industry, the propensity for people to start firms should correspondingly also vary across industries.

Although a huge number of studies have focused on the entry behavior of firms, a virtual void of knowledge exists about what happens to firms after they enter. The purpose of chapter 4 is to fill this void by examining the post-entry performance of new firms. In particular, new firms are

20. See Klein (1977).

tracked for a decade subsequent to entering to identify what shapes the likelihood of survival and growth. Just as the underlying technological regime is found to influence the propensity for people to start new firms in an industry, it is also found to affect the post-entry performance. That is, a greater dispersion of beliefs about what should be done in an industry apparently is associated with more startup activity. But at the same time, the likelihood that any one particular new enterprise will prove to be viable is lower. Thus the greater degree of diversity in beliefs leads to a greater number of experiments, but a lower percentage of them will ultimately succeed.

The extent to which entrepreneurial firms, or new firms, account for an industry's economic activity, and why that varies across industries, is examined in chapter 5. In some sense, the presence of entrepreneurial firms is shaped by the subjects of the preceding two chapters—the degree to which new firms are started combined with their propensity to survive over time. Not only is it found that the role of such entrepreneurial firms varies considerably from industry to industry, but that it is influenced by the underlying technological regimes. The majority of new firms are not only very small, but they are so small as surely to be suboptimal, at least in many, if not most industries. How are they able to survive? One answer, found in chapter 3, is by growing. A somewhat different although complementary answer is suggested in chapter 6. New firms are able, at least to some extent, to offset their size-inherent cost disadvantages by pursuing a strategy of compensating factor differentials, whereby they both deploy and compensate input factors differently than do their larger and more established counterparts. For example, by pushing down the remuneration of labor and deploying it more intensively, new and small firms are able to lower the costs of production from what they would otherwise be. Apparently the greater the extent to which a firm suffers from size-related disadvantages, the greater the reliance tends to be on a strategy of compensating factor differentials.

In chapter 7 the question is posed, "Who Exits and Why?" The answer to this question, that is, to what degree do the exiting firms tend to be comprised of new entrants and to what extent by larger incumbents, helps to shed considerable light on the process of industry evolution. Two different models of industry evolution emerge. The first is aptly described by the metaphor of the revolving door, where the bulk of the exiting firms tend to be accounted for by new entrants. The second type is where incumbent enterprises tend to be displaced by newer firms.

Finally, in the last chapter, a summary and conclusions are presented. Although a major conclusion of this book is that the structure of industries is perhaps better characterized by a high degree of fluidity and turbulence, the patterns of industry evolution vary considerably from industry to industry. And what apparently shapes the evolution of firms particular to a specific industry is, as much as anything else, the knowledge conditions influencing innovative activity underlying that industry. Just as economists might be well advised to focus on change as the rule and not the exception, public policymakers should perhaps shift their perspective from a static to dynamic view of firms and industries.

2   Measurement: The Longitudinal Data Base

2.1   Introduction

Perhaps the greatest impediment to analyzing firm and industry evolution over time has been the lack of comprehensive and systematic longitudinal data bases (Kuznets, 1962). Industry evolution can be most effectively analyzed by linking the performance of firms and establishments over time, identifying when a firm is started, and then tracking its subsequent performance. But such data bases have been rare, other than on a small and restricted scale, and typically for only a handful of firms. So rare that, as is described in the second section of this chapter, in 1976 and again in 1980 the U.S. Congress mandated the establishment of just such a longitudinal data base, which would facilitate the analysis of dynamic aspects of businesses. In fact, it was the response of the newly established Office of Advocacy of the United States Small Business Administration that created the longitudinal data base that is used throughout this book—the Small Business Administration Data Base (SBDB). A particular attraction of this data base, besides its comprehensiveness and reliability, is that it links the performance of virtually every manufacturing business over time between 1976 and 1986.

Of course, the construction and maintenance of such a longitudinal data base is a painstaking and imperfect undertaking. Therefore, particular attention must be devoted not only to how the data base is constructed and organized, but also to systematic and random weaknesses inherent in the data base that introduce measurement error. Thus in the following section of this chapter the longitudinal data base is introduced and described. In the third section, the major inherent measurement flaws are documented, along with the procedures used to edit the raw data files to correct, at least to some extent, for these errors. A comparison with several other major data bases is made in the fourth section to check for reliability. And in the fifth section a brief note is presented on the other major data base used in this book to measure innovative activity.

2.2 The Longitudinal Data Base

With the enactment of Public Law 94-305 on June 4, 1976, or what is called *The Small Business Act*, the U.S. Congress mandated the creation of an Office of Advocacy within the Small Business Administration which, under Title II of the act, was charged with the "Study of Small Business."[1] In particular, paragraph one of Section 202 dictated that the first of ten "primary functions" shall be to: "Examine the role of small business in the American economy and the contribution which small business can make in improving competition, encouraging economic and social mobility for all citizens, restraining inflation, spurring production, expanding employment opportunities, increasing productivity, promoting exports, stimulating innovation and entrepreneurship, and providing an avenue through which new and untested products and services can be brought to the marketplace."[2]

Following the establishment of the Office of Advocacy in the Small Business Administration, it became obvious that the implementation of *The Small Business Act* and, in particular, Section 202 (mandating a comprehensive and systematic examination of the population of American businesses) was not only ambitious but greatly exceeded the resources normally associated with the creation of a new office. At the heart of the problem was a deficiency of data, especially a comprehensive and systematic longitudinal data base tracking, in principle, the population of U.S. businesses over time. At that time, only the Census of Manufactures provided such a data base; however, it was only implemented twice a decade and the longitudinal aspects were weak, meaning it was not always possible to link businesses between census years.

To reinforce its commitment to establishing a comprehensive and systematic examination of U.S. businesses within a dynamic context, the U.S. Congress enacted Public Law 96-302 in 1980, amending the *Small Business Act*. In addition to passage of the *Small Business Economic Policy Act* of 1980 (Title III, Section 301),[3] the Congress also amended the *Small Business Act* in Title IV, requiring "Small Business Economic Research and Analysis," under which Section 401 mandates that the agency shall be responsible for

---

1. Public Law 94-305, *90 Stat. 668*, 4 1976 June.
2. For a similar concept in the United Kingdom, see the Bolton Report (1971).
3. Public Law 96-302, *94 Stat. 849*, 2 July 1980.

"establishing and maintaining an external small business economic data base for the purpose of providing the Congress and the Administration information on the economic condition and the expansion or contraction of the small business sector."[4]

Confronted with such a strong congressional mandate, the Office of Advocacy of the Small Business Administration determined that the only way to fulfill its mission was to create a new comprehensive and systematic longitudinal data base. Thus, under the auspices of the SBA, the Small Business Data Base (SBDB), built around the United States Establishment and Enterprise (USEEM) file, was created. The USEEM file was constructed from business data acquired from Dun & Bradstreet (D & B). Thus, to understand the SBDB, it is imperative to understand the USEEM file and the underlying D & B data on which it is constructed.

D & B does not collect and organize data with scholarly research as a goal. Rather, in reporting the credit activities of businesses, D & B acquires information about the location, ownership, types of products, and size of almost all businesses in the United States. Coverage is particularly high in the manufacturing sector. Any business that either purchases or sells on credit is included in the D & B data. After acquiring the raw data records from D & B, the SBA contracted with the Brookings Institution to process the data, and in particular to match branch and subsidiary businesses to parent companies. Additionally, Brookings was given the task of organizing the enormous files, so that both summary data and well-defined subsets could be generated.[5]

The essential unit of observation in the SBDB is the establishment, defined as an economic entity operating at a specific and single location. An establishment in the manufacturing sector is commonly referred to as a plant. An establishment can either be an independently owned legal entity, in which case it is also an enterprise, or it can belong to a separate legal entity, in which case the establishment is a branch or subsidiary of some enterprise. In what can become confusing jargon, an enterprise is what is commonly referred to as a firm. An establishment may or may not also be an enterprise, depending upon its ownership status. This distinction is crucial to observe, because both establishments and enterprises are ana-lyzed in this book. And this distinction is particularly pronounced in the

---

4. *94 Stat. 849.*
5. For a more detailed description and documentation of the SBDB and the underlying USEEM and USELM files, as well as the raw D & B data records, see Boden and Phillips (1985), Brown and Phillips (1989), Harris (1983), Armington and Odle (1982 and 1983), Jacobson (1985), MacDonald (1985), U.S. Small Business Administration (1986 and 1987), and Armington, Harris, and Odle (1984).

manufacturing sector, which is our focus. In any case, the USEEM files of the SBDB link the ownership of each establishment to its parent entity.

The USEEM files of the SBDB provide biennial observations on about 4.5 million U.S. business establishments over the period 1976 to 1986. This covers a changing business population of more than 20 million establishments. Each record includes the establishment location in terms of state and county, employment, the primary and secondary four-digit standard industrial classification (SIC) industry, the starting year of the business, sales (in some cases only), organizational status and legal connection to other establishments, and the employment of the entire firm, if the establishment belongs to a multi-establishment enterprise.

2.3   File Editing

Storey and Johnson (1987) argue that because the underlying D & B data have been assembled by a commercial organization whose principal purpose is to provide credit rating information, the reliability of the data is probably enhanced. They point out that the data are not based on confidentiality but rather on publicly available information (for a fee). In addition, D & B has a commercial incentive to provide data that are both current and accurate. Similarly, the reporting establishments themselves have an incentive to provide accurate information to a credit rating company.

Nonetheless, careful analysis has identified a number of systematic weaknesses in the raw records provided by D & B (Armington and Odle, 1982 and 1983; Jacobson, 1985; MacDonald, 1985; McCauley, 1981; and Harris, 1983). Probably the most significant weakness in the raw D & B data records is missing branch records in some cases and missing enterprise headquarters in others. That is, the sum of employment in all enterprises (firms) does not equal the sum of employment in all establishments. This problem arises because a number of branch and subsidiary establishments are reported as being owned by an enterprise that was never recorded by D & B. Similarly, a number of enterprises report owning branch or subsidiary establishments that were never recorded in the D & B files. This discrepancy presumably arises because the D & B files are compiled on the basis of credit rating, so that branches and subsidiaries of multi-establishment firms do not always require credit independently from the parent firm.

In one of the first applications of the D & B data, Birch (1981) attempted to correct for missing headquarters (enterprises) by recalculating the total enterprise employment from the aggregation of the employment recorded in each affiliated establishment. The problem with his correction procedure is that it implicitly assumed that there were no missing branch and subsidiary establishments. By contrast, Armington and Odle (1982) implicitly assumed that there were no missing enterprise headquarters and recalculated the employment level of each affiliated establishment from the reported enterprise employment level. The result of these dichotomous attempts to reconcile the discrepancy between the aggregation of establishment data and enterprise data was that Birch tended to understate the extent of employment multi-establishment firms, and Armington and Odle tended to overstate it.

A second problem with the D & B raw data is uneven coverage across sectors; in particular, there is a systematic underrepresentation in industries in which establishments have a lower propensity to apply for credit (MacDonald, 1985). When coverage of the D & B records was compared to that of the *Census Bureau's County Business Patterns*, the U.S. Small Business Administration (1986) concluded that coverage is incomplete principally in certain sectors of retail trade and services. Industry sectors that are typically underrepresented by D & B include agriculture, department stores, eating and drinking establishments, credit agencies, insurance agencies, and medical, legal, educational, and social services.[6]

A third problem involves the updating of records in the data base. Some records are based on information that has not been updated. This bias is particularly pronounced in newer and smaller establishments. For example, Jacobson (1985) found that in several cases firms and establishments were not included in the data base until several years after they had been established. This leads to a slight understatement of the number of new business units, particularly in expanding industries, such as certain types of services, and in new industries, such as microcomputers and software-related industries.

To correct for at least some of these deficiencies in the raw D & B data records, the Brookings Institution in conjunction with the Small Business Administration and the National Science Foundation restructured, edited, and supplemented the original data files with data from other sources as well as with adjustment procedures. Specifically, a "family tree" was constructed for each enterprise, identifying each branch and subsidiary. These family trees were then used to reconcile the organizational status

---

6. In fact, most of these sectors actually list as many employees as does the *County Business Patterns* but fewer establishments. To some extent this is attributable to the inclusion by the County Business Patterns since 1983 of all establishments which closed during each year, most of which had no employees in the fourth quarter of the year.

and employment figures between member establishments of multi-estab-lishment enterprises. The employment figures for the entire enterprise are compared to those reported by the individual establishments. Any discrep-ancy arising between the employment reported for the entire firm and the aggregation of all the individual establishments is then corrected either by increasing the total amount of employment attributed to the entire enter-prise to be consistent with that reported by the individual establishment, or else by imputing proxy branch establishments to represent affiliates implied by the employment reported by the enterprise (U.S. Small Business Administration, 1986; Brown and Phillips, 1989).

Using the SBDB, table 2.1 shows the size distribution of firms and establishments, measured by employment, for 1986. Each number indicates the percentage of the total sector employment included in the respective firm- and establishment-size class. For example, according to the SBDB, in the entire economy 5.39 percent of all employment is accounted for by firms with fewer than five employees. Similarly, 6.46 percent of employ-ment occurred in establishments with fewer than five employees.

There are four important observations to make from table 2.1. First, the employment shares of the smaller firm-size classes generally exceed those of the corresponding establishment-size classes. This is because employ-ment in those establishments that are branches or subsidiaries of a multi-establishment enterprise is classified according to the entire employment of the enterprise for the firm-size distribution but not for the establishment-size distribution. However, for the larger firm- and establishment-size classes, the employment shares of the firms tend to exceed those of the establishments. This is because these firm-size classes include the employ-ment of many smaller establishments.

Second, the employment shares in certain sectors, such as wholesale trade and construction, tend to be relatively similar between the firm and establishment measures. In other sectors, such as manufacturing and trans-portation, this differential is much greater, which indicates a greater pres-ence of multi-establishment enterprises.

Third, table 2.1 shows that the 1986 share of employment accounted for by firms with fewer than 500 employees—one of the standard benchmarks used to measure small firms—was 49.76 percent. Similarly, the employ-ment share of firms with fewer than 100 employees, which is the standard alternative measure, was 35.07 percent. In manufacturing, 35.34 percent of employment was in firms with fewer than 500 employees, and 20.55 per-cent was in firms with fewer than 100 employees.

Finally, there clearly exists considerable variation in the role that small firms play across the various sectors of the economy. For example, in construction, over 85 percent of employment is accounted for by small firms. By contrast, in transportation, only about one-third of the workers are employed in small firms.

2.4   Reliability Comparisons

It should be emphasized that the SBDB data have been adjusted by the U.S. Small Business Administration in conjunction with the Brookings Institution and the National Science Foundation in order to edit the raw data in the original D & B files. To provide at least some comparison regarding the consistency of the SBDB with two of the major data bases, the Bureau of Labor Statistics (BLS)[7] and Bureau of the Census' *County Business Patterns*,[8] table 2.2 compares employment according to primary business sectors in 1980 and 1986. Certain sectors, such as services, finance, retail and wholesale trade, and manufacturing provide fairly consistent employment levels for 1980 and 1986. Considerably less consistency exists in the employment patterns reported in these three data sources in the agriculture and mining sectors. However, the manufacturing sector, the focus of this book, shows a marked similarity in employment trends across the three data bases.

Table 2.3 provides a dynamic comparison between the SBDB and BLS data bases, particularly establishment employment growth rates between 1976 and 1978. The two data sources identify considerable consistency in the overall growth rate for the entire economy. Further, employment

---

7. Data based on establishment records are compiled each month from mail questionnaires —form BLS 790, the report on Employment, Payroll, and Hours—by the Bureau of Labor Statistics, in cooperation with state agencies. Along with data collected from a separate household survey, the 790 data are published monthly in the Bureau of Labor Statistics' *Employment and Earnings.* Unemployment Insurance data on wages and employment are collected at the state level from all establishments (or, more precisely, "reporting units") participating in state unemployment insurance programs. These data are, in turn, amassed into a national data base by the Bureau of Labor Statistics.

8. *County Business Patterns* is a cross-sectional, establishment-based data base on employment and payroll, encompassing all establishments with employees covered by the Federal Insurance Contributions Act (FICA). The data in *County Business Patterns* are assembled and published annually by the Bureau of the Census. The *County Business Patterns* data are also based on IRS Form 941, the Employer's Quarterly Tax Return, and, for larger firms, the annual Company Organization Survey. The data from Form 941 provide information on the geographic location, employment, and payroll of virtually all establishments that are not exempt from Social Security regulations. For multi-establishment firms of over 250 employees, the Company Organization Survey shows the industry, county, and employment for each establishment.

Table 2.1
The size distribution of employment (%) for U.S. firms and establishments, 1986

	Number of employees											
	1–4	5–9	10–19	20–49	50–99	<100	100–499	<500	500–999	1,000–4,999	5,000–9,999	10,000 and over
All industries												
Firms	5.39	6.23	6.68	9.60	7.17	35.05	14.69	49.76	5.25	12.32	5.65	27.10
Establishments	6.46	7.72	10.69	16.98	12.41	54.27	23.22	77.49	7.12	11.22	2.43	1.74
Agriculture												
Firms	16.69	16.18	12.21	13.19	7.48	65.74	13.27	79.01	3.79	6.63	0.94	9.63
Establishments	18.10	16.97	13.21	19.75	10.08	78.10	14.21	93.32	3.55	3.58	0.56	0.00
Mining												
Firms	3.72	4.28	5.60	7.78	5.39	26.76	10.56	37.33	4.32	10.17	9.04	39.15
Establishments	5.13	5.80	9.03	16.75	11.77	48.48	23.94	72.42	8.35	17.14	2.09	0.00
Construction												
Firms	14.89	13.09	13.95	17.71	10.58	70.23	15.23	85.46	3.17	5.08	1.57	4.71
Establishments	15.57	13.69	15.03	23.78	13.07	81.29	14.16	95.45	1.86	1.90	0.80	0.00
Manufacturing												
Firms	1.30	2.40	3.59	6.95	6.31	20.55	14.78	35.34	5.63	13.48	5.78	39.78
Establishments	1.64	2.93	4.63	10.35	11.46	31.00	32.02	63.02	11.55	16.92	4.57	3.94
Transportation												
Firms	2.41	3.61	4.72	7.22	5.17	23.12	10.43	33.44	3.81	11.60	6.28	44.76
Establishments	3.39	5.18	8.47	15.95	12.60	45.59	26.58	72.17	8.00	13.84	2.85	3.13
Wholesale trade												
Firms	8.04	11.70	12.40	15.23	9.16	56.52	13.93	70.46	3.46	7.59	2.96	15.54
Establishments	10.56	15.67	20.62	21.36	10.79	79.00	14.44	93.44	2.92	2.29	0.64	0.71
Retail trade												
Firms	8.32	9.83	9.01	12.49	8.28	47.92	11.11	59.03	3.60	7.38	3.94	26.05
Establishments	10.02	12.08	16.37	24.42	13.93	76.82	17.88	94.69	2.75	1.99	0.31	0.26

Finance												
Firms	5.53	4.95	5.56	8.28	6.24	30.56	13.93	44.49	5.70	15.55	9.84	24.42
Establishments	7.25	8.33	18.17	17.06	9.01	59.82	17.09	76.90	6.64	12.87	2.86	0.73
Services												
Firms	4.89	5.20	5.63	7.88	6.81	30.41	18.72	49.13	7.27	16.56	6.95	20.10
Establishments	5.67	6.08	7.31	15.58	13.59	48.23	24.12	72.35	8.19	15.45	2.57	1.45

Source: U.S. Small Business Administration, Office of Advocacy, Small Business Data Base, USEEM file, version 8, 1988.
Note: The figures indicate the share of employment in each sector accounted for by firms and establishments within each respective size class. The data exclude government employment.

Table 2.2
A comparison of employment statistics among the SBDB, BLS, and Census data bases

	Small Business Administration (SBDB)			Bureau of Labor Statistics			Bureau of the Census		
	1980	1986	Percent change 1980–1986	1980	1986	Percent change 1980–1986	1980	1985	Percent change 1980–1985
U.S. total	82,070,988	91,180,151	11.10	74,487,000	83,332,000	11.87	74,276,927	82,467,724	11.0
Agriculture	811,161	944,517	16.44	NA	NA	NA	289,843	412,010	42.1
Mining	1,127,950	1,136,989	0.80	1,025,000	792,000	−22.73	996,007	847,143	−14.9
Construction	4,748,128	5,011,112	5.54	4,469,000	4,960,000	10.99	4,473,551	4,658,669	4.1
Manufacturing	24,417,344	22,875,373	−6.32	20,361,000	19,186,000	−5.77	21,151,842	19,141,756	−9.5
Transportation	5,872,312	6,160,075	4.90	5,156,000	5,286,000	2.52	4,631,152	4,884,297	5.5
Wholesale trade	5,498,665	6,261,744	13.88	5,281,000	5,853,000	10.83	5,215,520	5,724,864	9.8
Retail trade	15,010,569	17,142,789	14.20	15,292,000	17,878,000	16.91	15,045,287	17,549,841	16.6
Finance	5,736,238	7,098,779	23.75	5,162,000	6,305,000	22.14	5,278,404	6,370,787	20.7
Services	18,848,622	24,548,774	30.24	17,741,000	23,072,000	30.05	17,195,327	22,818,357	33.0

Sources: U.S. Small Business Administration, Office of Advocacy, Small Business Data Base, USEEM files, 1988; U.S. Department of Labor, Bureau of Labor Statistics, Employment and Earnings (March 1981 and March 1987); U.S. Department of Commerce, Bureau of the Census, County Business Patterns, U.S. Summary (1980 and 1985 issues).
NA = Not available.

growth rates in establishments with fewer than 500 employees are virtually identical. Both data bases indicate that the growth rates of smaller establishments exceeded that of establishments with at least 500 employees.

Although such similarities exist, there are also several substantial differences observed between the establishment growth rates recorded in these two different data bases. For example, the overall growth rates in the manufacturing and transportation sectors vary considerably between the SBDB and BLS. Most strikingly, the SBDB records a growth rate in employment of 3.17 percent in manufacturing, whereas the BLS indicates that employment shrank by 5.85 percent. Despite these differences, one important result emerges in both data bases. The employment growth of small plants in manufacturing was clearly greater than that of large plants over this time period.

Tables 2.2 and 2.3 compare the employment data of the SBDB with those from the BLS and *County Business Patterns* (Bureau of the Census), but it is also possible to compare the number of U.S. enterprises recorded by different data sources. One such major comparable source is *Enterprise Statistics*, which is a cross-sectional, establishment-based data source on employment, payroll, and sales. It provides data for the industries covered in the censuses of wholesale trade, retail trade, services, manufacturing, mining, and construction that are conducted every five years by the Bureau of the Census. The finance and transportation sectors are not included.[9]

The distribution of firms by sector for the SBDB (USEEM file) is compared to that using the *Enterprise Statistics* data for 1982, the middle year in the SBDB, in table 2.4. The distribution of firms according to sector is quite similar between the two data bases. Most important, the SBDB records 9.67 percent of its enterprises as belonging to the manufacturing sector; but according to *Enterprise Statistics* only 7.43 percent of the firms are reported to be in manufacturing.[10]

The distribution of firms according to employment size in 1982 is compared between the SBDB and *Enterprise Statistics* in table 2.5. The *Enterprise Statistics* and SBDB data sources reveal very similar, although not identical, distributions of firm size. For example, *Enterprise Statistics* records more than nine out of ten enterprises as having fewer than twenty employees,

---

9. The data collected in *Enterprise Statistics* are reported in the *General Report on Industrial Organization*, which furnishes data on employment, receipts, number of establishments, and legal form of ownership for all companies.
10. MacDonald (1986) found that Dun and Bradstreet tends to assign more small firms to manufacturing than does the Bureau of the Census (*Enterprise Statistics*). For the large firms that he examined, however, he found the two data sources to be quite similar.

Table 2.3
Employment growth rates (%) according to establishment size class

	Total, all size classes	Number of employees per establishment/reporting unit					
		< 10	10–19	20–99	100–499	< 500	500 and over
All industries							
SBDB	21.66	12.87	25.84	35.43	20.17	24.83	11.95
BLS	18.15	20.20	23.69	26.97	24.03	24.29	2.27
Mining							
SBDB	15.20	48.98	33.77	16.32	1.87	16.55	11.80
BLS	19.09	52.15	50.27	33.03	16.66	30.14	−5.39
Construction							
SBDB	13.71	6.88	22.55	26.58	1.73	15.26	−11.35
BLS	18.27	11.06	20.99	30.16	23.37	21.63	−22.58
Manufacturing							
SBDB	3.17	16.97	20.26	17.70	1.49	8.97	−5.42
BLS	−5.85	14.31	9.35	5.36	−2.91	1.33	−14.83
Transportation							
SBDB	14.87	21.02	38.72	20.07	−1.64	12.80	20.61
BLS	8.25	29.89	26.70	33.45	18.96	26.58	−11.58
Wholesale trade							
SBDB	26.05	21.34	26.89	22.93	31.29	24.57	51.59
BLS	17.37	24.84	16.18	16.56	17.44	18.33	5.25
Retail trade							
SBDB	22.43	−1.03	20.66	38.35	67.88	27.51	−28.44
BLS	23.54	6.33	14.79	31.28	51.47	27.23	4.43
Finance							
SBDB	34.40	26.21	12.36	48.87	29.51	29.87	52.06
BLS	32.82	21.70	30.97	32.80	36.21	31.26	37.37
Services							
SBDB	44.39	25.11	49.09	58.77	40.18	45.06	42.66
BLS	42.71	33.14	42.33	41.92	51.67	42.68	42.83

Sources: SBDB-U.S. Small Business Administration, Office of Advocacy, Small Business Data Base, USEEM file, version 9, 1989; BLS-U.S. Department of Labor, Bureau of Labor Statistics, unpublished data prepared under contract for the U.S. Small Business Administration, 1988, adapted from Brown and Phillips (1989).
Note: The data exclude agriculture, forestry, and fishing.

Table 2.4
The distribution of firms by sector for the SBDB (USEEM) and Enterprise Statistics data, 1982 (percentages in parentheses)

	Data source	
Sector	Small Business Administration	Enterprise Statistics
Mining	32,686	43,366
	(0.93)	(1.10)
Construction	505,995	499,388
	(14.35)	(12.64)
Manufacturing	341,015	293,556
	(9.67)	(7.43)
Transportation, communication, and public utilities	125,887	149,911
	(3.57)	(3.80)
Wholesale trade	394,406	326,492
	(11.18)	(8.27)
Retail trade	1,064,747	1,055,095
	(30.19)	(26.71)
Finance, insurances, and real estate	254,088	361,396
	(7.20)	(9.15)
Services	808,445	1,220,631
	(22.92)	(30.90)
Total	3,527,269	3,949,835
	(100.01)	(100.00)

Sources: U.S. Department of Commerce, Bureau of the Census, *1982 Enterprise Statistics*, ES82-1 (Washington, DC: U.S. Government Printing Office, October 1986, table 3), and U.S. Small Business Administration Small Business Database (USEEM file).
Note: The finance and transportation sectors are excluded from the *Enterprise Statistics*. They have been estimated in this table from the *1982 County Business Patterns*.

while the SBDB identifies a slightly smaller share of enterprises accounted for by the smallest firms.

Because table 2.5 reveals that the greatest discrepancy between data sources may occur within the smallest firm-size classes, table 2.6 compares the employment recorded in the *County Business Patterns*, Bureau of Labor Statistics, and SBDB for establishments with fewer than one hundred employees in 1977. Overall, the SBDB records less employment in small establishments than does the *County Business Patterns*, but more than does the BLS. Within the manufacturing sector, however, the SBDB records about 11 percent more employment in small establishments than does the *County Business Patterns*, and about 18 percent more than does the BLS.

Table 2.5
Distribution of firms according to employment size for the Enterprise Statistics and SBDB data, 1982

Number of employees in firm	Enterprise Statistics Number	Percent	Small Business Administration Number	Percent
1–9	3,886,375	91.3	3,181,834	87.9
20–99	320,370	7.5	362,500	10.0
1–99	4,206,745	98.8	3,544,334	97.9
100–499	42,468	1.0	63,452	1.8
1–499	4,249,213	99.8	3,607,786	99.6
500 +	7,030	0.2	13,350	0.4
Total	4,256,243	100.0	3,621,136	100.0

Sources: U.S. Department of Commerce, Bureau of the Census, *1982 Enterprise Statistics*, ES82-1 (Washington, DC: U.S. Government Printing Office, October 1986), and U.S. Small Business Administration Database.
Note: The totals of the SBDB (USEEM) and the Enterprise Statistics are not strictly comparable because the Enterprise Statistics exclude the finance and transportation sectors.

Table 2.6
Employment in all establishments having fewer than 100 employees for the SBDB (USEEM), BLS, and County Business Patterns

Industry	(1) County Business Patterns	(2) BLS	(3) Small Business Administration	(3)/(1)	(3)/(2)
Agricultural services, forestry, fisheries	231,609	259,512	249,210	1.076	.960
Mining	308,403	291,880	331,770	1.076	1.137
Construction	2,649,704	2,666,462	3,271,780	1.235	1.227
Manufacturing	4,842,964	4,563,429	5,390,850	1.113	1.181
Transportation, communication, public utilities	1,746,405	1,477,215	1,573,080	0.901	1.065
Wholesale trade	3,539,010	3,419,599	3,750,990	1.060	1.097
Retail trade	10,679,058	8,885,947	8,719,670	0.817	0.981
Finance, insurance, real estate	2,780,444	2,198,158	2,100,250	0.755	0.955
Services	7,510,565	6,719,852	6,176,970	0.822	0.919
Totals	34,288,162	30,482,054	31,564,570	0.921	1.036

Source: Small Business Administration, Office of Economic Research, unpublished report.

2.5   A Note on Measuring Innovative Activity

The measure of innovative activity used throughout this book comes from the Small Business Administration's Innovation Data Base (SBIDB). It is multidimensional in that the innovative output, measured in terms of numbers of innovations, or new products and processes introduced on the market for all firms—large small—is identified. As the first word in the title of this book suggests, measuring innovative activity plays a key role throughout this volume. Because it has been used extensively by Acs and Audretsch (1987, 1988, 1990, 1991) and by Acs, Audretsch, and Feldman (1992 and 1994), an explanation and documentation need not be repeated here. Rather, the reader is referred to complete documentation in chapter 2 and to appendix D of Acs and Audretsch (1990). Several points however, should be emphasized here.

First, measures of technological change have typically involved one of the three major aspects of the innovative process: (1) a measure of inputs into the process, such as R & D expenditures, or the share of the labor force accounted for by employees involved in R & D activities; (2) an intermediate output, such as the number of inventions that have been patented; or (3) a direct measure of innovative output. In this book we focus on the third type of measure, a measure of direct innovative output. Knowledge regarding both the determinants and the impact of technological change has been largely shaped by the empirical data available for analyses.[11]

A clear limitation in using R & D activity as a proxy measure for technological change is that R & D reflects only the resources devoted to producing innovative output, not the amount of innovative activity realized. That is, R & D is an input and not an output in the innovation process.[12] And, as Mansfield (1984) points out, not all efforts within a formal R & D laboratory are directed toward generating innovative output in any case; other types of output, such as imitation and technology transfer, are also common goals.

As systematic data measuring the number of inventions patented were introduced in the mid-1960s, many scholars interpreted this new measure

---

11. For a review of this literature, see Baldwin and Scott (1987), Scherer (1992), and Cohen and Levin (1989).

12. Kleinknecht (1987 and 1989), Kleinknecht and Verspagen (1989), and Kleinknecht et al. (1991) have systematically and persuasively shown that R & D measures tend to incorporate efforts made to generate innovative activity that are undertaken in a somewhat formalized way, mainly within formal R & D laboratories. Similar results have been found for Italy (Santarelli and Sterlacchini, 1990). See also Scheirer (1991).

not only as being superior to R & D but also as reflecting innovative output. However, patents are more a type of intermediate than innovative output measure. A patent reflects new technical knowledge, but it does not indicate whether this knowledge has a positive economic value. Only those inventions which have been successfully introduced into the market can claim that they are innovations as well. Although innovations and inventions are related, they are not identical. The distinction is that an innovation is "a process that begins with an invention, precedes with the development of the invention, and results in the introduction of a new product, process or service to the marketplace" (Edwards and Gordon, 1984, p. 1).

Beside the fact that many, if not most, patented inventions do not result in an innovation, a second important limitation of patent measures is that they do not capture all of the innovations actually made. In fact, many inventions that result in innovations are not patented. The tendency of patented inventions to result in innovations and of innovations to be the result of inventions that were patented combine into what F. M. Scherer (1983) has termed "the propensity to patent." Uncertainty about the stability of the propensity to patent across enterprises and across industries casts doubt upon the reliability of patent measures. According to Scherer (1983, pp. 107–108): "The quantity and quality of industry patenting may depend upon chance, how readily a technology lends itself to patent protection, and business decision-makers' varying perceptions of how much advantage they will derive from patent rights. Not much of a systematic nature is known about these phenomena, which can be characterized as differences in the propensity to patent."

Mansfield (1984, p. 462) has explained why the propensity to patent may vary so much across markets: "The value and cost of individual patents vary enormously within and across industries ... Many inventions are not patented. And in some industries, like electronics, there is considerable speculation that the patent system is being bypassed to a greater extent than in the past. Some types of technologies are more likely to be patented than others."

Thus, even as new and superior sources of patent data have been introduced, such as the new measure of patented inventions from the computerization by the U.S. Patent Office (Pakes and Griliches, 1980 and 1984; Hall et al., 1986; and Jaffe, 1986), the reliability and validity of these data as measures of innovative activity have been severely challenged. For example, Pakes and Griliches (1980, p. 378) warn that "patents are a flawed measure of innovative output; particularly since not all new innovations are patented and since patents differ greatly in their economic impact." In addressing the question, "Patents as indicators of what?", Griliches (1990, p. 1669) concludes: "Ideally, we might hope that patent statistics would provide a measure of the (innovative) output ... The reality, however, is very far from it. The dream of getting hold of an output indicator of inventive activity is one of the strong motivating forces for economic research in this area."

It was well into the 1970s before systematic attempts were made to provide a direct measure of innovative output in the United States. The data base for measuring innovative activity used throughout this book, the SBIDB, represents the most recent and most ambitious major data base in the United States providing a direct measure of innovative activity. While the reader is again referred to the 1990 Acs and Audretsch study (chapter 2), it should be emphasized that the measure of innovative activity is a direct measure compared to the more traditional measures of innovative inputs and intermediate inputs.

The SBIDB consists of 8,074 innovations commercially introduced in the United States in 1982. A private firm, The Futures Group, compiled the data and performed quality control analyses for the U.S. Small Business Administration by examining over one hundred technology, engineering, and trade journals spanning every industry in manufacturing. From the sections in each trade journal listing innovations and new products, a data base consisting of the innovations by four-digit standard industrial classification (SIC) industries was formed.

Because the innovations recorded in 1982 were the result of inventions made, on average, 4.3 years earlier, in some sense the innovation data base represents the inventions made around 1978 that were subsequently introduced as innovation to the market in 1982. The data were also checked for duplication. In fact, 8,800 innovations were actually recorded, but it was subsequently found that 726 of them appeared either in separate issues of the same journal or in different journals. Thus double-counting was avoided.

The innovation data were classified according to the industry of the origin based on the SIC code of the innovating enterprise (firm). The Futures Group assigned the innovation to an industry based on the information given in the trade journal. When no such information was given, and the relevant industry could not be determined from other sources, no industry was assigned to the innovation. The data were then classified into innovations by large firms, defined as firms with at least 500 employees, and innovations by small firms, defined as firms with fewer than 500 employees. For example, an innovation made by a subsidiary of a diversified firm would be classified by industry according to the SIC industry of the innovating subsidiary (establishment) and not by SIC industry of the parent firm (enterprise). However, the innovation would be classified by size according to the size of the entire firm and not just by the size of the subsidiary. Because sixty-seven innovations could not be classified according to firm size, the number of total innovations does not always equal the sum of the large- and small-firm innovations.

There are several important qualifications that should be made concerning the SBIDB. The trade journals report relatively few process, service, and management innovations and tend to capture mainly product innovations. The most likely effect of this bias is to underestimate the number of innovations emanating from large firms, since larger enterprises tend to produce more process innovations than do their smaller counterparts. However, because it was found that the large-firm innovations are more likely to be reported in trade journals than are small-firm innovations, the biases are perhaps somewhat offsetting.

One potential concern might be that the significance and "quality" of the innovations vary considerably between large and small firms. Based on 4,938 of the innovations, each innovation was classified by Edwards and Gordon (1984) according to one of the following levels of significance: (1) the innovation established an entirely new category of product; (2) the innovation is the first of its type on the market in a product category already in existence; (3) the innovation represents a significant improvement in existing technology; and (4) the innovation is a modest improvement designed to update an existing product.

The distribution of innovative significance according to firm size is shown in table 2.7. Although none of the innovations in the sample was in the highest level of significance, 80 were in the second level, 576 in the third level, and 4,282 were classified in the fourth level. Within each level of significance, the distribution between large- and small-firm innovations proved to be remarkably constant. In both the second and third significance categories, the large firms accounted for 62.5 percent of the innovations and the small firms for the remaining 37.5 percent. In the fourth significance category, the large firms accounted for a slightly smaller share of the innovations, 56.6 percent, and the small firms contributed the remaining 43.4 percent. A chi-square test for the hypothesis that there is no difference in the frequency of innovation with respect to innovative significance and firm size cannot be rejected at the 99 percent level of confidence. Thus, based on the classification of the significance level of innovations, there

Table 2.7
Distribution of large- and small-firm innovations according to significance levels (percentages in parentheses)

Innovation significance	Description	Number of innovations	
		Large firms	Small firms
1	Establishes whole new categories	0 (0.00)	0 (0.00)
2	First of its type on the market in existing categories	50 (1.76)	30 (1.43)
3	A significant improvement in existing technology	360 (12.70)	216 (10.27)
4	Modest improvement designed to update existing products	2,424 (85.53)	1,858 (88.31)
Total		2,834 (99.99)	2,104 (100.00)

Source: SBIDB.

does not appear to be a great difference in the "quality" and significance of innovations between large and small firms.

To provide a test for any biases that might arise in the assignment of the innovation significance classification, The Futures Group undertook telephone interviews based on a subset of 600 innovating companies that were randomly selected. Of these selected companies, 529 were reached and 375 telephone interviews were actually carried out. Of those selected companies not participating in the telephone interviews, the most frequent reason given was the inability of The Futures Group to contact the innovating firm or person responsible for the innovation. The respondents to the interviews tended to rate their innovation as being more important than the rating assigned by The Futures Group. For example, even though The Futures Group did not assign any innovations to the most significant category, twenty-five of the interviewed firms considered their innovation to be worthy of the highest significance rating. Confronted with this disparity in ratings, Edwards and Gordon (1984, p. 66) conclude, "The liberalism of the part of the respondents, especially in the assignation of 1's, may be attributed to product loyalty on the part of some respondents and, perhaps, unfamiliarity with other products on the market on the part of some of the non technical respondents. Alternatively, The Futures Group may really have underrated the innovations."

Table 2.8
Comparison of innovation data with R & D and patent measures[a]

Industry group	Total innovations	Patents	Patents/ innovation	Company R & D (million)	R & D (millions)/ innovation
Food and tobacco	206	311	1.51	272	1.32
Textiles and apparel	29	147	5.07	65	2.24
Lumber and furniture	83	50	0.60	37	0.45
Paper	61	292	4.79	150	2.46
Chemicals (excluding drugs)	332	3,492	10.52	1,260	3.80
Drugs	170	868	5.11	449	2.64
Petroleum	24	1,046	43.58	360	15.00
Rubber and plastics	129	637	4.94	287	2.22
Stone, clay, and glass	59	477	8.09	149	2.53
Primary metals	74	424	5.73	239	3.23
Fabricated metal products	340	450	1.32	246	0.72
Machinery (excluding office)	612	1,657	2.71	852	1.39
Computers and office equipment	566	1,045	1.85	1,054	1.86
Industrial electrical equipment[b]	444	836	1.88	210	0.47
Household appliances	64	232	3.63	78	1.22
Communications equipment	262	2,384	9.10	1,136	4.34

Motor vehicles and other transportation equipment[c]	152	5.32	809	11.78	1,791
Aircraft and engines	48	10.44	501	13.60	653
Guided missiles and ordnance	16	10.81	173	6.44	103
Instruments	736	1.84	1,351	0.89	652
Total[d]	4,407	3.90	17,182	2.28	10,043

Source: SBIDB.
a. Company R & D (1974) and patent (June 1976–March 1977) data are from Scherer (1983).
b. Includes SIC 361, 362, 364, and 367.
c. Includes SIC 371, 373, 374, 375, and 379.
d. Includes only industries in this table.

It is in fact possible to compare directly the two more traditional measures of technological change—that is, the number of patented inventions and R & D expenditures—with the direct measure of innovative output from the SBIDB. Table 2.8 compares the 1977 company R & D expenditures from the U.S. Federal Trade Commission's Line of Business Survey with the total number of innovations from the SBIDB, and the total number of patented inventions between June 1976 and March 1977 (from Scherer, 1983).[13]

A positive and fairly strong relationship exists between the ratio of patents per innovation and R & D expenditures (millions of dollars) per innovation. This is supported by the simple correlation coefficient of 0.74. In general, those sectors that tend to generate substantial innovative activity also tend to engage in relatively high patent and R & D activity. There are however, several striking differences among these three measures of technological change. For example, in table 2.8 the simple correlation of 0.746 between company expenditures on R & D and the total number of innovations suggests a considerably stronger link between R & D input and innovative output than that between patent activity and innovative output, where the correlation coefficient is only 0.467. In addition, the correlation between the output and intermediate output measures—that is, the number of innovations and the number of registered patents—is greater than that between the R & D measures and patents.[14]

An important conclusion arising from the comparison between these three main measures of technological change and from the above qualifications associated with each measure, is that R & D, patented inventions, and innovative output do not at all measure the same economic phenomena. Even though they are all certainly related to the greater process of technological change, each measure focuses only on one particular aspect.

As table 2.9 indicates, in the most innovative four-digit SIC industries, large firms, defined as enterprises with at least 500 employees, contributed more innovations in some instances, whereas in other industries small firms proved to be more innovative. For example, in both the electronic computing equipment and process control instruments industries, the small firms contributed the bulk of the innovations. By contrast, in the aircraft

---

13. The patents represent 59 percent of all patented inventions issued to U.S. corporations between June 1976 and March 1977, and 61 percent of patents issued to industrial corporations over the same period. For further explanation, see Scherer (1983).

14. For a further comparison between the patent and innovation measures, see Acs and Audretsch (1989c).

Table 2.9
Number of significant innovations for large and small firms in the most innovative industries, 1982

Industry	Total innovations	Large-firm innovations	Small-firm innovations
Electronics computing equipment	395	158	227
Process control instruments	165	68	93
Radio and TV communication equipment	157	83	72
Pharmaceutical preparations	133	120	72
Electronic components	128	54	73
Engineering and scientific instruments	126	43	83
Semiconductors	122	91	29
Plastics products	107	22	82
Photographic equipment	88	79	9
Office machinery	77	67	10
Instruments to measure electricity	77	28	47
Surgical appliances and supplies	67	54	13
Surgical and medical instruments	66	30	36
Special industry machinery	64	43	21
Industrial controls	61	15	46
Toilet preparations	59	41	18
Valves and pipe fittings	54	20	33
Electric housewares and fans	53	47	6
Measuring and controlling devices	52	3	45
Food products machinery	50	37	12
Motors and generators	49	39	10
Plastic materials and resins	45	30	15
Industrial inorganic chemicals	40	32	8
Radio and TV receiving sets	40	35	4
Hand and edge tools	39	27	11
Fabricated platework	38	29	9
Fabricated metal products	35	12	17
Pumps and pumping equipment	34	18	16
Optical instruments and lenses	34	12	21
Polishes and sanitation goods	33	13	19
Industrial trucks and tractors	33	13	20
Medicinals and botanicals	32	27	5
Aircraft	32	31	1
Environmental controls	32	22	10

Source: SBIDB.
Note: Large- and small-firm innovations do not always sum to total innovations, because several innovations could not be classified according to firm size.

Probably the best measure of innovative activity is the total innovation rate, which is defined as the total number of innovations per 1,000 employees in each industry. The large-firm innovation rate is defined as the number of innovations made by firms with at least 500 employees divided by the number of employees (thousands) in large firms. The small-firm innovation rate is analogously defined as the number of innovations contributed by firms with fewer than 500 employees divided by the number of employees (thousands) in small firms.

The innovation rates, or the number of innovations per 1,000 employees, have the advantage in that they measure large- and small-firm innovative activity relative to the presence of large and small firms in any given industry. That is, in making a direct comparison between large- and small-firm innovative activity, the absolute number of innovations contributed by large firms and small enterprises is somewhat misleading, since these measures are not standardized by the relative presence of large and small firms in each industry. Hence the innovation rates are presumably a more reliable measure of innovative intensity.

Table 2.10 shows the mean innovation rates for industries aggregated to broader industrial sectors. For example, in the food sector there was an average of 0.2119 innovations per 1,000 employees. Thus the mean innovation rate in the food sector was about three times as high as that in textiles, but only slightly higher than the innovation rate in clothing or lumber. The lowest innovation rates were in printing (0.0426), textiles (0.0740), rubber (0.1204), and transportation equipment (0.1250). The highest innovation rates were in instruments (1.3586), chemicals (0.7592), and non-electrical machinery (0.6039).

Table 2.10 also compares the large-firm and small-firm innovation rates for each of the manufacturing sectors. The large-firm innovation rate is highest in rubber (2.1814), which is almost 500 times greater than that for leather (0.0053). The small-firm innovation rate is the highest for instruments (2.9987), which is considerably greater than that for printing (0.0313).

In general, the large-firm and small-firm innovation rates do not seem to be closely related. Whereas the large-firm innovation rates are relatively high in rubber, instruments, and chemicals, the small-firm innovation rates are relatively high in instruments, chemicals, non-electrical machinery, and electrical equipment. And whereas the large-firm innovation rates are relatively low in leather textiles, printing, and petroleum, the small-firm innovation rates are relatively low in printing, food, rubber, and paper. Some striking contrasts emerge between the large-firm and small-firm innovation rates. Whereas the large-firm innovation rate is the greatest in the rubber

Table 2.10
Innovation rates for large and small firms, by two-digit SIC sector, 1982

Sector	Total innovations	Large-firm innovations	Small-firm innovations
Food	0.2119	0.2555	0.1361[a]
	(0.1741)	(0.3120)	(0.1905)
Textiles	0.0740	0.0295	0.1669[a]
	(0.0612)	(0.0646)	(0.1723)
Apparel	0.1253	0.0639	0.1439
	(0.1553)	(0.1222)	(0.2076)
Lumber	0.1400	0.0506	0.1415
	(0.2179)	(0.0680)	(0.2662)
Furniture	0.3053	0.2412	0.2592
	(0.2917)	(0.3759)	(0.2243)
Paper	0.1616	0.1931	0.1214
	(0.1651)	(0.2821)	(0.2691)
Printing	0.0426	0.0468	0.0313
	(0.0350)	(0.0452)	(0.0552)
Chemicals	0.7592	0.6272	1.3547[a]
	(0.5945)	(0.6297)	(0.5641)
Petroleum	0.3386	0.0476	0.6173
	(0.3797)	(0.0824)	(0.6591)
Rubber	0.1204	2.1814	0.1129
	(0.0787)	(4.1868)	(0.1779)
Leather	0.1356	0.0053	0.1793[a]
	(0.1487)	(0.0106)	(0.1695)
Stone, clay, and glass	0.2130	0.1625	0.2696
	(0.1640)	(0.2116)	(0.1979)
Primary metals	0.1586	0.1624	0.3336
	(0.2905)	(0.3394)	(0.8319)
Fabricated metal products	0.3224	0.2878	0.3619
	(0.3109)	(0.3357)	(0.3862)
Machinery (non-electrical)	0.6039	0.4860	1.1491[a]
	(0.6728)	(0.5673)	(1.7965)
Electronics	0.3713	0.2719	0.7948[a]
	(0.3510)	(0.3263)	(0.7912)
Transportation equipment	0.1250	0.1182	0.1911
	(0.1289)	(0.1868)	(0.3349)
Instruments	1.3586	0.7442	2.9987[a]
	(0.9939)	(0.5367)	(2.5253)

Source: SBIDB.
Note: Innovation rates are defined as the number of innovations divided by employment (thousands of employees). Standard deviations are listed in parentheses.
a. The difference between the large- and small-firm innovation rates is statistically significant at the 90% level of confidence.

sector, the small-firm innovation rate is almost the lowest. Similarly, although the large-firm innovation rate is relatively low in the petroleum sector, the small-firm innovation rate is relatively high.

It is clear from table 2.10 that the difference in innovation rates between large and small firms varies considerably across industries. The small-firm innovation rate exceeds the large-firm innovation rate in fourteen of the industrial sectors, but the large-firm innovation rate exceeds the small-firm innovation rate in four of the sectors. An obvious question that arises when confronted with the disparate innovative strengths and weaknesses of large and small enterprises across different manufacturing sectors is, "What accounts for the differences in the relative innovative advantage of large and small firms?" In a series of studies, Acs and Audretsch (1987, 1988, and 1990) found that not only does market structure influence the total amount of innovative activity, but also the relative innovative advantage of large and small enterprises. The differences between the innovation rates of large and small firms can generally be explained by (1) the degree of capital intensity; (2) the extent to which an industry is concentrated; (3) the total amount of innovative activity in the industry; and (4) the extent to which an industry is comprised of large firms. In particular, the relative innovative advantage of large firms tends to be promoted in industries that are capital intensive, advertising intensive, concentrated, and highly unionized. By contrast, in industries that are highly innovative and comprised predominantly of large firms, the relative innovative advantage was found to be held by small enterprises.[15]

2.6 Conclusions

The statistical inferences made throughout the following five chapters are only as good as the underlying data base. In this chapter the longitudinal data base enabling the analysis of firm and industry evolution was introduced. Critical qualifications concerning the applicability of this longitudinal data base were provided, along with a description of some of the major procedures implemented to edit the raw data in the files. In addition, this data base was compared to more traditional sources of data that have been used to measure the economic activities of establishments on a broad basis. Such comparisons reveal that even though while differences certainly exist the SBDB is generally in line with the other major data bases measuring business activities.

---

15. To put the findings in the context of the broader literature, see Baldwin and Scott (1987) and Cohen and Levin (1989).

3 New Firms

3.1 Introduction

Professor Coase (1937) of the University of Chicago was awarded a Nobel
Prize for explaining why a firm should exist. But why should more than
one firm exist in an industry?[1] One answer is provided by the traditional
economics literature focusing on industrial organization. An excess level of
profitability induces entry into the industry. And this is why the entry of
new firms is interesting and important—because the new firms provide an
equilibrating function in the market, in that the levels of price and profit
are restored to the competitive levels.

In this chapter a somewhat different lens through which to view the
entry of new firms is suggested. A model is proposed that refocuses the
unit of observation away from firms deciding whether to increase their
output from a level of zero to some positive amount in a new industry, to
individual agents in possession of new knowledge that, due to uncertainty,
may or may not have some positive economic value. In fact, it is the
uncertainty inherent in new economic knowledge, combined with asymmetries across agents with respect to its expected value, that potentially
leads to a gap between the valuation of that knowledge.

To appropriate the value of that new knowledge, an economic agent can
either effectively sell it to an incumbent firm—typically through an employment contract—or use it to launch a new firm. Of course, an important
insight of Arrow (1962 and 1983), Stigler (1961), Williamson (1975), and
more recently Milgrom and Roberts (1988, 1990, and 1991) is that a firm's
decisionmaking process is made within the context of that firm's organization, that is, within a hierarchical bureaucracy.

---

1. Coase (1937, p. 23) himself asked, "A pertinent question to ask would appear to be (quite
apart from the monopoly considerations raised by Professor Knight), why, if by organizing
one can eliminate certain costs and in fact reduce the cost of production, are there any
market transactions at all? Why is not all production carried on by one big firm?"

That new economic knowledge is inherently asymmetric is an insight that dates back at least to Schumpeter (1911) and Knight (1921). For example, Schumpeter (1911) emphasized that an innovation is the result of new economic knowledge that is embodied in an individual. This led him to observe that, "The function of entrepreneurs is to reform or revolutionize the pattern of production by exploiting an invention, or more generally, an untried technological possibility for producing a new commodity or producing an old one in a new way ... To undertake such new things is difficult and constitutes a distinct economic function, first because they lie outside of the routine tasks which everybody understands, and secondly, because the environment resists in many ways" Schumpeter (1942, p. 13).

Because new economic knowledge is inherently asymmetric, a divergence in beliefs between an incumbent firm, or more exactly stated, the decisionmakers embedded in the hierarchical organization of an incumbent firm, and an individual agent can emerge with respect to the potential economic value of that new knowledge. This leads to the prediction that the greater the extent to which knowledge asymmetries exist, the more likely new economic knowledge will result in the agent deciding that she or he must start a new enterprise in order to appropriate the expected economic value of that new knowledge.

Therefore, new firms are expected to be more pervasive in industries characterized by what is termed as the *entrepreneurial technological regime*, or where the underlying knowledge conditions tend to be particularly asymmetric. By contrast, under the *routinized technological regime*, less knowledge asymmetry tends to result in innovative activity occurring within the boundaries of the incumbent enterprises. There is less incentive for an agent to resort to starting a new firm to appropriate the potential economic value of her or his new economic knowledge, and therefore presumably less startup activity under the rountinized technological regime.

Based on a large panel data base enabling the examination of the startup of new firms within both a cross section and time series context, there is considerable evidence consistent with the hypothesis that new-firm startups are shaped by the underlying knowledge conditions. There tends to be less startup activity in industries better characterized by the routinized technological regime. By contrast, in those industries more closely conforming to the entrepreneurial technological regime, new-firm startups clearly play a more important role. These findings provide at least some support for the view that the entry of new firms is not only shaped by the decisionmaking process of individuals, but that new entrants represent, at least in some cases, not merely smaller replica of the existing incumbent enterprises but also agents of change.

3.2   Why Firms Exist

Before tackling the questions of why new firms would come into existence and how this relates to technological change and the evolution of industries, it is appropriate first to understand why firms should exist at all. In fact, what has become known as the theory of the firm is one of the major topics of modern microeconomics.[2] But to say that the topic draws a significant portion of the attention and energy of the economics profession is not to say that there is anything approaching unanimity about the subject. Thus, in reflecting, "What does economics have to say about the role of the business firm in a market economy?" Sidney Winter (1991, p. 179) concludes that, "I think we must acknowledge that the present state is one of incoherence."

At least part of the reason for this state of incoherence is attributable to what Edith Penrose (1959, p. 10) observed some three decades ago: "A 'firm' is by no means an unambiguous clear-cut entity; it is not an observable object physically separable from other objects, and it is difficult to define except with reference to what it does or what is done within it. Hence each analyst is free to choose any characteristics of firms that he is interested in, to define firms in terms of those characteristics, and to proceed thereafter to call the construction so defined a 'firm'. Herein lies a potential source of confusion." Still, a number of schools of thought, or focal points, have emerged in economic discourse on the theory of the firm.

There are three major categories, or schools of thought, with respect to the theory of the firm that are relevant here.[3] The first views the firm in the context of a production function—that is, by combining inputs to produce outputs.[4] The second view focuses on the firm in terms of the information and transactions it processes and is able to process. And the third view is evolutionary in that it considers the firm as a repository of knowledge.

This first school of thought, or view of the firm, considers firms as possessing a specific capability for transforming inputs into outputs generally through a process characterized by a production function. Firms are assumed to be solitary actors which reach decisions rationally. In particular, the goal of the firm is to maximize profit or, in terms of invested resources,

---

2. See, for examples, Kreps (1991) and Milgrom and Roberts (1987 and 1988).

3. Others can be found in Holmstrom and Tirole (1989).

4. Nelson and Winter (1982, pp. 6–11) refer to the production-function view of the firm as the "orthodox" viewpoint in economic theory. According to Winter (1991, p. 180), "Orthodox economic theory is the theoretical view that dominates the leading textbooks of intermediate microeconomics, together with the extensions and elaborations of that basic viewpoint found in more advanced work."

the present value of a stream of profits over time. Of particular importance here is the assumption that firms produce in markets for homogeneous commodities. Both inputs and outputs are typically purchased and sold on a spot market. And technology is considered to be exogenous. Beyond anything else, this view of the firm focuses on how an exogenous technology and production process transforms inputs into outputs.

The second view of the firm dates back at least to Coase (1937), who redirected the focus of attention away from the production process and toward transactions as the unit of analysis. Coase's answer to the question, "What is a firm?" was that a firm is a form of coordination of economic activity by authority, that is by administration, rather than by contract on an exchange market. Coase recognized that there are different ways of organizing transactions, or what has been more recently termed as "modes of governance" for transactions. These different organizational structures or modes of governance incur differing costs, and it is the costs of transactions that will ultimately dictate the organizational form. Thus Coase (1937, p. 38) concluded that, "The main reason why it is profitable to establish a firm would seem to be that there is a cost of using the price mechanism." That is, firms come into existence because the costs of coordinating economic activities through the market exceed the costs of administering those activities within the boundaries of the firm. What sets the limits of the firm's boundaries? Here, too, Coase (1937, p. 30) was unequivocal, "The question always is, will it pay to bring an extra exchange transaction under the organizing authority? At the margin, the costs of organizing within the firm will be equal either to the costs of organizing in another firm or to the costs involved in leaving the transaction to be 'organized' by the price mechanism."

For Williamson (1975), as well, the unit of observation is the transaction.[5] Williamson makes two key behavioral assumptions regarding human action, both of which follow from the notion that it is people or economic agents who engage in transactions. That is, goods or services are transferred a a result of human action: "Transaction cost economics characterizes human nature as we know it by reference to bounded rationality and opportunism. The first acknowledges limits on cognitive competence. The second substitutes subtle for simple self-interest seeking" (Williamson, 1985, p. 44). Because rationality is bounded and economic agents engage in opportunistic behavior additional costs are incurred in making transactions.

---

5. According to Williamson (1985, p. 1), "A transaction occurs when a good or service is transferred across a technologically separable interface. One stage of activity terminates and another begins."

As for Coase, Williamson (1985, p.46) concludes that the motivation to minimize costs of transaction shapes the emerging organizational structures that ultimately govern the costs of transactions, or what has become known as the governance structures:

Economizing on bounded rationality takes two forms. One concerns decision processes, and the other involves governance structures. The use of heuristic problem-solving ... is a decision process response. Transaction cost economics is principally concerned, however, with the economizing consequence of assigning transactions to governance structures in a discriminating way. Confronted with the realities of bounded rationality, the costs of planning, adapting, and monitoring transactions need expressly to be considered. Which governance structures are more efficacious for which types of transactions? *Ceteris paribus*, modes that make large demands against cognitive competence are relatively disfavored.

Thus "the modern corporation is mainly to be understood as the product of a series of organizational innovations that have had the purpose and effect of economizing on transaction costs" (Williamson, 1985, p. 273). This leads Williamson (1985, p. 13) to conclude that, "the firm is more usefully regarded as a governance structure."

The third school of thought on the theory of the firm considers the repository of knowledge to be the most distinguishing feature of a firm. In fact, this view dates back at least to Alfred Marshall (1920, p. 115), who defined capital largely in terms of knowledge and organization, "Capital consists in a great part of knowledge and organization: and of this some part is private property and the other part is not. Knowledge is our most powerful engine of production; it enables us to subdue Nature and force her to satisfy our wants. Organisation aids knowledge."

Edith Penrose (1959, pp. 31–32) similarly attributed the distinguishing characteristic of an enterprise to the knowledge embedded in the firm, "The productive activities of a firm are governed by what we shall call its 'productive opportunity', which comprises all of the productive possibilities that its entrepreneurs see and can take advantage of ... It is clear that this opportunity will be restricted to the extent to which a firm does not see opportunities for expansion, is unwilling to act upon them, or is unable to respond to them." According to Penrose, the source of these ideas is the experience and knowledge generated within the firm.

Penrose's view focusing on the characteristic of firm-specific knowledge as the distinguishing feature of a firm was a predecessor to the evolutionary theory developed by Nelson and Winter. At the heart of their theory are three concepts underlying the evolution of industries—routine, search, and, selection. The organizational knowledge of each firm is stored in its routines. A routine refers to the "regular and predictable" (Nelson and Winter, 1982, p. 14) aspects regulating the behavior of the firm. Thus Nelson and Winter (1982, p. 99) argue that, "It is easy enough to suggest that a plausible answer to the question, 'Where does the knowledge reside?' is 'In the organization's memory.' But where and what is the memory of an organization? We propose that the routinization of activity in an organization constitutes the most important form of storage of the organization's specific operational knowledge."

The notion of a routine emerges as an organizational mechanism for dealing with Simon's (1984) bounded rationality. That is, confronted with incomplete information, and ill-equipped for digesting an abundance of information—much of it certain—organizations resort to their routines in guiding not only actions but, beyond everything else, the decision-making process. As the agents employed by a firm accumulate experience and knowledge, they incorporate them into the routines characterizing the firm. Nelson and Winter (1982, p. 36) assume that, although these routines may change in the long run, they are stable over the short and medium run. Most importantly, the routines are stable enough to yield predictions as to how a given firm will cope with a change in its external environment.

According to Nelson and Winter (1982), the firm can engage in actively searching for new economic knowledge. This function is distinct from that embedded in routines: "Organizations that are involved in the production or management of economic change as their principal function—organizations such as R & D laboratories and consulting firms—do not fit neatly into the routine operation mold" (Nelson and Winter, 1982, p. 97). The two key distinguishing features of search are irreversibility and uncertainty. Still, Nelson and Winter (1982, p. 247) incorporate a routine-like structure in the search mechanism: "The decision maker is viewed as having a set of decision rules ... these rules determine the direction of 'search'."

The third key element in Nelson and Winter's (1982) evolutionary theory involves selection, which is determined partially by the external environment. Nelson and Winter (1982, p. 19) characterize the selection mechanism as, "Search and selection are simultaneous, interacting aspects of the evolutionary process: the same prices that provide selection feedback also influence the directions of search. Through the joint action of search and selection, the firms evolve over time, with the condition of the industry in each period bearing the seeds of its condition in the following period."

3.3   The Traditional View of Entry

After summarizing the state of knowledge with respect to entry, Mueller (1991) concludes that at least five different forms of entry can be distinguished, only one of which involves a newly created firm.[6] Still, a new-firm startup not only represents the entry of a firm, but as Dunne, Roberts, and Samuelson (1988 and 1989) show, it is by far the most prevalent and common form of entry. Which is to say that if the standard theories about why firms enter industries—and why the propensity to enter may vary from industry to industry—are about anything, they are about the startup of new firms.

Why do firms enter an industry? The traditional view to be found in the literature of industrial organization[7] is that a level of profitability in excess of long-run equilibrium induces entry into the industry. And this is why the entry of new firms is interesting and important in the traditional theory—the new firms provide an equilibrating function in the market, in that the levels of price and profit are restored to their long-run competitive levels.

In this traditional theory, outputs and inputs in an industry are assumed to be homogeneous. That is, the entry of new firms is about business as usual—it is just that with the new entrant there is more of it. For example, Geroski (1991a, p. 65) assumes that,

If we think of entry as an error-correction mechanism which is attracted by and serves to bid away excess profits, it is natural to suppose that entry will occur whenever profits differ from their long-run levels. Given this maintained hypothesis, observations of actual entry rates and current (or expected post-entry) profits can be used to make inferences about the unobservable of interest—long-run profits. In particular, entry in an industry is hypothesized to occur whenever expected post-entry profits exceed the level of profits protected in the long run.

This leads to the traditional model of entry:

$$E_{jt} = \lambda(P_{jt} - b_j) + u_{jt},\tag{3.1}$$

where E_{jt} represents entry in industry j at time t, P_{jt} represents expected post-entry profits, and b_j represents the level of profits protected in the

---

6. The other four types are (1) entry by an existing firm that builds a new plant in the industry; (2) entry by an existing firm that purchases a plant or firm already existing in the industry; (3) entry by an existing firm that alters the product mix in an existing plant; and (4) entry by a foreign-owned firm in one of the above ways.

7. See, for examples, Geroski (1989b, 1990, 1991a, 1991c, and 1992).

long run by entry barriers b_j, and u_{jt} represents stochastic disturbance. In this standard model of entry, which theoretically dates back to Bain (1956) and empirically to Orr (1974), λ measures the speed with which entrants respond to excess profits, and has the dimension of a flow per unit of time. The level of profits which can be sustained in perpetuity without attracting entry is b_j, and serves as the limit to what Geroski (1991a, pp. 65–66) terms as "limit profits" and is a natural measure of the height of barriers to entry.

The point to be emphasized here is that this traditional model assumes that the impact that the new entrant has on the market, and on equilibrium price and industry profits, is through the additional amount of output that is contributed. And the fundamental motivation for entering an industry, either through a new firm or through diversified entry (Schwalbach, 1987), as reflected in equation (3.1), is that profits exceed their long-run equilibrium level, even after accounting for structural barriers to entry. In fact, little consensus has emerged in the growing plethora of studies trying to link industry profitability, growth, and structural barriers to entry rates, as implied by equation (3.1).

The level of industry profitability was found to have only a weak positive impact on entry in studies by Orr (1974) and Duetsch (1984), whereas Khemani and Shapiro (1986) found past profits to be a strong determinant of entry.[8] And five of the six country studies contained in Geroski and Schwalbach (1991) found a positive link between industry profitability and entry.

As equation (3.1) implies, a positive relationship has generally been found to exist between industry growth rates and entry rates. Presumably higher rates of growth enable incumbent enterprises to raise prices (Bradburd and Caves, 1982), thereby inducing more entry, or else raise expectations about future profits. For example, in five of the six country studies (Germany, Norway, Portugal, Belgium, and Korea) contained in Geroski and Schwalbach (1991) entry rates were found to be positively influenced by industry growth rates. Only for the United Kingdom did a negative relationship emerge between entry rates and industry growth.

One of the most startling results that has emerged in empirical studies is that entry by firms into an industry is apparently not substantially deterred or even deterred at all in capital-intensive industries in which scale economies play an important role (Austin and Rosenbaum, 1990; Siegfried and

---

8. While Orr (1974) used net entry as the dependent variable, the dependent variable in Khemani and Shapiro (1986) was de novo gross plant entry, net of exit, plant openings by incumbents, mergers, and diversification.

Evans, 1992). For example, Acs and Audretsch (1990, chapter 5; 1989a and 1989b) found that even small firms are not significantly deterred from entering industries that are relatively capitalintensive.

Empirical evidence in support of the model represented by equation (3.1) is ambiguous at best, leading Geroski (1991c, p.282) to conclude, "Right from the start, scholars have had some trouble in reconciling the stories told about entry in standard textbooks with the substance of what they found in their data. Very few have emerged from their work feeling that they have answered half as many questions as they have raised, much less that they have answered most of the interesting ones."

Perhaps one reason for this trouble is the inherently static model used to capture an inherently dynamic process. Manfred Neumann (1993, pp. 593–594) has criticized this traditional model of entry, as found in the individual country studies contained in Geroski and Schwalbach (1991), because they

are predicated on the adoption of a basically static framework. It is assumed that startups enter a given market where they are facing incumbents which naturally try to fend off entry. Since the impact of entry on the performance of incumbents seems to be only slight, the question arises whether the costs of entry are worthwhile, given the high rate of exit associated with entry. Geroski appears to be rather sceptical about that. I submit that adopting a static framework is misleading ... In fact, generally, an entrant can only hope to succeed if he employs either a new technology or offers a new product, or both. Just imitating incumbents is almost certainly doomed to failure. If the process of entry is looked upon from this perspective the high correlation between gross entry and exit reflects the inherent risks of innovating activities ... Obviously it is rather difficult to break loose from the inherited mode of reasoning within the static framework. It is not without merit, to be sure, but it needs to be enlarged by putting it into a dynamic setting.

3.4 Asymmetric Information, Transaction Costs, and the Principal-Agent Relationship

The starting point for most theories of innovation is the firm. The relative innovative advantages of large and small firms are then analyzed by comparing factors such as the cost of and access to finance, scale economies in production and marketing, and access to a supply of new technological knowledge that has the potential for being transformed—through innovative activity—into new economic knowledge. In such theories the firms are exogenous and their performance in generating technological change is endogenous.[9] For example, in the most prevalent model found in the litera-

---

9. See, for example, Williamson (1975), Scherer (1984 and 1991), Cohen and Klepper (1991, 1992a, and 1992b), and Arrow (1962 and 1983).

ture of technological change, the model of the knowledge production function introduced by Zvi Griliches (1979), firms exogenously exist and then engage in the pursuit of new economic knowledge as an input into the process of generating innovative activity.[10]

Here I propose shifting the unit of observation away from exogenously assumed firms to individuals—agents confronted with new knowledge and the decision whether and how to act upon that new knowledge.[11] Of course, agents can and do work for firms, and even if they do not, they can potentially be employed by an incumbent firm. In fact, in a model of perfect information with no agency costs, any positive economies of scale or scope will ensure that, in the absence of monopoly rents being earned by the incumbent firm, no incentive will exist for an agent to start a firm. If an agent has an idea for doing something different than is currently being practiced by the incumbent enterprises—both in terms of a new product or process and in terms of organization—the idea, which we will term here as an innovation, will be presented to an incumbent enterprise. Because of the assumption of perfect knowledge, both the firm and the agent would agree upon the expected value of the innovation. But to the degree that any economies of scale or scope exist, the expected value of implementing the innovation within the incumbent enterprise will exceed that of taking the innovation outside of the incumbent firm to start a new enterprise. Thus the incumbent firm and the inventor of the idea would be expected to reach a bargain splitting the value added to the firm contributed by the innovation. The payment to the inventor—either in terms of a higher wage or some other means of remuneration—would be bounded between the expected value of the innovation if it is implemented by the incumbent

---

10. See also Jaffe (1986 and 1989), Acs, Audretsch, and Feldman (1992 and 1994), and Feldman (1994a and 1994b).

11. Winter (1991) points out that J. de V. Graaf (1957, p. 16) characterized the "clash" between focusing on the firm and on the individual as, "When we try to construct a transformation function for society as a whole from those facing the individual firms comprising it, a fundamental difficulty confronts us. There is, from a welfare point of view, nothing special about the firms actually existing in an economy at a given moment of time. The firm is in no sense a 'natural unit'. Only the individual members of the economy can lay claim to that distinction. All are potential entrepreneurs. It seems, therefore, that the natural thing to do is to build up from the transformation function of men, rather than the firms, constituting an economy. If we are interested in eventual empirical determination, this is extremely inconvenient. But it has conceptual advantages. The ultimate repositories of technological knowledge in any society are the men comprising it, and it is just this knowledge which is effectively summarized in the form of a transformation function. In itself a firm possesses no knowledge. That which is available to it belongs to the men associated with it. Its production function is really built up in exactly the same way, and from the same basic ingredients, as society's."

enterprise on the upper end, and by the return that the agent could expect to earn if she used it to launch a new enterprise on the lower end. Or, as Frank Knight (1921, p. 273) observed more than seventy years ago, "The laborer asks what he thinks the entrepreneur will be able to pay, and in any case will not accept less than he can get from some other entrepreneur, or by turning entrepreneur himself. In the same way the entrepreneur offers to any laborer what he thinks he must in order to secure his services, and in any case not more than he thinks the laborer will actually be worth to him, keeping in mind what he can get by turning laborer himself."

Kihlstrom and Laffont (1979), Evans and Leighton (1989, 1990a, and 1990b), Holmes and Schmitz (1990), Evans and Jovanovic (1989), Jovanovic (1994), and Blanchflower and Meyer (1994) have all reinterpreted Knight's theory of the decision confronting each economic agent to become either an employee in an incumbent enterprise or an entrepreneur, that is start a new firm, in terms of a model of income choice:[12]

$$Pr(e) = f(P_i - w), \tag{3.2}$$

where the probability of an agent starting a new firm is $Pr(e)$, the expected profits accruing from such a new firm are represented by P_i, and w is the wage that the agent would earn if she or he chooses to be employed by an incumbent enterprise. In fact, the model of income choice has served as the underlying framework for estimating those individual characteristics shaping the choice individuals make between starting a new firm or being an employee in an incumbent firm (Evans and Leighton, 1989, 1990a, and 1990b; Evans and Jovanovic, 1989; Blanchflower and Meyer, 1994).

But, of course, as Knight (1921), and later Arrow (1962) and Stigler (1961) were among the first to emphasize, new economic knowledge is anything but certain. Not only is new economic knowledge inherently risky, but substantial asymmetries exist across agents both between and within firms (Milgrom and Roberts, 1987). Which is to say that the expected value of a new idea—or what has been termed loosely here as a potential innovation—is likely to be anything but unanimous between the inventor of that idea and the decisionmaker, or group of decisionmakers,[13] of the firm confronted with evaluating proposed changes or innovations. In fact, it is because information is not only imperfect but also asymmetric that Knight (1921, p. 268) argued that the primary task of the firm is to process

---

12. See also Vivarelli (1991), Santarelli and Sterlacchini (1994), and Foti and Vivarelli (1994).
13. For example, as of 1993 a proposal for simply modifying an existing product at IBM had to pass through 250 layers of decisionmaking to gain approval ("Überfördert und Unregierbar," *Der Spiegel*, No. 14, 1993, p. 127).

imperfect information in order to reach a decision: "With the introduction of uncertainty—the fact of ignorance and the necessity of acting upon opinion rather than knowledge—into this Eden-like situation (that is a world of perfect information), its character is entirely changed ... With uncertainty present doing things, the actual execution of activity, becomes in a real sense a secondary part of life; the primary problem or function is deciding what to do and how to do it."[14]

Alchian (1950) pointed out that the existence of knowledge asymmetries would result in the inevitability of mistaken decisions in an uncertain world. Later, Alchian and Demsetz (1972) attributed the existence of asymmetric information across the employees in a firm as resulting in a problem of monitoring the contribution accruing from each employee and seeing the rewards correspondingly. This led them to conclude that, "The problem of economic organization is the economical means of metering productivity and rewards" (Alchian and Demsetz, 1972, p. 783).

Combined with the bureaucratic organization of incumbent firms to make a decision, the asymmetry of knowledge leads to a host of agency problems, spanning incentive structures, monitoring, and transaction costs. It is the existence of such agency costs, combined with asymmetric information that not only provides an incentive for agents with new ideas to start their own firms, also at a rate that varies from industry to industry, depending on the underlying knowledge conditions of the industry.

Coase (1937) and later Williamson (1975) argued that the size of an (incumbent) enterprise will be determined by answering what Coase (1937, p. 30) articulated as, "The question always is, will it pay to bring an extra exchange transaction under the organizing authority?" In fact, Coase (1937, p. 24) pointed out that, "Other things being equal, a firm will tend to be larger the less likely the (firm) is to make mistakes and the smaller the increase in mistakes with an increase in the transactions organized." And both Coase (1937) and Williamson (1975) were quick to note that an

---

14. Knight (1921, pp. 268 and 295) emphasizes that the existence of imperfect information leads to the two most important characteristics of firms, "In the first place, goods are produced for a market, on the basis of entirely impersonal prediction of wants, not for the satisfaction of the wants of the producers themselves. The producer takes the responsibility of forecasting the consumers' wants. In the second place, the work of forecasting and at the same time a large part of the technological direction and control of production are still further concentrated upon a very narrow class of the producers, and we meet with a new economic functionary, the entrepreneur ... When uncertainty is present and the task of deciding what to do and how to do it takes the ascendancy over that of execution the internal organisation of the productive groups is no longer a matter of indifference or a mechanical detail. Centralisation of this deciding and controlling function is imperative, a process of "cephalization" is inevitable."

obvious source causing an increase in transaction costs is uncertainty and imperfect information. According to Coase (1937, p. 27), "The fact of uncertainty means that people have to forecast future wants. Therefore, you get a special class springing up who direct the activities of others to whom they give guaranteed wages. It acts because good judgement is generally associated with confidence in one's judgement."

The basic agency problem (Alchian and Demsetz, 1972; Jensen and Meckling, 1976; Holmstrom and Milgrom, 1987; Holmstrom and Tirole, 1979; and Milgrom, 1988) arises in the context of an organization responding to an agent who possesses potentially new economic knowledge. In fact, it may even be the task of that agent within the context of a bureaucratic organization to search out, either through production or acquisition, such economic knowledge. Because the principal is not able to directly observe either the efforts or the outcome of the agent, both monitoring and incentive problems, as well as possible hostage problems, emerge. Notice that if either information asymmetries or a divergence in risk preferences along the lines described in Kihlstrom and Laffont (1979) exists then the principal and the agent will tend to value any given proposed project differently. Further, the agent will have a clear incentive to exaggerate the expected value of a potential innovation along with the amount of effort required by her to develop and implement it.

If the principal introduces some mechanism for monitoring, it can induce something about the agent's efforts from a particular signal. Alchian and Demsetz (1972) pointed out that a principal needs a monitor to meter inputs, particularly effort. However, the riskier any project might be, the less able the principal is to infer from monitoring. That is, the costs of monitoring rise and the expected value of the project falls as risk increases. This, in turn, reduces the incentive for the agent to develop risky projects, or at least their likelihood of being approved and implemented by an incumbent firm.

Holmstrom (1989) and Milgrom (1988) have pointed out the existence of a "bureaucratization dilemma," where, "To say that increased size brings increased bureaucracy is a safe generalization. To note that bureaucracy is viewed as an organizational disease is equally accurate" (Holmstrom, 1989, p. 320). Milgrom (1988) has argued that bureaucratic rules are a rational way for organizations to limit investments by agents in influence activities; and Tirole (1986) and Milgrom and Roberts (1991) have pointed out that bureaucratic decisionmaking is a mechanism to avoid collusion among coalitions of subordinates and bosses, because the integrity of the evaluation of subordinates depends on the incentives facing the monitor. Bureaucratic decisionmaking favoring nondiscretionary over discretionary rules reduces such collusions.

To minimize agency problems and the cost of monitoring, bureaucratic hierarchies develop objective rules. In addition, Kreps (1991) has argued that such bureaucratic rules promote internal uniformity and that a uniform corporate culture, in turn, promotes the reputation of the firm. These bureaucratic rules, however, make it more difficult to evaluate the efforts and activities of agents involved in activities that do not conform to such bureaucratic rules. As Holmstrom (1989, p. 323) points out, "Monitoring limitations suggest that the firm seeks out activities which are more easily and objectively evaluated. Assignments will be chosen in a fashion that are conducive to more effective control. Authority and command systems work better in environments which are more predictable and can be directed with less investment in information. Routine tasks are the comparative advantage of a bureaucracy and its activities can be expected to reflect that."

Williamson (1975, p. 201) has also emphasized the inherent tension between hierarchical bureaucratic organizations and entrepreneurial activity, "Were it that large firms could compensate internal entrepreneurial activity in ways approximating that of the market, the large firm need experience no disadvantage in entrepreneurial respects. Violating the congruency between hierarchical position and compensation appears to generate bureaucratic strains, however, and is greatly complicated by the problem of accurately imputing causality." This leads Williamson (1975, pp. 205–206) to conclude that,

I am inclined to regard the early stage innovative disabilities of large size as serious and propose the following hypothesis: An efficient procedure by which to introduce new products is for the initial development and market testing to be performed by independent inventors and small firms (perhaps new entrants) in an industry, the successful developments then to be acquired, possibly through licensing or merger, for subsequent marketing by a large multidivision enterprise ... Put differently, a division of effort between the new product innovation process on the one hand, and the management of proven resources on the other may well be efficient.

The degree to which agents and incumbent firms are confronted with knowledge asymmetries and agency problems with respect to seeking out new economic knowledge and (potential) innovative activity would not be expected to be constant across industries. This is because the underlying knowledge conditions vary from industry to industry. In some industries new economic knowledge generating innovative activity tends to be relatively routine and can be processed within the context of incumbent hierarchical bureaucracies. In other industries, however, innovations tend to come from knowledge that is not of a routine nature and therefore tends to be rejected by the hierarchical bureaucracies of incumbent corporations. Nelson and Winter (1974, 1978, and 1982) described these different underlying knowledge conditions as reflecting two distinct technological regimes—the entrepreneurial and routinized technological regimes: "An entrepreneurial regime is one that is favorable to innovative entry and unfavourable to innovative activity by established firms; a routinized regime is one in which the conditions are the other way around" (Winter, 1984, p. 297). At least some empirical evidence was provided by Acs and Audretsch (1987, 1988, and 1990) supporting the existence of these two distinct technological regimes.

Gort and Klepper (1982) posited, and found evidence, that the relative innovative advantage between newly established enterprises and incumbent firms depends on the source of information generating innovative activity. If information based on nontransferable experience in the market is an important input in generating innovative activity, then incumbent firms will tend to have the innovative advantage over new firms. This is consistent with Winter's (1984) notion of the routinized regime, where the accumulated stock of nontransferable information is the product of experience within the market, which firms outside of the industry, by definition, cannot possess.

By contrast, when information outside of the routines practiced by the incumbent firms is a relatively important input in generating innovative activity, newly established firms will tend to have the innovative advantage over the incumbent firms. Arrow (1962), Mueller (1976), and Williamson (1975) have all emphasized that when such information created outside of the incumbent firms cannot be easily transferred to those incumbent firms—presumably due to the type of agency and bureaucracy problems analyzed above—the holder of such knowledge must enter the industry to exploit the market value of her or his knowledge.

Thus, when the underlying knowledge conditions are better characterized by the routinized technological regime, there is likely to be relatively little divergence in the evaluation of the expected value of a (potential) innovation between the inventor and the decisionmaking bureaucracy of the firm. Under the routinized regime a great incentive for agents to start their own firms will not exist, at least not for the reason of doing something differently. When the underlying knowledge conditions more closely adhere to the entrepreneurial technological regime, however, a divergence in beliefs between the agent and the principal regarding the expected value of a (potential) innovation is more likely to emerge. Therefore, it is under the entrepreneurial regime where the startup of new firms is likely to play a more important role, presumably as a result of the motivation to appropriate the value of economic knowledge; due to agency problems, this knowledge cannot be easily and costlessly transferred to the incumbent enterprise.

The analytical framework supporting the decision of how best to appropriate the value of new economic knowledge confronting an individual economic agent seems useful when considering the actual decision to start a new firm taken by entrepreneurs. For example, Chester Carlsson started Xerox after his proposal to produce a (new) copy machine was rejected by Kodak. Kodak based its decision on the premise that the new copy machine would not earn very much money, and, in any case, Kodak was in a different line of business—photography. It is perhaps no small irony that this same entrepreneurial startup, Xerox, decades later turned down a proposal from Steven Jobs to produce and market a personal computer, because they did not think that a personal computer would sell, and, in any case, they were in a different line of business—copy machines (Carrol, 1993). After seventeen other companies turned down Jobs for virtually identical reasons, including IBM and Hewlett Packard, Jobs resorted to starting his own company, Apple Computer (Rose, 1989).

Similarly, IBM turned down an offer from Bill Gates, "the chance to buy ten percent of Microsoft for a song in 1986, a missed opportunity that would cost $3 billion today."[15] IBM reached its decision on the grounds that "neither Gates nor any of his band of thirty some employees had anything approaching the credentials or personal characteristics required to work at IBM."[16] In fact, even as recently as 1991, IBM clung to the belief, reflected in an executive's memo, that "the technical superiority of IBM's OS/2 and Presentation Manager over DOS and Windows 3.0 is universally unquestioned" (Ichbiah and Knepper, 1993, p. 244).

Divergences in beliefs with respect to the value of a new idea need not be restricted to what is formally known as a product or even a process innovation. Rather, the fact that economic agents choose to start a new firm due to divergences in the expected value of an idea applies to the sphere of managerial style and organization as well. One of the most vivid examples involves Bob Noyce, who founded Intel. Noyce had been employed by Fairchild Semiconductor, which is credited with being the pio-

---

15. "System Error," The Economist, 18 September 1993, p. 99.
16. Paul Carrol, "Die Offene Schlacht," Die Zeit, No. 39, 24 September 1993, p. 18.

neering semiconductor firm. In 1957, Noyce and seven other engineers quit en masse from Schockley Semiconductor to form Fairchild Semiconductor, an enterprise that in turn is considered the start of what is today known as Silicon Valley (Cringley, 1993, p. 36). Although Fairchild Semiconductor had "possibly the most potent management and technical team ever assembled" (Gilder, 1989, p. 89), "Noyce couldn't get Fairchild's eastern owners to accept the idea that stock options should be part of compensation for all employees, not just for management. He wanted to tie everyone, from janitors to bosses, into the overall success of the company … This management style still sets the standard for every computer, software, and semiconductor company in the Valley today … Every CEO still wants to think that the place is being run the way Bob Noyce would have run it" (Cringley, 1993, p. 39). That is, Noyce's vision of a firm excluded the dress codes, reserved parking places, closed offices, and executive dining rooms, along with the other trappings of status that were standard in virtually every hierarchical and bureaucratic U.S. corporation. But when he tried to impress this vision upon the owners of Fairchild Semiconductor,[17] he was flatly rejected. The formation of Intel in 1968 was the ultimate result of the divergence in beliefs about how to organize and manage the firm.

The key development at Intel was the microprocessor, which has been described as a computer on a chip, in that it has a central processing unit (CPU), is programmable, and could readily be connected to memory chips and input-output devices. When Ted Hoff approached IBM and DEC with his new microprocessor in the late 1960s, "IBM and DEC decided there was no market. They could not imagine why anyone would need or want a small computer; if people wanted to use a computer, they could hook into time-sharing systems" (Palfreman and Swade, 1991, p. 108).

3.5 New-Firm Startups Over Time and Across Industries

Studies examining the determinants of entry generally suffer from two well-known limitations. First, while several notable exceptions exist (Dunne, Roberts, and Samuelson, 1988 and 1989), the most common measure of entry used in studies attempting to empirically identify the determinants of entry has been the change in the number of firms over a given period, or what has become referred to as "net entry."[18] Measuring the change in the

---

17. Fairchild Semiconductor was actually controlled by an eastern firm, Fairchild Camera and Instrument of Syosset, New York.
18. For examples of this literature, see Orr (1974), Duetsch (1984), and Baldwin and Gorecki (1985, 1987, and 1989).

number of firms does not account for enterprises that exited from the industry during the relevant time period. That is, given an amount of gross entry, the measure of net entry will increase as the number of exits from the industry decreases. Thus it is quite conceivable that an industry could have a negative amount of net entry, if many firms actually entered the industry (i.e., if gross entry was positive), but even more firms exited from the industry. Because the pattern of industry exits varies across industries, the extent to which net entry deviates from actual gross entry will also vary substantially from industry to industry.

The second limitation is that entry has typically been measured over a single time period. Although it has been possible to measure the number of new-firm startups at the aggregate macroeconomic level (Highfield and Smiley, 1987), it has not been systematically done at the disaggregated industry level.[19]

These two limitations have made it virtually impossible to disentangle the macroeconomic influences on new-firm startups from the microeconomic influences. All that can be concluded from the existing literature is that both are probably important. To overcome these traditional data limitations, I rely upon the U.S. Small Business Administration's Small Business Data Base (SBDB), which was documented in chapter 2. The annual number of new-firm startups is aggregated to major manufacturing sectors and shown for alternate years between 1976 and 1986 in table 3.1. The share of the total number of enterprises and in the sector accounted for by new-firm startups is listed in parentheses. Three major points from table 3.1 should be emphasized. First, the number of new-firm startups and their share of the total number of enterprises vary considerably across manufacturing sectors.

Second, the number of startups varies substantially from year to year. That is, in 1976 there were 11,154 new-firm startups in all of U.S. manufacturing; this fell by nearly one-quarter to 8,525 startups in 1980, and by nearly two-thirds to 4,239 in 1982. By 1984 the number of manufacturing startups had more than doubled to 10,055, which was nearly again at the 1976 and 1978 levels. This volatility in the number of new-firm startups is attributable, at least to some extent, to macroeconomic fluctuations. This is reflected by the fluctuations in annual growth rates of real gross national product (GNP) of 4.9 percent in 1976, 5.3 percent in 1978, −0.2 percent

19. Yamawaki (1991) examines the determinants of net entry into 135 three-digit Japanese manufacturing industries for five one-year periods between 1980 and 1984. However, he was not able to identify new-firm startups from his measure of net entry.

in 1980, -2.5 percent in 1982, 6.8 percent in 1984, and 2.8 percent in 1986.[20] The extent of startup activity for manufacturing as a whole corresponds quite closely to these macroeconomic fluctuations. In addition, there is also a clear tendency for the number of startups within each manufacturing sector to reflect the phase of the business cycle.

The third major point from table 3.1 is that, although no industrial sector is immune from the influences of macroeconomic fluctuations, the impact varies considerably from sector to sector. New-firm startups in certain sectors, such as petroleum, textiles and apparel, and communications are apparently quite susceptible to the prevailing phase of the business cycle, at least over this period of time. By contrast, in the computer and food sectors, the number of startups seems to be less vulnerable to macroeconomic fluctuations. Just as the strong intertemporal tendency toward fewer startups in the transportation (other) sector probably reflects a longer-term decline, the pronounced tendency toward an increase in the number of startups in computers seems to suggest long-term sectorial expansion.

3.6   The Model

The dependent variable in the model to be estimated is based on the panel of data described in section 3.5, in which the unit of observation is the number of new-firm startups in a given four-digit SIC industry for a given year over the period 1976–1986, for alternate years. The theory from section 3.4 of this chapter suggests that the propensity for new firms to be started will be shaped by the underlying technological regime. But that is not to say that the technological regime is the only factor influencing new-firm startups. A rich and expansive literature has developed linking the entry of firms to the existence of scale economies and capital intensity.[21] This literature points to an immediate application to the model of an agent and bureaucratic hierarchy deciding how to deal with new economic information. The greater the extent of scale economies and capital requirements for establishing a new firm, the higher the cost will be to the agent for starting a new firm. That is, for any given gap in the expected value of a (potential) innovation arising between the agent and the decisionmaking bureaucracy of the incumbent firm, the agent will be less likely to decide to start a new firm as the startup costs rise.

---

20. The annual growth rates of real gross national product are from the U.S. Department of Commerce, Bureau of Economic Analysis.

21. For recent examples, see the individual country studies contained in Geroski and Schwalbach (1991) as well as Siegfried and Evans (1992).

Table 3.1
New-firm startups by industrial sector

	1976	1978	1980	1982	1984	1986
Food	474	481	374	209	480	535
	(2.53)	(2.67)	(2.15)	(1.22)	(2.79)	(3.09)
Textiles and apparel	1,172	1,254	854	491	1,026	992
	(4.03)	(4.20)	(2.95)	(1.69)	(3.41)	(3.34)
Lumber and furniture	1,325	1,375	868	425	1,060	1,106
	(3.71)	(3.70)	(2.28)	(1.12)	(2.75)	(2.79)
Paper	126	191	101	50	149	152
	(2.97)	(4.24)	(2.20)	(1.11)	(3.19)	(3.15)
Chemicals	322	390	384	164	332	335
	(2.95)	(3.52)	(2.54)	(1.45)	(2.85)	(2.83)
Industrial	91	99	98	41	85	84
	(3.62)	(3.76)	(3.69)	(1.55)	(3.12)	(3.09)
Drugs and medicinals	34	54	22	26	48	49
	(2.75)	(4.47)	(1.82)	(2.11)	(3.60)	(3.50)
Other	123	154	116	65	130	138
	(2.39)	(3.00)	(2.24)	(1.23)	(2.42)	(2.52)
Petroleum	41	42	57	11	43	46
	(3.21)	(3.16)	(4.01)	(0.76)	(3.02)	(3.17)
Rubber	430	469	312	158	382	385
	(4.72)	(4.78)	(2.97)	(1.44)	(3.26)	(3.18)
Stone, clay, and glass	545	493	292	133	337	358
	(3.86)	(3.41)	(2.00)	(0.93)	(2.41)	(2.58)
Primary metals	168	179	141	79	195	201
	(2.97)	(3.07)	(2.36)	(1.32)	(3.22)	(3.25)
Ferrous metals	85	90	61	45	102	110
	(3.21)	(3.28)	(2.24)	(1.67)	(3.70)	(3.80)
Nonferrous metals	83	89	80	34	93	91
	(2.76)	(2.89)	(2.47)	(1.04)	(2.82)	(2.76)
Fabricated metal products	962	1,042	782	362	913	877
	(3.19)	(3.30)	(2.37)	(1.07)	(2.65)	(2.52)
Machinery	1,519	1,731	1,407	586	1,433	1,314
	(3.14)	(3.38)	(2.60)	(1.02)	(2.43)	(2.22)
Office and computers	50	66	62	43	118	100
	(4.73)	(5.27)	(4.14)	(2.21)	(4.58)	(3.64)
Other machinery, non-electrical	1,469	1,665	1,345	543	1,315	1,214
	(3.10)	(3.34)	(2.56)	(0.98)	(2.33)	(2.15)
Electrical equipment	635	620	461	274	665	606
	(4.41)	(3.98)	(2.88)	(1.62)	(3.63)	(3.21)
Radio and TV equipment	79	82	53	21	43	49
	(5.02)	(4.63)	(3.00)	(1.15)	(2.38)	(2.73)
Communications equipment	128	94	74	48	168	119
	(5.27)	(3.59)	(2.77)	(1.62)	(5.02)	(3.40)
Electronic components	193	204	163	110	233	211
	(4.83)	(4.64)	(3.40)	(2.10)	(3.98)	(3.46)
Other	235	240	171	95	221	227
	(3.67)	(3.54)	(2.52)	(1.39)	(3.03)	(3.04)

Table 3.1 (cont.)

	1976	1978	1980	1982	1984	1986
Motor vehicles	147	149	116	57	147	148
	(4.55)	(4.31)	(3.11)	(1.49)	(3.62)	(3.33)
Other transport equipment	247	250	142	76	191	127
	(5.31)	(5.23)	(3.17)	(1.76)	(4.30)	(2.99)
Aircraft and missiles	26	36	26	13	33	42
	(2.50)	(3.24)	(2.09)	(0.94)	(2.19)	(2.68)
Instruments	312	323	226	160	308	353
	(3.94)	(3.72)	(2.41)	(1.60)	(2.79)	(3.01)
Scientific and measuring	130	120	104	66	145	141
	(4.56)	(3.63)	(2.76)	(1.55)	(2.99)	(2.72)
Optical, surgical, and photographic	182	203	122	94	163	212
	(3.59)	(3.78)	(2.18)	(1.63)	(2.63)	(3.24)
Other manufacturing	2,703	2,703	2,082	1,081	2,361	2,435
	(3.62)	(3.48)	(2.67)	(1.35)	(2.81)	(2.82)
Total manufacturing	11,154	11,728	8,525	4,329	10,055	10,012
	(3.56)	(3.60)	(2.56)	(1.27)	(2.86)	(2.80)

Source: SBIDB.
Note: The share (percentage) of the total number of firms accounted for by new-firm startups is indicated in the parentheses.

To measure the extent to which scale economies exist in an industry (Caves and Porter, 1977), we rely on a common proxy measure of the minimum efficient scale (MES), developed and applied by Comanor and Wilson (1967), who measured the MES as the mean size of the largest plants accounting for one-half of the industry value-of-shipments. Along with the 1977 proxy for scale economies, we include a measure of the 1977 capital intensity, defined as gross assets divided by the labor force.[22]

As mentioned in section 3.4, a second traditional explanation for why entry varies across industries has been variations in expected profitability. Although expected profitability is virtually impossible to measure, it has been generally positively associated with industries experiencing higher growth rates (Bradburd and Caves, 1982). Thus we measure industry growth as the annual percentage change in value-of-shipments. Presumably the extent of new-firm startups will be greater in industries exhibiting greater rates of growth.

---

22. White (1982) points out that higher capital-labor ratios tend to be associated with greater scale economies. This is partially because capital equipment tends to be "lumpy" in nature. Also, by enabling firms to take advantage of increased specialization and greater rates of utilization, the use of larger machines tends to reduce costs per unit of output.

Although the above measures have been the main focus of most prior studies focusing on the entry behavior of firms, it was argued in section 3.4 that the underlying knowledge conditions that shape the decisionmaking process at the level of the individual economic agent to choose between pursuing an innovation within an incumbent firm or starting a new firm results in a propensity for people to start firms in a manner that systematically reflects the underlying technological regime. While the concept of technological regimes does not lend itself to precise measurement, the major conclusion of Acs and Audretsch (1987, 1988, and 1990) was that the existence of these distinct regimes can be inferred by the extent to which small firms are able to innovate relative to the total amount of innovative activity in an industry. That is, when the small-firm innovation rate is high relative to the total innovation rate, the technological and knowledge conditions are more likely to reflect the entrepreneurial regime. The routinized regime is more likely to exhibit a low small-firm innovation rate relative to the total innovation rate.

Using the innovation data base described in chapter 2, the total innovation rate is defined as the total number of innovations recorded in 1982 divided by industry employment. The small-firm innovation rate is defined as the number of innovations contributed by firms with fewer than 500 employees divided by small-firm employment. The rates are used to standardize the amount of innovative and small-firm innovative activity in an industry for the size of that industry (as Acs and Audretsch do in their 1987 and 1990 studies). Since high small-firm innovation rates, given a total innovation rate, presumably reflect the entrepreneurial regime, the small-firm innovation rate is expected to have a positive influence on new-firm startups. By contrast, a high total innovation rate, given a small-firm innovation rate, which reflects the routinized regime, would be expected to lead to a lower number of new-firm startups.

Studies by Yamawaki (1991) and Highfield and Smiley (1987) have shown that the extent of entry is influenced by the business cycle. And certainly table 3.1 indicates that new-firm startups tend to exhibit procyclical tendencies. To capture these influences for a data set that contains a time series element, we include three measures that typically reflect the stage of the business cycle—macroeconomic growth, the interest rate, and the unemployment rate. To measure macroeconomic growth, the annual percentage change in real GNP is used. The average three-month interest rate paid on U.S. treasury bills should reflect the cost of capital. These three measures are taken from the 1989 *Economic Report of the President*. Both the growth rate of real GNP and the unemployment rate are expected to exert

Table 3.2
Regression results for new-firm startups

	(1)	(2)
Scale economies$_{(i)}$	0.043	0.004
	(5.27)**	(0.39)
Capital intensity$_{(i)}$	0.245	0.243
	(5.83)**	(5.63)**
Total innovation rate$_{(i)}$	−0.094	−0.098
	(−2.27)**	(−1.86)*
Small-firm innovation rate$_{(i)}$	6.002	4.263
	(2.45)**	(1.86)*
Industry growth$_{(it)}$	0.496	0.750
	(0.46)	(0.70)
Macroeconomic growth$_{(t)}$	0.576	0.573
	(5.59)**	(5.43)*
Interest rate$_{(t)}$	−0.437	−0.432
	(−2.88)**	(−2.77)**
Unemployment$_{(t)}$	−1.626	−1.655
	(−5.24)**	(−5.20)**
Industry sales$_{(it)}$	0.147	—
	(10.57)	
R^2	0.121	0.081
F	37.027**	26.702**
Sample size	2442	2442

Note: t-statistics listed in parentheses.
*Statistically significant at the 90 percent level of confidence for a two-tailed test.
**Statistically significant at the 95 percent level of confidence for a two-tailed test.

a positive influence on new-firm startups, and the interest rate is expected to be negatively related to the number of startups.

It should be emphasized that although these macroeconomic variables vary over time—but not across industries for any given year—most of the industry-specific variables are measured only at one point in time. It is implicitly assumed that variables such as the total innovation rate and the small-firm innovation rate, along with the measures of capital intensity and scale economies in an industry are invariant over a relatively short time period. Only the measure of industry growth varies over time and across industries.

3.7 Results

The regression results based on pooled cross-section estimation using the number of new-firm startups in each industry for each year as the dependent variable are reported in table 3.2. It should be emphasized that the subscript i denotes variables that are measured only at one point in time within a cross-sectional context, while the subscript t denotes those variables that are constant across industries but vary over time. Those variables with a subscript it have both industry- and time-specific components. Because the dependent variable, the number of new-firm startups for a particular industry in a given year, does not control for variations in market size, an additional variable—industry value-of-shipments—is included in the first equation to account for variations in size across industries.

There is no evidence that the existence of scale economies or capital intensity serves to deter the startup of new firms. Although this result is somewhat startling, it is certainly consistent with the same findings in a number of the individual country studies included in Geroski and Schwalbach (1991), as well as in Acs and Audretsch (1989a, 1989b, and 1990, chapter 5), Austin and Rosenbaum (1990), and Siegfried and Evans (1992).

The regression results are consistent with the central hypothesis of this chapter—that new-firm startups are shaped by the underlying knowledge conditions in an industry. As the negative and statistically significant coefficient of the total innovation rate and the positive and statistically significant coefficient of the small-firm innovation rate indicate, new-firm startups tend to be lower in industries that are best characterized by the routinized regime—that is, where the overall innovation rate of the industry is high but the small-firm innovation rate is low. On the other hand, new-firm startups tend to be greater in industries that are best characterized by the entrepreneurial regime, where for any given level of innovative output, the small-firm innovation rate is particularly high.

Contrary to the findings in most of the traditional studies linking entry to market structure (Orr, 1974 and Geroski and Schwalbach, 1991), new-firm startups are not significantly influenced by the growth rate at the industry level. However, macroeconomic growth clearly influences startup activity. In fact, all of the variables reflecting the business cycle influence new-firm startups. The startup of new firms is found to be greater during periods of strong macroeconomic growth and low unemployment. At the same time, high interest rates, presumably reflecting the cost of capital, are found to exert a negative influence on startup activity.

3.8   Conclusions

Neither the theory nor the results of this chapter contradict previous studies linking the entry behavior of new firms to industry specific characteristics. Indeed, our findings that growth is an important determinant of entry (albeit at the aggregated macroeconomic level and not at the disaggregated industry level) are certainly consistent with the conclusions of virtually every study in the literature. We have argued here, however, that there is another industry-specific characteristic that shapes entry behavior that has generally been overlooked in the literature—the knowledge conditions underlying the industry. It is the existence of asymmetric information in the context of agency costs and bureaucratic decisionmaking that leads agents to value an anticipated innovation differently from the decisionmaking bureaucracy of an incumbent organization. But the extent to which asymmetric information between agents and principals exists is not at all constant across industries. Rather, these underlying knowledge conditions vary from industry to industry and can be characterized alternatively by the routinized technological regime and the entrepreneurial technological regime.

The evidence from a large panel data set used throughout this book lends support to the hypothesis that the startup of new firms is influenced by the underlying knowledge conditions or what has been termed as the technological regime. Because in industries better characterized by the routinized regime, new-firm startups tend to be less important. Presumably in these industries there is less divergence in beliefs about the expected value of an anticipated innovation. Under the routinized regime innovative activity tends to occur within the incumbent enterprises, and there is less of an incentive for an agent to start a new firm to exploit the expected value of her or his economic knowledge.

By contrast, under the entrepreneurial regime asymmetric information leads to a divergence in beliefs regarding the expected value of anticipated innovations. Thus it is under the entrepreneurial regime that agents resort to starting a new firm in order to appropriate the expected value of their knowledge. The findings of this chapter are consistent with this view because new-firm startups are significantly greater in industries characterized by the entrepreneurial regime than in industries characterized by the routinized regime.

The industrial organization literature has generally considered entry to be an important economic phenomenon because it is the mechanism by which market equilibrium is restored. The focus has been on firms which, by entering, restore prices and profits back to their equilibrium levels of output. Under this view, entry is about business as usual, it is just that the new entrant supplies more of it. By contrast, in this chapter I have shifted the focus away from firm to individual economic agents confronted by maximizing the value of new economic knowledge. Because new economic knowledge is not only imperfect but also asymmetric, agents must decide whether to pursue their anticipated innovation within the boundaries of an incumbent enterprise or start a new firm.

Focusing on the individual possessing uncertain knowledge leads to an additional economic role for the new entrant—not just to equilibrate the market by increasing the supply of the product already produced by the incumbent firms—but rather by doing something different and thereby serving as an agent of change. This role is reminiscent of the concepts of "voice" and "exit" introduced and popularized by Albert O. Hirschman (1970). An agent in possession of new economic knowledge may be unable to exercise "voice" in the context of the decisionmaking hierarchy of an incumbent firm, that is, to actualize her potential innovation within the boundaries of an incumbent enterprise. This drives her to choose instead to exercise "exit"—out of the incumbent enterprise, and ultimately to start a new business entity.

An important insight is that the implicit model of technological change currently dominating the literature, the model of the knowledge production function introduced by Griliches (1979)—that firms exogenously exist and then engage in the pursuit of new knowledge—is perhaps somewhat misguided, or in any case not complete. It is because new knowledge held by individual agents, which here is treated as exogenous, is not being utilized within the context of the incumbent enterprises, that endogenously leads economic agents to the decision to start a new firm.

4   Survival and Growth

4.1   Introduction

Two empirical results that have emerged consistently in the literature pose something of a puzzle to industrial organization economists. The first, which has received considerable attention at least since the seminal study by Herbert Simon and Charles Bonini (1958) more than three decades ago, is the persistence of an asymmetric firm-size distribution predominated by small enterprises. Ijiri and Simon (1977, p. 2) characterize this "regularity in social phenomena that is both striking and observable in a number of quite diverse situations. It is a regularity in the size distribution of firms."[1] In fact, virtually no other economic phenomenon has persisted as consistently as the skewed asymmetric firm-size distribution. Not only is it almost identical across every manufacturing industry, but it has remained strikingly constant over time (at least since the Second World War) and even across developed industrialized nations (Acs and Audretsch, 1993).

The persistence of this skewed asymmetric firm-size distribution is consistent with the common observation in industrial organization that the bulk of firms in most industries are operating at a suboptimal level of output.[2] The second puzzling result, which is somewhat more tentative, is the emergence of a number of studies—including chapter 3 in this book—that have found that the entry of new firms into an industry is apparently not

---

1. Ijiri and Simon (1977, pp. 1–2) observe that, "Nature, as it presents itself to the physical scientist, is full of clearly defined patterns ... The patterns that have been discovered in social phenomena are much less neat. To be sure, economics has evolved a highly sophisticated body of mathematical laws, but for the most part, these laws bear a rather distinct relation to empirical phenomena ... Hence, on those occasions when a social phenomenon appears to exhibit some of the same simplicity and regularity of pattern as is seen so commonly in physics, it is bound to excite interest and attention."
2. See, for examples, the studies by Weiss (1963 and 1976), Scherer (1973), and Pratten (1971).

substantially deterred in industries where scale economies play an important role.[3]

These findings raise two troubling questions, "Why is it that the preponderance of enterprises in virtually every U.S. manufacturing industry are small, and how are they able to remain viable if so many of them are operating at a suboptimal scale of output?", and "Why are entrepreneurs not more noticeably deterred from entering industries characterized by substantial scale economies?"

The purpose of this chapter is to shed some light on these questions, not by examining the entry process itself—as was done in chapter 3—but rather by investigating what happens to new firms subsequent to entering. By focusing on the post-entry performance of new firms, the process of firm selection and industry evolution over time can be inferred. In particular, I focus on the ability of new firms to grow and survive over time subsequent to their startup.

The theory of firm selection and industry evolution, first proposed by Jovanovic (1982), is used in the second section of this chapter to deduce four major hypotheses about the factors shaping the post-entry performance of new firms. These hypotheses generally revolve around the pressure exerted on new firms to grow in order to close the gap between their startup size and an efficient scale of operations, as well as around the technological environment, which dictates the likelihood that the firm will be producing, or even attempting to produce, a viable product. In the third section I employ the SBDB longitudinal data base to examine the growth and survival patterns of new firms in U.S. manufacturing established in 1976. A logit regression model for new-firm survival and growth rate equations is estimated in the fourth section to test the four major hypotheses about the factors determining new-firm growth and survival.

In the fifth section the semiparametric hazard duration model is estimated, enabling me to test the hypothesis that the rate of hazard confronting new establishments is influenced not only by their evolution over time, but also by the extent of scale economies, the technological environment, as well as particular establishment characteristics, such as startup size and ownership structure.

Finally, in the sixth section a summary and conclusions are provided. The answer to the question, "What happens to new businesses subsequent to entry?" is "It depends." The results of this chapter make it clear that key

---

3. In addition to chapter 3, see for examples Acs and Audretsch (1989a, 1989b, and 1990, chapter 5), Siegfried and Evans (1992), Austin and Rosenbaum (1990), and a number of the country studies contained in Geroski and Schwalbach (1991), as summarized in Cable and Schwalbach (1991).

elements of industry evolution—the likelihood of survival, rate of growth, and rate of hazard confronting new businesses—are invariably shaped by specific factors external to the establishment, such as the presence of scale economies and the technological environment, as well as factors internal to the establishment, such as the startup size and the ownership structure. In particular, I find considerable evidence supporting the dynamic view of the selection process of new firms. Although an asymmetric firm-size distribution comprised of mostly small firms may persist over time, the individual suboptimal scale firms themselves tend not to persist over time. Either they succeed and grow, thereby reducing scale disadvantages, or they face a diminished likelihood of survival. Firm size and the extent of scale economies in an industry apparently play key roles in this dynamic process, because they determine the extent to which new firms need to grow in order to become viable enterprises and ultimately survive.

4.2   Firm Selection

One of the main points emerging from the previous chapter is that knowledge asymmetries can result in individual agents deciding to start a new firm. Divergences in the expected value regarding new knowledge suggest that some agents will value a given idea (potential innovation) more than other agents, including those involved in the decisionmaking process of incumbent firms. When such divergences occur, and ultimately an agent chooses to exercise what Albert O. Hirschman (1970) has termed as "exit" rather than "voice," and depart from an incumbent firm to launch a new enterprise, who is right, the departing agents or those agents in the organizational hierarchy who, by assigning the new idea a relatively low value, have effectively driven the agent with the potential innovation away? Ex post the answer may not be too difficult. But given the uncertainty inherent in new knowledge, the answer is anything but easy a priori.

Thus, when a new firm is launched, its prospects are shrouded in uncertainty. If the new firm is built around a new idea, i.e., potential innovation, it is uncertain whether there is sufficient demand for the new idea or if some competitor will have the same or even a superior idea. Even if the new firm is formed to be an exact replica of a successful incumbent enterprise, it is uncertain whether sufficient demand for a new clone, or even for the existing incumbent, will prevail in the future. Tastes can change. And new ideas emerging from other firms will certainly influence those tastes.

Finally, an additional layer of uncertainty pervades a new enterprise. It is not known how competent the new firm really is, in terms of management, organization, and workforce. At least incumbent enterprises know something about their underlying competencies from past experience. Which is to say that a new enterprise is burdened with uncertainty as to whether it can produce and market the intended product as well as sell it. In both cases the degree of uncertainty will typically exceed that confronting incumbent enterprises.

This initial condition of not just uncertainty, but greater degree of uncertainty vis-à-vis incumbent enterprises in the industry is captured in the theory of firm selection and industry evolution proposed by Boyan Jovanovic (1982). Jovanovic presented a model in which the new entrants, referred to as entrepreneurs by Jovanovic, face costs that are not only random but also differ across firms. A central feature of the model is that a new firm does not know what its cost function is, that is its relative efficiency, but rather discovers this through the process of learning from its actual post-entry performance. In particular, Jovanovic (1982) assumed that entrepreneurs are unsure about their ability to manage a new-firm startup and therefore their prospects for success. Although entrepreneurs may launch a new firm based on a vague sense of expected post-entry performance, they only discover their true ability—in terms of managerial competence and of having based the firm on an idea that is viable on the market—once their business is established. Those entrepreneurs who discover that their ability exceeds their expectations expand the scale of their business, whereas those discovering that their post-entry performance is less than commensurate with their expectations will contract the scale of output and possibly exit from the industry. Thus Jovanovic's (1982) model is a theory of "noisy" selection, where efficient firms grow and survive and inefficient firms decline and fail.

The role of learning in the selection process has been the subject of considerable debate. On the one hand is what has been referred to as the "Larackian" assumption that learning refers to adaptations made by the new enterprise. In this sense, those new firms that are the most flexible and adaptable will be the most successful in adjusting to whatever the demands of the market are. As Nelson and Winter (1982, p. 11) point out, "Many kinds of organizations commit resources to learning; organizations seek to copy the forms of their most successful competitors."[4] In fact, Pakes and

---

4. Merton et al. (1952) introduced several pathbreaking theories about how organizations can learn and change. And Scott (1987), Simon (1957), Simon and Bonini (1958), and Cyert and March (1963) developed general theories of decisionmaking within organizations. These theories were generally interdisciplinary, linking sociology, political science, and economics. Perow (1961 and 1967) and Thompson (1967) explored how organizations adjust to demands imposed by uncertainty in technical and environmental circumstances. Burns and Stalker (1961) argued that "bureaucratic or mechanistic systems of production

Erikson (1987) extend Jovanovic's (1982) original theory by incorporating strategies that entrepreneurs can pursue to accelerate the learning process, such as investing in knowledge-creating activities like R & D.

On the other hand is the interpretation that the role of learning is restricted to discovering if the new firm "has the right stuff" in terms of the product it is producing as well as the way it is being produced. Under this interpretation the new enterprise is not necessarily able to adapt or adjust to market conditions, but receives information based on its market performance with respect to its "fitness" in terms of meeting demand most efficiently vis-à-vis rivals. The theory of organizational ecology proposed by Michael T. Hannan and John Freeman (1989) most pointedly adheres to the notion that, "We assume that individual organizations are characterized by relative inertia in structure." That is, firms learn not in the sense that they adjust their actions as reflected by their fundamental identity and purpose, but in the sense of their perception. What is then learned is whether the firm has "the right stuff," but not how to change that "stuff."

In fact, it is not crucial for the theory in this book to distinguish between the two types of learning. But it is a theme I will return to throughout this book; because the role of learning clearly is crucial to the process of firm selection and ultimately industry evolution.

In any case, Jovanovic's (1982) theory of firm selection is particularly appealing in view of the rather startling size of most new firms. For example, in the next section of this chapter I show that the mean size of the more than 11,000 new-firm startups in U.S. manufacturing in 1976 was less than eight workers per firm. While the minimum efficient scale (MES) varies substantially across industries, and even to some degree across various product classes within any given industry,[5] the observed size of most new firms is sufficiently small to ensure that the bulk of new firms will be operating at a suboptimal scale of output. Why would an entrepreneur start a new firm that would immediately be confronted by scale disadvantages? An implication of Jovanovic's (1982) theory is that firms may begin at a small—even suboptimal scale of output—and then, if merited by subsequent performance, expand. Those firms that are successful will grow, whereas those that are not successful will remain small and may ultimately

---

tend to break down in the face of complex and changing technologies and tend to be replaced with more fluid "organic" systems of production." The contingency theory developed by Lawrence and Lorsch (1967) argues that environmental uncertainty causes different parts of an organization to seek solutions, which lead to structural change.

5. Ross and Bradburd (1988) show that there is considerable heterogeneity within four-digit SIC industries.

be forced to exit from the industry if they are operating at a suboptimal scale of output.

An important ingredient in determining whether a new firm is successful may be its ability not just to replicate the exact products and production methods of the incumbent—that is, to engage in "business as usual"—but rather to do something different from the incumbent firms—that is, to serve as an "agent of change." One of the key findings in the previous chapter was that innovation apparently is an important mechanism and motivation for the entry of new firms in an industry.

Subsequent to entering an industry, a firm must decide whether to maintain its output (Q_{it}), expand, contract, or exit.[6] Three different strands of literature have identified several major influences shaping the decision to exit an industry. The first, and most obvious strand of literature (Weiss, 1964, 1976, 1979, and 1991; and Caves et al., 1975) suggests that the probability of a business exiting will tend to increase as the gap between its level of output and the minimum efficient scale (MES) level of output increases.[7] That is, given a long-run average cost function and MES in an industry, the smaller the scale at which an enterprise operates, the greater will be its cost disadvantage. Conversely, for any business of a given size, higher levels of the MES will result in a greater cost disadvantage. As the gap between the size of the business and the MES increases, and the cost disadvantage confronting the business correspondingly increases, the likelihood of exit increases.

Of course, as a second strand of literature points out, to the extent that prices become elevated above long-run average costs in an industry, the cost disadvantage confronting a suboptimal scale business is diminished. An important finding of Bradburd and Caves (1982) is that industry growth can contribute to elevated price-cost margins. Thus the likelihood of exit for any given suboptimal scale business will tend to diminish in markets where growth is greater.

The third strand of literature points to the role that the technological environment plays in shaping the decision to exit. As Dosi (1982 and 1988) and Arrow (1962) argue, an environment characterized by more frequent innovation may also be associated with a greater amount of uncertainty regarding not only the technical nature of the product but also the demand for that product. As technological uncertainty increases, the likelihood that

---

6. Several important theoretical models have been recently introduced, including Reynolds (1988), Ghemawat and Nalebuff (1990), and Baden-Fuller (1989).

7. For example, Weiss (1976, p. 126) argues that, "In purely competitive long-run equilibrium, no suboptimal capacity should exist at all."

the business will be able to produce a viable product and ultimately be able to survive tends to decrease.

Putting these three strands together suggests that the probability of a firm remaining in business in period t, or $P(Q_{it} > 0)$, is essentially determined by the extent to which a firm is burdened with an inherent size disadvantage, and the probability of producing an innovation or some other growth-inducing activity i is

$$P(Q_{it} > 0) = f(i_{it}, c(Q_{it}) - c(Q^*)), \qquad (4.1)$$

where $c(Q_{it})$ is the average cost of producing at a scale of output Q_i, and $c(Q^*)$ is the average cost of producing at the MES level of output, or the minimum level of production required to attain the minimum average cost, Q^*. Thus, in deciding whether to remain in or exit out of the industry, a firm will weigh the extent to which it is confronted by a scale disadvantage against the likelihood of innovating or otherwise growing.

One of the main points to be emphasized is that, as firm size grows relative to the MES level of output, the more likely the firm is to decide to remain in the industry. This suggests that either an increase in the startup size of the firm or a decrease in the MES level of output should increase the likelihood of survival. It also implies that, given a level of MES output in an industry, the greater the size of the firm, the less it will need to grow in order to exhaust the potential scale economies. Notice that this hypothesis is strikingly contradictory to the more typical and traditional theory that growth will be positively related to size for new firms, since larger (new) firms are presumed to have more financial muscle (Dunkelberg and Cooper, 1990).

The rather ambiguous role of innovative activity should also be emphasized. On the one hand, a greater perceived likelihood of innovating (i) will lead the firm to remain in an industry, even if other factors, such as the gap between the firm's size and the MES level of output resulting in a cost differential of $c(Q_{it}) - c(Q_i^*)$, would otherwise have led the firm to exit out of the industry. Seen from this perspective, firms in a highly innovative environment will tend to have a lower propensity to exit, ceteris paribus, as long as the perceived likelihood of innovative activity is relatively high. On the other hand, the likelihood that the firm will actually end up producing a viable product for which there is sufficient demand will clearly be lower in more innovative environments. A paradox could be that new firms may have a greater likelihood of innovating in an industry characterized by what Scherer (1991) has termed as a high "technological opportunity class" than in an industry characterized by a low "technological opportunity class." Yet, the likelihood that the firm will emerge with a viable and marketable product is greater in the low technological opportunity class, where the product design is relatively standard and lower in the high technological opportunity class, where the product design is considerably more volatile.

That is, the actual innovative activity of the firm, I_{it}, and not the likelihood of that innovative activity, i_{it}, will ultimately shape its actual level of output in period t, Q_{it}, so that

$$Q_{it} = \overline{Q}_{it} + Q(I_t), \tag{4.2}$$

where $\overline{Q}_{it}$ is a factor of the firm's output in the previous period,

$$\overline{Q}_{it} = Q_{i0} + \lambda Q_{it-1}, \tag{4.3}$$

and Q_0 is an autonomous level of output and λ is a factor representing the portion of the previous period's output that can be maintained in the market the next period (this could be zero in some cases). Factors such as market growth presumably influence the value of λ. That is, if market growth is sufficiently high, a new firm may be able to grow enough so that $Q_{it} = Q_i^*$, even in the absence of innovative activity.

An important implication of the above process is that firms are more likely to be operating at a suboptimal scale of output if the underlying technological conditions are such that there is a greater chance of making an innovation or otherwise growing. If firms successfully learn and adapt, or are just plain lucky, they grow into viably sized enterprises. If not, they stagnate and may ultimately exit from the industry. This suggests, as we found in the previous chapter, that entry and the startup of new firms may not be greatly deterred in the presence of scale economies. As long as entrepreneurs perceive that there is some prospect for growth and ultimately survival, such entry will occur. Thus, in industries where the MES is high, it follows from the observed general small size of new-firm startups that the growth rate of the surviving firms would presumably be relatively high.

At the same time, firms not able to grow and attain the MES level of output would presumably be forced to exit from the industry, resulting in a relatively low likelihood of survival. In industries characterized by a low MES, neither the need for growth, nor the consequences of its absence are as severe, so that relatively lower growth rates but higher survival rates would be expected. Similarly, in industries where the probability of innovating is greater, more entrepreneurs may actually take a chance that they will succeed by growing into a viably sized enterprise. In such industries, one would expect that the growth of successful enterprises would be greater, but that the likelihood of success (in terms of producing the right product the most efficiently)—and therefore survival—would be correspondingly lower.

Summarizing the above arguments, the theory of firm selection leads to the following predictions, or hypotheses concerning the likelihood of survival and the growth rates of those surviving new firms:

1. Firm growth should be greater but the probability of firm survival lower in industries with higher scale economies;

2. Firm growth rates should be lower but the likelihood of firm survival greater for larger firms;

3. Firm growth should be greater but the probability of firm survival lower in industries characterized by a greater amount of innovative activity (that is, those industries in a higher technological opportunity class); and

4. Both firm growth and the likelihood of survival should be greater in high-growth industries.

4.3   Post-Entry Performance of New Firms

The greatest impediment to analyzing the post-entry performance of new firms has been the lack of longitudinal data bases that identify the actual startup and closure dates of firms. That is, although a number of studies have identified the determinants of firm entry, there have only been a handful that actually track the performance of firms subsequent to entering the industry.[8] As discussed in chapter 2, the U.S. Small Business Administration's Small Business Data Base (SBDB) both identifies the formation of new firms and establishments (plants in manufacturing) as well as tracks their subsequent performance over time, and thus is well suited for such a longitudinal study.

The most basic unit of observation in the SBDB is the establishment, which is defined as a particular economic entity operating at a specific and single geographic location. Although most establishments, especially new ones, are legally independent and therefore represent enterprises or firms, the SBDB identifies the legal status of others as being owned by a parent firm through either a branch or subsidiary relationship. An important

---

8. See, for examples, Dunne, Roberts, and Samuelson (1988 and 1989), Evans (1987a and 1987b), Phillips and Kirchhoff (1989), Mata (1994a and 1994b), Wagner (1992 and 1994), Albach (1984), Albach et al. (1984), Arrighetti (1994), Audretsch (1991), Baldwin and Gorecki (1991), Mahmood (1992), and Audretsch and Mahmood (1994 and 1995).

feature of the SBDB is that the ownership of establishments is linked to any parent firm. This makes it possible to distinguish between (1) single-establishment firms, in which case the establishment is an independent legal entity; (2) a branch or subsidiary belonging to a multi-establishment firm; or (3) the headquarters of a multi-establishment firm.

Two aspects of the dynamic post-entry performance of new firms can be identified using the SBDB—their ability to survive and grow over time. The starting point for measurement in this chapter was to extract from the SBDB all records identifying the startup of a new firm in 1976. The bulk of these firms consisted of establishments, although some are the headquarters of new multiplant firms. New establishments belonging to existing firms, either within or outside the industry in the case of diversified entry, were not extracted since these do not represent new firms. Restricting the analysis only to the startup of a new firm and not to new establishments has the advantage of controlling for the age of the firm as well as its ownership status. Just as Evans (1987a and 1987b) and Dunne, Roberts, and Samuelson (1988 and 1989) found that growth rates vary systematically with the age of the firm, Audretsch (1991), Audretsch and Mahmood (1994 and 1995), and Mahmood (1992) identified the propensity to exit as being inversely related to firm age.

Those new firms which become a legal subsidiary or branch plant belonging to another enterprise subsequent to the startup year, presumably through acquisition or merger, are left in the analysis. Removal of such records from the analysis would create a bias if the determinants of their post-entry performance, that is survival and growth, are systematically different from those for firms which remain legally independent. Also, if a firm established in 1976 subsequently exited from its initial (four-digit SIC) industry of operations and entered a new industry, it is still considered to be in existence. Thus there are two relevant outcomes in this chapter available for new firms subsequent to startup—either survival or the cessation of operations.

As table 4.1 shows, the mean size of the cohort of new firms in 1976 was about eight employees, with a fairly large standard deviation.[9] The mean size of new firms was somewhat larger for those firms still existing in 1982, 1984, and 1986 than for those new enterprises ceasing to exist within the first four years of being established. That is, those firms surviving for a longer period of time tend to exhibit a slightly larger initial startup size

---

9. It should be noted that there are actually more new-firm startups in 1976 recorded in the SBDB, but only those records containing full information about firm size in all of the years could be used.

Table 4.1
Evolution of mean firm size (employment) according to survival status of cohort (standard deviation in parentheses)

Cohort	N	Year					
		1976	1978	1980	1982	1984	1986
New-firm startups in 1976	11,314	7.63 (11.68)	—	—	—	—	—
Firms still existing in 1978	8,266	7.51 (11.74)	10.70 (19.61)	—	—	—	—
Firms still existing in 1980	6,165	7.27 (11.68)	10.57 (19.74)	12.68 (23.69)	—	—	—
Firms still existing in 1982	4,045	7.92 (12.45)	11.80 (20.29)	14.65 (25.05)	15.95 (28.02)	—	—
Firms still existing in 1984	3,099	7.98 (12.53)	12.15 (20.22)	15.63 (26.69)	17.23 (29.74)	19.27 (34.99)	—
Firms still existing in 1986	2,509	7.94 (12.48)	12.01 (19.76)	15.32 (25.91)	17.05 (29.13)	19.32 (34.64)	20.95 (37.23)

Note: Growth rate (%) from previous period listed in parentheses.

than those firms ceasing operations within several years subsequent to establishment. Table 4.1 also suggests that the mean size of firms in existence throughout the sample period tends to be greater than those not surviving. For example, in 1978 the group of firms surviving throughout the entire sample period exhibited a mean size of 12.01 employees, which is considerably greater than the mean size of 10.70 employees for all firms still in existence as of 1978. In fact, firms that survived until 1984 and 1986 were noticeably larger than those ceasing operations before 1984 in every year for which a comparison is possible.

Not only does the initial startup size of surviving firms tend to be larger, but as table 4.2 shows, the growth rates also tend to be higher. That is, between 1976 and 1980 the employment growth of all new firms averaged 74.42 percent. However, for those firms that survived throughout the entire sample period (1976–1986), the mean growth rate between 1976 and 1980 was substantially greater, 92.95 percent. There are two important trends that should be emphasized in table 4.2. First, the growth rate in each subperiod of time tends to be greater for the cohort of firms surviving the longest. Second, the growth rates tend to diminish over time for each cohort of firms still in existence. Taken together, tables 4.1 and 4.2 suggest two important features that are common among firms still surviving a decade subsequent to establishment—they tend to be slightly larger when they start and they tend to grow faster, particularly within the first few years subsequent to establishment.

Table 4.2
Mean firm growth rate (%) over time, according to survival status of cohort

Cohort	N	Period				
		1976–78	1976–80	1976–82	1976–84	1976–86
Firms still existing in 1978	8,266	12.48	—	—	—	—
Firms still existing in 1980	6,165	45.39	74.42 (19.96)	—	—	—
Firms still existing in 1982	4,045	48.99	84.97 (24.15)	101.39 (8.87)	—	—
Firms still existing in 1984	3,099	52.26	95.85 (28.64)	115.91 (10.24)	141.48 (11.84)	—
Firms still existing in 1986	2,509	51.26	92.95 (27.56)	114.74 (11.29)	143.32 (13.31)	163.85 (8.44)

Note: Growth rate (%) from previous period listed in parentheses.

The general tendencies exhibited for all new manufacturing firms in tables 4.1 and 4.2 could be the result of compositional differences across industries. That is, if industries where the propensity to survive is relatively high also tend to be comprised of large firms, then variations in firm size and survival rates across industries could result in the tendencies observed in tables 4.1 and 4.2, even if they did not hold for many, or even most industries. Thus in table 4.3 the mean size, growth, and survival of new firms established in 1976 are compared across major industrial sectors.[10] There are five important points emerging from table 4.3. First, the startup size varies somewhat across manufacturing sectors. For example, in printing the startup size is relatively low, with new firms averaging fewer than five employees, whereas in primary metals new firms had a mean startup size of nearly ten employees.

Second, the survival of new firms over both a two-year and a ten-year period varies substantially across sectors. Third, the startup size of firms in cohorts surviving throughout the entire ten-year sample period tends to be considerably greater than those firms ceasing operations. Only in four sectors—paper, printing, petroleum, and instruments—did the initial mean size of the surviving firms not exceed that of all new firms. It should be pointed out that specific industries in the paper, printing, and instrument sectors tend to be predominantly characterized by a relatively low MES. And in 1981 the petroleum industry was subjected to the removal of regulations which had promoted the existence of suboptimal capacity refineries.

---

10. The major industrial sectors correspond to two-digit SIC industries. The tobacco sector (SIC 21) has been excluded from table 4.3 due to a deficiency of observations.

Fourth, the mean growth rates of firms vary considerably across sectors, both within two years subsequent to startup, as well as within a decade of being established. Thus, the fifth point from table 4.3 is that the variation in the 1986 mean size of surviving firms across sectors is much greater than the variation in either the 1976 mean startup size or the mean size of the survivors in 1978. From table 4.3 it can be concluded that the importance of startup size and subsequent growth to the likelihood of survival varies considerably across industrial sectors. This points to the key role that industry-specific characteristics play in shaping the post-entry performance of new firms.

4.4   Firm Growth and Survival

To test the four main hypotheses stated at the end of section 4.2, the post-entry performance of new firms established in 1976 is measured over two relatively short-run time periods, 1976–1978 and 1976–1980, and three relatively long-run time periods, 1976–1982, 1976–1984, and 1976–1986. This was done for several reasons. First, in the major studies relating firm size to firm growth, it has never been clear what the appropriate time span should be (Evans, 1987a and 1987b; Hall, 1987; and Mansfield, 1962). Should the assumption of equal growth rates underlying Gibrat's Law be valid over a period of days, weeks, months, or years? Second, and perhaps even more important, there is no reason to assume that the evolutionary process of firm selection remains constant, at least for any given cohort of new firms. That is, at some point in time, firms that are growing will approach and even attain the MES level of output. As they approach the MES scale of output, the cost disadvantages will tend to decrease, and once they have attained it they will disappear. Thus growth as a prerequisite for survival may be something close to the rule for new and suboptimal scale firms, but this is less likely to be the case for firms that are approaching and have attained the MES level of output.

Within each of the selected time periods two regression equations are estimated. The first is an ordinary least squares (OLS) regression equation, which is estimated for growth and is defined as the firm size, measured in terms of employment, in the last year of the period divided by firm size in 1976. The second regression equation uses the logit method of estimation, and predicts the probability of the firm surviving over the sample period. Each firm established in 1976 is assigned a value of zero if it ceases operations, and one if it survives. It should be emphasized that even within each of the five time periods considered, the sample of firms included to estimate

Table 4.3
Mean size and growth (%) of 1976 startups compared in 1978 and 1986 according to industrial sector (standard deviation in parentheses)

| | 1976 | | Cohort 1978 | | | | 1986 | | | |
| | N | Size | N | 1976 size | 1978 size | Growth (%) | N | 1976 size | 1986 size | Growth (%) |
Sector										
Food	475	8.92 (13.18)	320	8.42 (12.60)	9.73 (13.42)	15.56	78	9.58 (15.72)	14.78 (21.30)	54.28
Textiles	310	12.54 (16.91)	209	12.17 (16.95)	19.25 (32.40)	58.17	52	14.12 (16.80)	44.86 (74.73)	218.41
Apparel	894	13.90 (17.04)	616	14.70 (17.86)	21.07 (28.89)	43.33	142	16.44 (20.62)	41.80 (60.43)	154.26
Lumber	805	7.08 (10.03)	582	6.79 (10.27)	10.08 (16.06)	48.45	171	7.87 (11.65)	17.50 (31.04)	122.36
Furniture	543	7.44 (10.51)	381	7.56 (10.38)	12.34 (25.02)	63.23	100	8.84 (13.34)	28.60 (50.31)	223.53
Paper	134	9.23 (11.09)	96	8.66 (9.50)	13.49 (14.61)	55.77	37	7.51 (7.63)	24.92 (21.18)	231.82
Printing	1,818	4.76 (6.40)	1,400	4.43 (5.42)	5.43 (6.73)	22.57	515	4.38 (4.96)	11.71 (17.57)	167.35
Chemicals	336	6.36 (8.01)	240	6.50 (8.06)	8.60 (11.05)	32.30	66	7.00 (9.27)	16.92 (22.96)	141.71
Petroleum	47	7.77 (9.95)	26	6.96 (8.94)	12.31 (19.25)	76.87	4	4.25 (2.95)	12.75 (15.77)	200.00
Rubber and plastics	442	7.43 (9.44)	333	7.53 (9.77)	11.83 (16.28)	57.10	117	8.94 (11.11)	24.20 (25.85)	170.69

Industry									
Leather	122	7.22 (11.29)	85	8.14 (9.26)	11.56 (27.38)	42.0	21	13.76 (20.36)	25.86 (37.26)	87.94
Stone, clay, glass	560	7.42 (9.91)	412	7.21 (9.26)	10.39 (27.38)	44.11	121	7.72 (9.95)	13.19 (23.13)	70.85
Primary metals	161	9.88 (13.95)	122	9.93 (15.08)	13.93 (17.39)	40.28	42	13.29 (18.27)	32.98 (38.44)	148.16
Fabricated metal products	976	7.85 (11.13)	723	7.66 (11.28)	10.57 (15.10)	37.98	239	8.97 (13.42)	18.43 (26.97)	105.46
Machinery (non-electrical)	1,535	5.79 (8.06)	1,196	5.82 (8.44)	8.51 (14.81)	46.22	452	5.86 (8.05)	17.31 (24.68)	195.39
Electrical equipment	645	6.99 (9.81)	465	6.92 (9.98)	11.13 (15.92)	60.84	116	8.59 (13.46)	37.86 (60.66)	330.75
Transportation equipment	413	7.68 (10.24)	281	7.51 (10.40)	13.24 (31.35)	76.30	56	8.62 (9.34)	18.14 (26.29)	126.18
Instruments	316	6.76 (9.32)	245	6.55 (9.01)	9.69 (13.41)	47.94	75	6.03 (6.85)	36.05 (83.01)	497.84
Miscellaneous	780	6.37 (9.30)	532	6.38 (9.44)	8.30 (17.66)	30.09	105	7.58 (10.40)	17.88 (23.37)	135.88

the OLS growth regression and the logit survival regression is not the same. This is because growth can be measured only for surviving firms, whereas the survival equations include both surviving and exiting firms. Thus there are the same number of observations, 11,322, in each of the logit regressions estimating survival, regardless of the time period, while the number of observations used to estimate firm growth declines as the number of surviving firms decreases, from 8,300 in the 1976–1978 period, to 2,534 in the 1976–1986 period.[11]

The number of employees in 1976 is taken as the size measure of the firm. As the startup size increases relative to the MES level of output, the degree to which a firm needs to grow in order to exhaust scale economies decreases. This would suggest that firm size should be positively related to the likelihood of survival but negatively related to the post-entry growth rate.

To reflect the technological opportunity class, or the degree to which technological change plays a role in the industry, I include the total innovation rate, which was introduced and defined in the previous chapter as the number of innovations made in a four-digit SIC industry in 1982 divided by employment (thousands). Measurement of the MES level of output is similarly identical to that used in chapter 3, where I adapted the standard Comanor-Wilson proxy, defined as the mean size of the largest plants in each industry accounting for one-half of the industry value-of-shipments, 1977. As the MES increases, the more a firm of any given size must grow in order to realize maximum efficiency. Thus a positive relationship is expected to emerge between the proxy measure of the MES level of output and post-entry firm growth. At the same time, the economic consequences of not growing become greater for a firm of a given size as the MES increases. This suggests that the likelihood of survival should be negatively related to the extent of scale economies in the industry.

An important qualification of the impact that scale economies have on post-entry performance is that to the extent that capital investments represent sunk costs, firms will have a lower propensity to exit from industries that are capital intensive (Caves and Porter, 1976). A positive relationship would therefore be expected to emerge between the 1977 capital-labor ratio and the likelihood of survival. At the same time, if the propensity to exit tends to decrease with capital intensity, ceteris paribus, then the

---

11. It should be noted that the number of observations used to estimate the regression equations in tables 4.4 and 4.5 do not match the number of observations in tables 4.1, 4.2, and 4.3, due to observations for firms in four-digit SIC industries for which there are not corresponding data for the explanatory variables.

growth rate should be negatively related to capital intensity. That is, the cohort of firms electing not to exit out of the industry would include some low-growth firms that, due to sunk investments, decide to remain in the industry even though they would have exited in the absence of such sunk investments. Thus the overall effect should be to lower the growth rate observed for surviving enterprises in industries where capital intensity is relatively high, after controlling for the extent of scale economies.

On the presumption that all firms in an industry will tend to grow along with high rates of industry growth, both the probability of survival and the post-entry firm growth rates should be positively related to industry growth. Industry growth is measured as the value-of-shipments at the end of the relevant time period divided by 1976 value-of-shipments. It should be pointed out that this measure changes along with the relevant time period considered.

As was described in section 4.3, although none of the cohort of new firms are legally owned by another entity at the beginning of the time period, some of the 1976 new-firm startups are in fact the headquarters for a new multiplant firm. The post-entry performance of such firms may vary for a number of reasons. First, the post-entry performance of the entire firm will be influenced by the performance in each of the separate establishments, not all of which may be in the same industry. Second, although such multiplant firms are listed as new startups, there is a greater chance that they are the result of some reorganizational activity, and that at least some of them may in fact be "less new" than the single-establishment startups. Third, and perhaps most important, the number of employees for the entire firm entered in the "firm size" variable will actually overstate the actual size of the individual plants. That is, the gap between the MES level of output and what is recorded as the firm size will tend to be less than the actual gap between the MES level of output and the size of individual plants. The measure of firm size will tend to systematically overstate the size of the actual plants comprising the entire firm, so that the likelihood of survival will tend to be systematically lower than would be predicted by the firm size variable, while at the same time the growth rates will tend to be systematically higher. In any case, a dummy variable taking on the value of one for multiplant new firms was created to control for such cases. The systematic overstatement of firm size for multiplant enterprises should result in a negative coefficient in the survival (logit) regression and a positive coefficient in the growth rate regression.

The results for the estimated regression of new-firm growth and likelihood of survival are shown in table 4.4 for the short run (1976–78 and

Table 4.4
Regressions of new-firm growth and survival in the short run (t-statistics in parentheses)

	Time period			
	1976–1978		1976–1980	
	Growth (OLS)	Survival (Logit)	Growth (OLS)	Survival (Logit)
Size	−0.001	0.002	−0.002	0.002
	(−2.72)	(2.41)	(−2.63)	(2.69)
Total innovation rate	0.052	0.013	0.299	−0.056
	(0.64)	(0.23)	(2.10)	(−0.95)
Scale economies	0.001	−0.002	0.001	−0.007
	(3.07)	−(4.74)	(0.75)	(−4.60)
Capital intensity	0.008	0.003	0.002	0.003
	(3.05)	(2.33)	(0.38)	(1.99)
Industry growth[a]	0.153	0.222	0.51	0.392
	(1.06)	(2.19)	(3.03)	(5.74)
Multiplant dummy	0.773	−0.504	1.456	−0.490
	(4.61)	(−3.89)	(5.02)	(−3.77)
Intercept	1.393	−1.539	1.368	−1.854
	(6.99)	(−10.96)	(5.09)	(−16.51)
R^2	0.059	—	0.080	—
F	9.28	—	8.39	—
Log-likelihood	—	−5,986	—	−5,971
N	8,300	11,322	6,210	11,322

a. Corresponds to the relevant time period.

1976–80) and table 4.5 for the long run (1976–82, 1976–84, and 1976–86). Regardless of the time period considered, startup size is negatively related to firm growth but positively related to the likelihood of survival. The results concerning innovative activity are somewhat more ambiguous. Post-entry growth is positively related to the amount of innovative activity in the industry in all of the time periods analyzed (although the effect is not statistically significant in the very short run). This is consistent with the hypothesis that new firms that survive tend to grow faster in innovative industries. Other than in the very short run, the coefficient of innovative activity in the survival equations is negative, but in any case is too small to be statistically significant.

The growth rate of new firms tends to be positively related to the extent of scale economies in the short run, but beyond the 1976–78 time period the coefficient is not statistically significant. The likelihood of new-firm survival is clearly reduced in the presence of scale economies. While this

Table 4.5
Regressions of new-firm growth and survival in the long run (*t*-statistics in parentheses)

	Time period					
	1976–1982		1976–1984		1976–1986	
	Growth (OLS)	Survival (Logit)	Growth (OLS)	Survival (Logit)	Growth (OLS)	Survival (Logit)
Size	−0.002	0.002	−0.002	0.002	−0.002	0.002
	(−2.50)	(2.57)	(−2.90)	(2.58)	(−2.03)	(2.64)
Total	0.562	−0.048	1.276	−0.047	1.834	−0.034
innovation	(2.66)	(−0.81)	(3.86)	(−0.79)	(4.60)	(−0.59)
rate						
Scale	0.002	−0.002	0.002	−0.002	0.002	−0.002
economies	(1.63)	(−4.68)	(1.00)	(−4.93)	(0.63)	(−4.80)
Capital	−0.006	0.004	−0.018	0.004	−0.017	0.004
intensity	(−0.96)	(2.39)	(−1.72)	(2.42)	(−1.26)	(2.63)
Industry	0.453	0.206	0.425	0.164	0.332	0.153
growth[a]	(3.90)	(4.60)	(2.21)	(5.05)	(1.60)	(5.44)
Multiplant	1.546	−0.490	1.786	−0.486	1.074	−0.487
dummy	(3.45)	(−3.78)	(2.46)	(−3.75)	(1.13)	(−3.75)
Intercept	1.706	−1.598	2.748	−1.574	3.266	−1.582
	(5.37)	(−18.40)	(6.22)	(−21.33)	(6.105)	(−22.67)
R^2	0.12	—	0.11	—	0.12	—
F	6.02	—	7.01	—	6.00	—
Log-likelihood	—	−5,978	—	−5,976	—	−5,970
N	4,076	11,322	3,130	11,322	2,534	11,322

a. Corresponds to the relevant time period.

negative effect is statistically significant in both the short and long run, it may be possible to reconcile the results between the strong short-run but weak long-run impact of scale economies on growth and the consistent strong influence exerted by the measure of MES on the probability of survival. It should be recalled that only surviving firms are included in the regressions estimating firm growth, whereas both surviving firms and enterprises ceasing to exist are included in the regressions estimating the likelihood of survival. In the first period analyzed, the results suggest that of those firms surviving until 1978, growth tended to be greater for firms in industries characterized by a high MES level of output. Those firms not subsequently surviving until 1980, which based on tables 4.1, 4.2, and 4.3 had a distinct tendency not to grow as fast as the surviving firms, were not included in the estimation of the regression for the 1976–80 period. That is, firms not surviving to the subsequent time period, which as tables 4.1,

4.2, and 4.3 showed to be the low-growth firms, are constantly being dropped from the estimating equations for each extended time period. The significance of the scale economies measure only in the short run may suggest that surviving firms tend to grow the fastest within the first several years subsequent to startup, after which time any remaining scale disadvantages are no longer so significant. Because the logit survival estimation includes both surviving firms and enterprises that have ceased to exist, the impact that scale economies had on the original cohort of 11,322 new startups in 1976 is reflected even as the estimating period is extended into the long run. This would imply that while the probability of survival remains negatively influenced by the extent of scale economies, the conditional probability of a firm remaining in existence, given that it has survived the first several years, may tend not to be significantly influenced by the extent of scale economies.

As is the case for the measure of scale economies, the capital-labor ratio has a positive and statistically significant impact on growth only in the very short run. The positive coefficient of capital intensity in the logit regressions examining survival in every time period is consistent with the hypothesis that, holding constant the other factors, and in particular the degree of scale economies, the propensity for new firms to exit from the industry tends to fall as capital intensity rises. This supports the hypothesis that sunk costs, at least to the degree that they are represented by capital intensity (after controlling for the extent of scale economies), reduce the propensity for new firms to exit the industry.

Finally, the positive coefficient of the multiplant dummy variable in the growth regressions and the negative coefficient in the survival (logit) regressions presumably reflects the systematic tendency for the measure of firm size to systematically overstate the actual size of subsidiary plants of a multiplant enterprise. The negative coefficient in the logit regressions indicates that the likelihood of such new multiplant enterprises surviving is actually systematically lower than is predicted given the measure of firm size. Similarly, firm growth (of the surviving firms) is apparently systematically greater for new multiplant enterprises than is predicted given the measure of firm size. These results are consistent with the interpretation that the actual gap between the MES level of output and the size of the relevant establishment is systematically greater than is being measured using the number of employees of the entire enterprise to measure size.

The results in tables 4.4 and 4.5 generally provide considerable evidence supporting the dynamic view of the selection process of new firms. Apparently new firms are under pressure to grow. The force of this pressure is dictated, at least to some extent, by the inherent cost disadvantages emerging from the gap between the size of the enterprise and the MES level of output. As this gap increases, the pressure on the firm to expand, either through innovative activity or some other mechanism, is greater. Therefore, both firm size and the extent of scale economies play key roles in this dynamic selection process; because they determine the extent to which new firms need to grow in order to become viable enterprises and ultimately survive.

4.5   Semiparametric Hazard Duration Model

An alternative method for analyzing survival is to estimate a semiparametric hazard duration function (Lawless, 1982). Two important functions are the survival and hazard functions. The survival function gives for each time period the share of those establishments founded in 1976 which still existed. The hazard function gives for each time point the risk of failure, that is, the (conditional) probability that an establishment will exit in the next time interval, on the condition that this establishment had survived up to the beginning of the time interval.

The survival of new enterprises was analyzed in section 4.4. Because some new enterprises are actually the headquarters of multiplant firms, this ownership structure had to be accounted for and was found to significantly influence the propensity for new enterprises to survive as well as influence their growth rates. By contrast, in this section I will use the establishment as the fundamental unit of observation. Since over 90 percent of the new establishments opened in 1976 were, in fact, independent enterprises, this distinction is not relevant for the bulk of new businesses.

As table 4.6 shows, the SBDB identifies 12,251 new plants that were established in U.S. manufacturing in 1976.[12] The subsequent survival rates for these establishments included in the cohort are then tracked throughout the remainder of the period using the longitudinal data base. One of the most striking features of table 4.6 is the skewed size distribution of newly established plants. While 11,662 (95.19 percent) had fewer than 50 employees during their startup year, only 589 (4.89 percent) had at least 50 employees.[13] As was found in the previous section for new-firm startups,

---

12. The number of new establishments in each of the broad industry sectors does not equal the total number of new plant startups in manufacturing because of the omission of the tobacco sector from table 4.6.

13. The usual classification of small firms is enterprises with fewer than 500 employees (Brown and Phillips, 1989). However, due to the skewed distribution, this size criterion is not practical when examining new establishment startups.

Table 4.6
Plant startup size and numbers of surviving new small plants (and percentage surviving) by sector and year, 1976–1986

Sector	Startup size	Year					
		1976	1978	1980	1982	1984	1986
Food	Large	57	47 (82.5)	41 (71.9)	35 (61.4)	29 (50.9)	26 (45.6)
	Small	504	367 (72.8)	293 (58.1)	208 (41.3)	157 (31.2)	129 (25.6)
Textiles	Large	38	30 (79.9)	24 (63.2)	16 (42.1)	13 (34.2)	12 (31.6)
	Small	303	221 (72.9)	161 (53.1)	108 (35.6)	86 (28.4)	72 (23.8)
Apparel	Large	96	80 (83.3)	69 (71.9)	55 (57.3)	46 (47.9)	38 (39.6)
	Small	851	603 (70.9)	459 (53.9)	313 (36.8)	236 (27.7)	179 (21.0)
Lumber	Large	31	24 (77.4)	19 (61.3)	17 (54.8)	11 (35.5)	7 (22.6)
	Small	821	619 (75.4)	525 (64.0)	356 (43.4)	276 (33.6)	230 (28.0)
Furniture	Large	21	14 (66.7)	13 (61.9)	13 (61.9)	11 (52.4)	10 (47.6)
	Small	559	409 (73.2)	317 (56.7)	197 (35.2)	162 (29.0)	135 (24.2)
Paper	Large	11	6 (54.6)	5 (45.5)	5 (45.5)	5 (45.5)	5 (45.5)
	Small	145	111 (76.6)	88 (60.7)	72 (49.7)	63 (43.5)	59 (40.7)

Printing	Large	25	21 (84.0)	15 (60.0)	13 (52.0)	12 (48.0)	11 (44.0)
	Small	1,877	1,541 (82.1)	1,307 (69.6)	975 (51.9)	832 (44.3)	736 (39.2)
Chemicals	Large	16	14 (88.9)	11 (68.8)	10 (62.5)	9 (56.3)	9 (56.3)
	Small	360	265 (73.6)	210 (58.3)	155 (43.1)	127 (35.3)	110 (30.6)
Petroleum	Large	5	3 (60.0)	3 (60.0)	2 (40.0)	1 (20.0)	1 (20.0)
	Small	51	34 (66.7)	24 (47.1)	20 (39.2)	14 (27.5)	12 (23.5)
Rubber	Large	27	23 (85.2)	17 (63.0)	13 (48.2)	12 (44.4)	8 (29.6)
	Small	450	352 (78.2)	293 (65.1)	216 (48.0)	187 (41.6)	162 (36.0)
Leather	Large	7	7 (100.0)	6 (85.7)	6 (85.7)	4 (57.1)	4 (57.1)
	Small	122	87 (71.3)	74 (60.7)	39 (32.0)	30 (24.6)	27 (22.1)
Stone, clay, glass	Large	20	17 (85.0)	16 (80.0)	12 (60.0)	10 (50.0)	10 (50.0)
	Small	595	472 (79.3)	371 (62.4)	272 (45.7)	276 (36.3)	173 (29.1)
Primary metals	Large	24	22 (91.7)	20 (83.3)	19 (79.2)	19 (79.2)	19 (79.2)
	Small	180	144 (80.0)	116 (64.4)	83 (46.1)	73 (40.6)	63 (35.0)
Fabricated metal products	Large	59	51 (86.4)	39 (66.1)	34 (57.6)	28 (47.5)	24 (40.7)
	Small	1,009	789 (78.2)	659 (65.3)	508 (50.4)	427 (42.3)	360 (35.7)

Table 4.6 (cont.)

Sector	Startup size	Year					
		1976	1978	1980	1982	1984	1986
Machinery (non-electrical)	Large	54	50 (92.6)	41 (75.9)	37 (68.5)	33 (61.1)	32 (59.3)
	Small	1,595	1,296 (81.3)	1,094 (68.6)	848 (53.2)	734 (46.0)	621 (38.9)
Electrical equipment	Large	39	31 (79.5)	26 (66.7)	2 (56.4)	20 (51.3)	18 (46.2)
	Small	674	519 (77.0)	400 (59.4)	273 (40.5)	221 (32.8)	184 (27.3)
Transportation equipment	Large	21	16 (76.2)	12 (57.1)	11 (52.4)	9 (42.9)	9 (42.9)
	Small	440	318 (72.3)	243 (55.2)	154 (35.0)	111 (25.2)	93 (21.1)
Instruments	Large	11	10 (90.0)	9 (81.8)	9 (81.8)	8 (72.7)	8 (72.7)
	Small	328	260 (80.0)	210 (64.6)	151 (46.5)	126 (38.8)	115 (35.4)
Miscellaneous	Large	27	19 (70.4)	16 (59.3)	13 (48.2)	10 (37.0)	10 (37.0)
	Small	799	578 (72.3)	440 (55.1)	272 (34.0)	201 (25.2)	158 (19.8)
Total	Large	589	485 (82.3)	401 (68.1)	343 (58.2)	290 (49.2)	261 (44.3)
	Small	11,662	8,987 (77.1)	7,286 (62.5)	5,221 (44.8)	4,280 (36.7)	3,618 (31.0)

Note: The survival rate is defined as the number of firms surviving in an industry in a given year, as a percentage of the total number of new firms established in 1976.

at least some, if not most, of these new plants are likely to be too small at their time of establishment to be operating at anything approaching the MES level of output. Still, it should be emphasized that the startup size varies considerably across industries. For example, in the non-electrical machinery sector the mean startup size was only 5.79 employees. Similarly, in printing the average startup size was 4.79 employees. By contrast, in primary metals the mean startup size was 9.88 employees, and in paper it was 9.23 employees.

Table 4.6 also shows that new plants tend to be established at a relatively larger scale in the primary metals, textiles, apparel, food, and petroleum sectors, where the number of larger plants established was at least one-tenth as great as the number of smaller plant startups. By contrast, new plants in the printing, non-electrical machinery, instruments, and leather sectors consisted mostly of establishments with fewer than 50 employees.[14]

The likelihood of a plant exiting is also apparently related to establishment size. A change in establishment ownership is not counted as exit. Rather, exit is defined as a cessation of manufacturing operations. Of the large plants established in 1976, 45.7 percent had exited by 1986. By contrast, 69.0 percent of the small plants established had exited during this same ten-year period. However, the exit rate of the smaller plants did not exceed that of their larger counterparts in every manufacturing sector. For example, the ten-year exit rate of the larger startups actually exceeded that of the smaller establishment startups in the lumber, petroleum, and rubber sectors.

The observation by Evans (1987a and 1987b), Hall (1987), Phillips and Kirchhof (1989), Audretsch (1991 and 1994), Mahmood (1992), and Audretsch and Mahmood (1993, 1994, and 1995) that the probability of a business exiting an industry increases with the time period considered, but decreases with increasing age, is confirmed for these data at the establishment level. That is, the (cumulative) exit rate tends to increase as the time interval considered also increases, but the conditional probability of an establishment exiting decreases with the amount of time it has already survived. These two tendencies hold regardless of the size of the initial plant startup.

---

14. It should be noted that these comparisons of startup size are on an employee basis. A comparison based on sales could yield somewhat different results due to variations in capital intensity and therefore sales-employee ratios across manufacturing industries. However, it should be emphasized that the employment criterion is the most common measure used to distinguish establishment and enterprise size.

Although not included in table 4.6, establishment size in the startup year is apparently strongly influenced by ownership status. There is a distinct tendency for the startup size of independent establishments to be smaller than that of subsidiaries and branches of incumbent firms. The mean startup size of independent plants established in 1976 was 9.55 employees. By contrast, the mean startup size of branch and subsidiary establishments was 58.9 employees. This disparity in startup size exists across individual manufacturing sectors as well as for manufacturing as a whole.

One of the major findings of section 4.4 is that the cohort of new firms that ultimately survived grew faster than their counterparts that exited, especially during the first several years subsequent to startup. Table 4.7 similarly compares employment growth rates between exiting plants and establishments that survived throughout the entire ten-year period. For example, the first column shows the mean growth rates between 1976 and 1978 for establishments that subsequently exited prior to 1980, and the second column shows the mean growth rate for plants which survived until 1986. As was found for new-firm startups in the previous section, growth and survival are apparently closely related. The mean growth rate of those establishments ultimately surviving throughout the entire period exceeds that of exiting firms for each matched subperiod. For example, establishments that still existed in 1978 but had exited by 1980 had a mean growth rate of 36.2 percent between 1976 and 1978. By contrast, the growth rate of establishments surviving throughout the period was 44.8 percent between 1976 and 1978.

The techniques of survival analysis, as developed by Lawless (1982), are used to compute the survival and hazard functions that are presented in table 4.8 and figures 4.1 and 4.2. While the first column in table 4.8 provides the survival and hazard rates for all establishments founded in 1976, the second column includes only those establishments that were identified as being a branch or subsidiary of an existing multi-establishment enterprise. The survival and hazard rates for all new firms, but not branches and subsidiaries, are indicated in the third column. Finally, only those new establishments representing single-establishment firms (excluded are not only new subsidiaries and branches of multiplant firms, but also establishments that are headquarters of new multi-establishment enterprises) are included in the sample analyzed in the last column.

The extent to which the technological environment, or what Scherer terms as the "technological opportunity class," influences the ability of new establishments to survive is shown in table 4.9. Those 944 establishments opened in 1976 in industries with an R & D/sales ratio of at least 5 percent

Table 4.7
Employment growth rates (%) in exiting plants and 1986 survivors

| | 1976–78 | | 1976–80 | | 1976–82 | | 1976–84 | | 1976–86 |
| | Exiting plants | 1986 survivors | Exiting plants | 1986 survivors | Exiting plants | 1986 survivors | Exiting plants | 1986 survivors | 1986 survivors |
Sector									
Food	11.4	8.4	44.9	22.5	106.7	27.5	64.4	32.6	44.8
Textiles	34.0	62.0	50.0	100.4	143.0	92.9	86.6	116.3	115.5
Apparel	39.2	39.1	57.4	131.7	35.5	132.6	164.2	181.8	176.0
Lumber	34.2	36.3	66.9	44.7	25.3	48.0	112.5	82.1	98.0
Furniture	59.4	68.7	68.4	121.7	27.5	150.3	99.0	179.9	213.7
Paper	28.8	48.1	72.0	73.7	263.7	101.9	83.3	157.3	205.7
Printing	21.7	32.7	23.9	69.2	39.3	96.1	131.3	127.4	160.4
Chemicals	6.7	20.5	48.9	33.5	34.5	79.0	131.7	135.9	113.9
Petroleum	44.0	12.1	46.3	3.0	72.7	−15.2	78.9	−24.2	6.1
Rubber	44.7	51.6	34.4	89.6	151.0	109.8	104.3	138.0	160.5
Leather	67.4	9.4	82.4	74.5	18.7	135.2	158.3	130.9	134.2
Stone, clay & glass	37.6	36.7	91.2	65.7	5.4	53.7	44.6	73.9	95.5
Primary metals	2.6	21.7	103.6	48.7	69.1	48.2	191.0	52.8	76.2
Fabricated metal products	20.1	41.7	26.1	78.4	80.5	94.4	146.5	105.1	125.0
Machinery (non-electrical)	36.6	54.6	52.4	109.4	101.8	136.4	135.5	140.4	177.6
Electrical equipment	48.1	73.9	39.8	166.2	125.5	174.6	176.3	272.5	279.5
Transportation equipment	125.1	113.6	62.1	140.1	125.3	186.8	60.1	252.1	273.4
Instruments	45.0	46.0	84.0	137.7	16.0	269.2	232.0	339.7	420.4
Total	36.2	44.8	51.2	90.3	66.0	106.1	127.2	135.2	154.8

Table 4.8
Life table of establishments founded in 1976

Time interval	Survival rate	Hazard rate	Survival rate	Hazard rate	Survival rate	Hazard rate	Survival rate	Hazard rate
1976–1978	1.000	0.000	1.000	0.000	1.000	0.000	1.000	0.000
1978–1980	0.775	0.254	0.800	0.222	0.774	0.225	0.776	0.252
1980–1982	0.631	0.205	0.632	0.234	0.631	0.204	0.633	0.202
1982–1984	0.441	0.354	0.479	0.274	0.439	0.358	0.441	0.358
1984–1986	0.374	0.164	0.427	0.116	0.372	0.166	0.373	0.166
1986	0.316	0.166	0.361	0.167	0.314	0.166	0.316	0.165
Number of observations	12,251		590		11,661		11,154	
Sample	All establishments		Branches		All firms		Single-establishment firms	

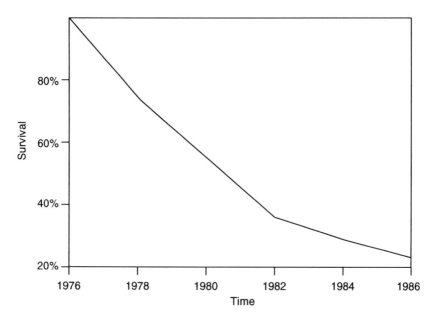

Figure 4.1
Survival rates for new establishments

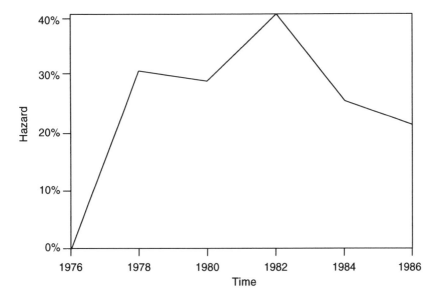

Figure 4.2
Hazard rates for new establishments

Table 4.9
Life table according to technological environment

	High-tech[a]		Moderate-tech[b]		Low-tech[c]	
Time interval	Survival rate	Hazard rate	Survival rate	Hazard rate	Survival rate	Hazard rate
1976–1978	1.000	0.000	1.000	0.000	1.000	0.000
1978–1980	0.786	0.239	0.789	0.235	0.763	0.268
1980–1982	0.627	0.225	0.647	0.196	0.618	0.209
1982–1984	0.427	0.379	0.471	0.315	0.421	0.381
1984–1986	0.354	0.187	0.410	0.139	0.351	0.181
1986	0.303	0.155	0.347	0.165	0.296	0.168
Number of observations	944		4,751		6,556	

a. Includes industries where R & D/sales $\geq$ 5%.
b. Includes industries where 1% < R & D/sales < 5%.
c. Includes industries where R & D/sales $\leq$ 1%.

are included in the "high-technological" opportunity class. By contrast, those 6,556 new establishments in industries with an R & D/sales ratio less than 1 percent are classified as being in a "low-technological" opportunity class. The remaining 4,751 establishments started in 1976 are considered to be in the "moderate-technological" opportunity class. Table 4.9 shows that the mean survival rates of establishments in the high- and low-technological opportunity classes are considerably less than the mean survival rate for new establishments in the moderate-technological opportunity class.

The Cox-Regression model (Cox, 1972 and 1975; Kiefer, 1988) captures the effects of the covariates (or explanatory variables) upon death (hazard rates) rather than upon times to death. In addition, it corrects for the problem of censored data.

The model is defined in terms of $h(t; x)$, where h is the hazard rate for a business, and x is a vector of covariates. The hazard model is given by,

$$h(t; x) = h_0(t) \cdot \exp(\beta x') \tag{4.4}$$

or

$$\ln[h(t; x)/h_0(t)] = \beta x' \tag{4.5}$$

where β is a vector of unknown regression coefficients and $h_0(t)$ is an unknown non-negative baseline hazard rate. The second exponential term incorporates the covariates vector x. Estimates of the regression parameters are obtained as follows: let $t_1 < t_2 < \cdots t_k$ represent distinct times to death among n observed survival times.

The conditional probability that the ith firm exits at time t_i^* with a covariate vector x_i, given that a single exit has occurred at t_i, is given as the ratio of the hazards,

$$\exp(\beta x_i') \Big/ \sum_{j \in R_i} \exp(\beta x_i'), \tag{4.6}$$

where $j \in R_i$ corresponds to those establishments that are just at risk prior to time t_i. The baseline hazard rate is assumed to be the same for all the observations, and hence it cancels out.

The partial likelihood function derived from Cox (1972 and 1975) is obtained by multiplying these probabilities together for each of the k incidences of exit,

$$PL(\beta, x_1, \ldots, x_n) = \prod_{\substack{k \\ j \in R_i}} [\exp(\beta x_i') / \sum \exp(\beta x_i')]. \tag{4.7}$$

Maximization of the partial likelihood function yields estimators of β with properties similar to those of usual maximum likelihood estimators, such as asymptotic normality.

The estimated regression coefficient indicates the relationship between the covariate and the hazard function. A positive coefficient increases the value of the hazard function and therefore indicates a negative relationship with survival. A negative coefficient has the reverse interpretation.

In the case of ties among the time until exit, Breslow (1974) proposed to maximize the following likelihood function,

$$PL(\beta, x_1, \ldots, x_n) = \prod_{j=1}^{k} \left[\exp(\beta s_i') \Big/ \sum_{i \in R_i} \exp(\beta x_i') m_i \right]. \tag{4.8}$$

where m_i is the number of exits at t_i and s_i is the vector sum of covariates of the m_i businesses. The SBDB data base introduced in chapter 2 satisfies these criteria, because they provide enough of the censored observations and ties so that the hazard duration function can be estimated with equation 4.5.

The semiparametric hazard duration model, or the Cox-Regression technique, is used to test the hypotheses presented in section 4.2 that the exposure to risk of new establishments is influenced by the extent to which a gap exists between the MES in the industry and the initial startup size of the establishment, market growth, and the technological environment. The measures of the MES, initial startup size market growth, and the technological opportunity class are the same ones used in section 4.5.

One of the most striking findings to emerge in the previous section is that the likelihood of new-firm survival is lower in markets characterized by a high technological opportunity class, or where innovative activity plays an especially important role. However, this measure of the technological opportunity class, although reflecting the overall importance of innovative activity in the industry, does not distinguish between the two technological regimes—the routinized technological regime and the entrepreneurial technological regime—introduced in chapter 3. According to Winter (1984), the entrepreneurial regime is particularly conducive to innovative activity by established businesses, whereas the routinized regime tends to impede innovations from entrants. In fact, one of the major conclusions of chapter 3 is that startup activity varies substantially between the routinized technological regime and the entrepreneurial technological regime. Startups play a more important role under the entrepreneurial regime than under the routinized regime. That is, under the entrepreneurial regime new entrants are more likely to enter an industry in the hopes of successfully innovating. However, as was found in the previous section for new firms, those new startups that are unable to innovate or adapt in some other manner that enhances growth at least to the MES level of output will be forced to exit from the industry. Thus, under the entrepreneurial regime, or where innovative activity tends to emanate more from the small firms than from their larger counterparts, the hazard rate is expected to be greater than under the routinized regime, where the large firms tend to have the innovative advantage, and new businesses are less likely to enter an industry with the hopes of pursuing an innovative strategy.

Here I employ the same measures of the technological regime as were introduced by Acs and Audretsch (1987 and 1990) and used in chapter 3. When the small-firm innovation rate is large relative to the total innovation rate, the industry is better characterized by the entrepreneurial regime. By contrast, the routinized regime is more reflective of the underlying technological conditions when the total innovation rate is high relative to the small-firm innovation rate.

In addition, the ownership structure of the establishment is captured by including a dummy variable taking on the value of one for branches and subsidiaries that belong to a multi-establishment enterprise and zero for establishments that represent newly established firms. As suggested above, the hazard rate for newly established firms is expected to be greater than for new plants opened by existing enterprises. An established firm's new plant is presumably founded by a managerial unit that is better informed about economic conditions and also has an established managerial competence.

Table 4.10
Semi-parametric hazard duration function

Independent variables	(1)	(2)	(3)	(4)
Scale economies	0.004	0.004	0.005	0.004
	(2.02)	(2.03)	(2.53)	(2.13)
Startup size	−0.002	−0.001	−0.002	—
	(−3.23)	(−3.09)	(−3.25)	
Growth	−1.393	−1.390	−1.445	−1.404
	(−3.15)	(−3.14)	(−3.27)	(−3.17)
R & D/sales	0.020	0.020	−0.002	0.002
	(1.57)	(1.59)	(−0.12)	(1.61)
Total innovation rate	—	—	0.088	—
			(2.32)	
Small-firm innovation rate/	0.006	0.006	—	—
total innovation rate	(1.67)	(1.74)		
Branch dummy	0.086	—	0.083	0.092
	(1.14)		(1.09)	(1.22)
Number of observations	7,070	7,070	7,070	7,070
Chi square	37.1	35.8	37.2	34.6
Log of likelihood	−39,310	−39,310	−39,310	−39,310

Note: t-statistics in parentheses.

Using all 7,070 manufacturing establishments that were founded in 1976 and for which compatible industry characteristics could be matched, the Cox-Regression model was estimated, and the results are shown in table 4.10. The positive and statistically significant (at the 95 percent level of confidence) coefficient of the measure of the MES suggests that new establishments face a greater rate of hazard in industries where scale economies play an important role than in markets where the MES is relatively low.[15] The startup size of the establishment is apparently negatively related to the hazard rate. That is, new establishments that are larger experience a lower risk of failure, at least within ten years subsequent to startup.

The negative coefficient of the industry growth variable confirms the hypothesis that the hazard rate tends to be lower for establishments founded in high growing industries and greater for those in industries with low or even negative growth. A higher technological opportunity class, as reflected by the total innovation rate and the industry R & D/sales ratio, is associated with a higher rate of hazard, as indicated by the positive coefficients.

15. It should be noted that the MES is measured in terms of thousands of dollars, so that an increase in the MES of one thousand dollars results in an increase in the hazard rate of 0.004.

Perhaps most striking is the positive and statistically significant coefficient of the small-firm innovation rate divided by the total innovation
rate, suggesting that under the entrepreneurial regime the hazard rate confronting new establishments tends to be higher than it is under the routinized
regime. That is, in industries where small firms tend to be particularly
innovative relative to the innovative activity of the entire industry, the
exposure to risk confronting those new establishments is greater.

Finally, the coefficient of the branch dummy is positive but the t-statistic
cannot be considered to be significantly different from zero. In any case,
there is little evidence supporting the hypothesis that the hazard rate of
new branches and subsidiaries belonging to existing multi-establishment
firms is any less than that for new-plant startups. Omitting the branch
dummy variable in the second equation of table 4.10 leaves the coefficients
of the other explanatory variables virtually unaffected.

In equation (3) both the total innovation rate and the R & D/sales ratio
are included to capture the technological opportunity class. While the positive coefficient of the total innovation rate reinforces the conclusion that
the new-establishment hazard rate is greater in high-technology environments, the coefficient of the R & D/sales ratio becomes negative and
cannot be considered statistically significant. This is probably attributed to
the high simple correlation between the two measures found by Acs and
Audretsch (1990, chapter 2).

One possible explanation for the insignificance of the branch dummy
variable is that the startup size of branches and subsidiaries tends to be
greater than that of new firms. However, when the startup size variable is
omitted from the regression in equation (4), the coefficient of the branch
dummy variable remains virtually unchanged.

Although the results from table 4.10 suggest that, after controlling for
scale, technological, and startup size effects, the extent to which new establishments are exposed to risk does not significantly differ between new
branches and subsidiaries of existing enterprises and new-firm startups, it is
certainly possible that the establishment ownership status affects the relationships multiplicatively or in an interactive manner. Therefore, the first
two equations in table 4.11 contain all new firms in equation (1) and new
branches and subsidiaries of existing enterprises in equation (2).

There are five important points to emphasize in comparing the determinants of the hazard functions between new-firm startups and the opening
of new plants by existing firms. First, the hazard rate tends to be higher in
the presence of scale economies for new-firm startups but not for branches
and subsidiaries. Second, newly established firms can apparently reduce

Table 4.11
Semiparametric hazard duration function according to ownership and technological environment

Independent variables	New firms (1)	Branches (2)	All establishments		
			High-tech (3)	Moderate-tech (4)	Low-tech (5)
Scale economies	0.014	0.003	−0.004	0.009	0.015
	(2.15)	(0.39)	(−1.30)	(3.25)	(3.74)
Startup size	−0.003	−0.001	−0.001	−0.001	−0.001
	(−3.07)	(−0.99)	(−0.62)	(−2.42)	(−2.18)
Growth	−1.621	2.540	−1.538	−0.864	−0.726
	(−3.49)	(1.28)	(−1.32)	(−1.30)	(−0.94)
R & D/sales	0.027	−0.041	0.033	0.001	0.350
	(2.08)	(−0.77)	(1.33)	(0.04)	(6.87)
Small-firm innovation rate/total innovation rate	0.005	0.008	0.005	0.019	0.005
	(1.35)	(1.24)	(0.50)	(1.23)	(1.14)
Number of observations	6,492	322	810	3,388	2,872
Chi square	40.9	4.5	3.9	23.5	62.7
Log of likelihood	−35,646	−1,132	−3,530	−16,768	−14,487

Note: t-statistics in parentheses.

their hazard rate by increasing the startup size. The rate of hazard of new establishments belonging to multiplant firms is not significantly influenced by the initial plant size.

Third, although a high market growth rate reduces the exposure to risk confronting new firms, it has no apparent effect on branches and subsidiaries. Similarly, the hazard rate confronting new-firm startups is significantly and positively related to R & D intensity; and R & D/sales apparently exerts no influence on the ability of new plants opened by existing firms to survive. Finally, the impact of the technological regime, or the relative innovative advantages of large and small firms, on the hazard rate is virtually identical, regardless of ownership status.

In general, the distinct differences between the two hazard rate functions suggest that new-firm startups are much more influenced by the external environment and in particular, by the extent of scale economies and the technological environment than are new branches and subsidiaries of existing firms. Perhaps the importance of the initial startup size of new firms is attributable to its role as a mechanism for offsetting otherwise inherent scale and technology disadvantages. By contrast, the startup size contributes little toward reducing the exposure to risk confronting new branches and subsidiaries, which apparently are able to exploit the advantage of belonging to an established multiplant firm.

Because of the important role that technology plays, the Cox-Regression model is also used to estimate the hazard duration function for new establishments in high-technology, moderate-technology, and low-technology industries.[16] There are two important results emerging from equations (3), (4), and (5) in table 4.11. First, although the existence of scale economies tends to raise the hazard rate confronting new establishments in low- and moderate-technology industries, this is clearly not the case in high-technology industries. Second, the startup size is apparently important in reducing the hazard rate for new establishments in low- and moderate-technology industries, but the exposure to risk confronting new establishments is not influenced by startup size in high-technology industries. This would suggest that in a high-technology environment, initial size and scale considerations do not seem to play an important role in the ability of the establishment to survive. Rather, innovation is presumably the more important factor in such industries.

The conclusion of Dunne et al. (1988) that the ownership structure of establishments affects their ability to survive is confirmed here. However, the results of the Cox-Regression estimation at the individual establishment level reveal that after controlling for scale, technological, and initial size effects, this ownership structure differential in hazard rates disappears. What does emerge is that the roles that scale economies, technology, and the startup size play apparently differ depending upon the ownership structure. That is, the hazard rate of new enterprises is greater in the presence of scale economies, a high-technology environment, and low market growth. A large startup size can at least somewhat offset these inherent disadvantages by reducing the exposure to risk. By contrast, the hazard rate confronting new branches and subsidiaries opened by existing firms does not appear to be significantly influenced by the existence of scale economies, technology, or the startup size. That the ten-year survival rate of the branches and subsidiaries established in 1976 is about 15 percent greater than that for the new firms can be attributed to the influence that scale economies, the technological environment, and initial startup size exert on new firms but not on new establishments belonging to multiplant enterprises.

---

16. The classification of industries according to the technological environment is identical to that used in table 4.9. It should be noted that all new establishments (both firms as well as branches and subsidiaries) are included in the sample used to estimate equations (3), (4), and (5).

Finally, the risk of failure confronting all new establishments is conditional upon the technological environment. The scale and startup size disadvantages confronting new establishments do not play an important role in high-technology industries, but rather only in low- and moderate-technology markets.

4.6   Conclusions

One of the striking findings to emerge from chapter 3 is that the entry of new firms is apparently promoted in industries where small firms tend to have the innovative advantage. The results of this chapter, however, strongly suggest that, although entry might be greater in such markets, new businesses are actually exposed to a greater degree of risk. Such industries, characterized by the entrepreneurial regime, are particularly turbulent. Not only is the propensity to enter relatively high, but the corresponding high rate of hazard reflects the high propensity of new businesses to fail within the first years of their existence. An important characteristic of the entrepreneurial regime, where small new entrants tend to contribute much of the innovative activity, is the accompanying high rate of firm failure and turbulent industry structure.

The results from this chapter shed at least some light on the seeming paradox posed by the findings in the industrial organization literature that (1) the bulk of firms in an industry are not only very small, but also sufficiently small so as to operate at a suboptimal scale of output in most industries, and (2) as was found in chapter 3, even new firms are not deterred from entering industries where scale economies play an important role. A dynamic view of the process of firm selection and industry evolution is that new firms typically start at a very small scale of output. Because this level of output may be suboptimal in that the MES level has not been attained, the firm must grow in order to survive.

The empirical evidence presented in this chapter supports such a dynamic view of the role of new firms in manufacturing; because the post-entry growth of surviving firms, at least in the first few years, tends to be spurred by the extent to which there is a gap between the MES level of output and the size of the firm. At the same time, the likelihood of any new firm surviving tends to decrease as this gap increases. Firms starting in industries characterized by a high degree of innovative activity may face a greater prospect of growth, but they are burdened with a somewhat lower likelihood of survival. In general, with some variations depending upon whether a short- or long-run time horizon is being considered, the impact of firm size, scale economies, and innovative activity tends to by asymmetrical with respect to firm growth and survival. Factors that promote firm growth tend to reduce the probability of survival, and vice versa. Only the market growth rate exerts something of a symmetrical influence on both firm growth and survival.

While Lucas (1978) attempted to explain the pervasiveness of small and suboptimal scale enterprises in the firm-size distribution with a static theory, viewed through a dynamic lens, the often observed asymmetric size distribution of firms becomes more understandable. According to this view, the answer to the question, "How are such small and suboptimal enterprises able to be viable?" is, "They are not—at least not by remaining small and suboptimal." Rather, such new suboptimal scale firms are engaged in the selection process, whereby the successful enterprises grow and ultimately approach or attain the optimal size, whereas the remainder stagnate and may ultimately be forced to cease operations. Thus the persistence of an asymmetric firm-size distribution skewed toward small enterprises and the large presence of suboptimal scale enterprises presumably reflects a continuing process of entry into industries and not necessarily the survival of such small and suboptimal enterprises over a long period of time. That is, although the skewed size distribution of firms persists with remarkable stability over time, it does not appear to be a constant set of small and suboptimal scale firms that is responsible for this skewness.

5   Entrepreneurship

5.1   Introduction

Among the most remarkable characteristics of the literature on entrepreneurship is the lack of convergence toward a singular definition of what actually constitutes entrepreneurial activity. While Richard Cantillion (1931) and Frank Knight (1921) associated entrepreneurship with risk taking, Joseph Schumpeter (1942) focused on the innovative aspects of entrepreneurship. More recently Schultz (1975 and 1980) defined entrepreneurship as the ability to deal with disequilibrium, but within the context of equilibrium models.[1] According to T. W. Schultz (1980, p. 443), "What entrepreneurs do, has an economic value. This value accrues to them as a rent, i.e., a rent which is a reward for their entrepreneurial performance. This reward in earned. Although this reward for the entrepreneurship of most human agents is small, in the aggregate in a dynamic economy it accounts for a substantial part of the increases in national income." And Israel Kirzner (1985, p. 118) has extended the views of Friedrich von Hayek (1945) and Ludwig Mises (1951)[2] that (1) the market is an entrepreneurial process; (2) a learning process is central to the market; and (3) entrepreneurial activities are creative acts of discovery. This led him to focus on the exploitation of profit opportunities as being intrinsic to entrepreneurship. According to Kirzner (1985, pp. 63–64), "In the single-period case

---

1. For example, Schultz (1980, p. 443) writes that, "The substance of my argument is that disequilibria are inevitable in a dynamic economy. These disequilibria cannot be eliminated by law, by public policy, and surely not by rhetoric. A modern dynamic economy would fall apart were it not for the entrepreneurial actions of a wide array of human agents who reallocate their resources and thereby bring their part of the economy back into equilibrium. Every entrepreneurial decision to reallocate resources entails risk."
2. Mises (1951, p. 13) defined an entrepreneur using the following criterion: "There is a simple rule of thumb to tell entrepreneurs from non-entrepreneurs. The entrepreneurs are those on whom the incidence of losses on the capital employed falls."

alertness can at best discover hitherto overlooked current facts. In the multiperiod case entrepreneurial alertness must include the entrepeneur's perception of the way in which creative and imaginative action may vitally shape the kind of transactions that will be entered into in future market periods."[3]

In more practical, empirical applications, defining entrepreneurship has produced a diversity of operational approaches, ranging from the "... carrying out of innovation" (Nelson, 1984, p. 646), to "... those individuals who respond to the opportunities for creating new products" (Holmes and Schmitz, 1990, p. 266), and finally to simply measuring the number of self-employed workers (Evans and Leighton, 1989, 1990a and 1990b, Evans and Jovanovic, 1989; Blanchflower and Oswald, 1990; and Blanchflower and Meyer, 1994). Although these operational definitions are sometimes overlapping, they can often be quite contradictory. For example, an important qualification in equating self-employment with entrepreneurship is that most of the self-employed are not engaged in anything resembling innovative activity. At the same time, as Acs and Audretsch (1988 and 1990) show, much and even most of innovative activity takes place within large corporations.

Still another dimension of entrepreneurship is the creation or establishment of new firms. Even though empirical studies of entry have recently blossomed,[4] their applicability to measuring and understanding the phenomenon of entrepreneurship is limited for two reasons. First, as pointed out in chapter 3 many of the studies have focused on net entry, or the total change in the number of firms within a specific time period, rather than on gross entry or the startup of new firms. Equally important, as Dunne, Roberts, and Samuelson (1988 and 1989), Cable and Schwalbach (1991), Baldwin and Gorecki (1989 and 1991), and Siegfried and Evans (1992) show, industry exit rates are highly correlated with industry entry rates. That is, high entry accompanied by high exit may indicate a type of revolving door, whereby a large proportion of the new firms in the industry are forced to exit within a few years subsequent to entry. In fact, as was shown in chapter 4, the majority of new firms fail within several years

---

3. For a rich review of the major schools of thought regarding entrepreneurship, see Hébert and Link (1989) and Baumol (1990).

4. See, for examples, the country studies contained in Geroski and Schwalbach (1991), Dunne, Roberts, and Samuelson (1988 and 1989), Siegfried and Evans (1992), Acs and Audretsch (1989a and 1989b), as well as some of the groundbreaking work, such as Orr (1974) and Duetsch (1975).

subsequent to the startup year.[5] Thus the importance or the role that new firms play in markets has not yet been explored in a systematic manner.

The purpose of this chapter is to provide a new operational measure of entrepreneurship—the extent to which an industry is comprised by new and young firms. This places the age of the enterprise as the central parameter defining entrepreneurial activity. In a sense it combines the propensity for new firms to enter an industry, relative to the stock of incumbent firms, with the propensity for the new entrants to survive the initial few years. In this sense the measure of entrepreneurial activity is analogous to the measure of the presence of small firms, or the shares of employment and sales accounted for by small firms, which were the focus of the pioneering study by Larry White (1982) and later by Acs and Audretsch (1990, chapter 4), Joachim Schwalbach (1989) for Germany, José Mata (1993a and 1993b) for Portugal, and Vassilis Droucopoulos and Stavros Thomadakis (1993) for Greece. But rather than focus on the employment or sales share of small firms, which confounds (small) enterprises of all ages, the focus is instead on the share accounted for by new firms, which we term here as entrepreneurial firms.

This new measure is then used to test the hypothesis that the extent of entrepreneurial activity—or the degree to which the industry is characterized by new firms—is determined by those factors found in chapters 3 and 4 to shape startup activity and the ability of new firms to survive. These factors include the extent of scale economies and the technological environment, as well as the competitive environment or the ability of incumbent firms, to retaliate against new entrants.

In the second section of this chapter the exact manner used to measure entrepreneurship is explained. In the third section the hypotheses suggesting why the extent of entrepreneurial activity would be expected to vary across industries are introduced. The empirical results, based on two different measures of entrepreneurial activity, are provided in the fourth section. Finally, in the last section a summary and conclusions are provided. In particular, we find that the absence of scale economies and capital intensity tends to promote entrepreneurial activity. In industries characterized by a high technological opportunity class, entrepreneurial firms are found to account for more of the enterprises but for less of the employment. Perhaps

---

5. The positive relationship between enterprise (and establishment) age and the likelihood of survival has also been found in Audretsch (1991 and 1994), Audretsch and Mahmood (1993, 1994, and 1995), Dunne, Roberts, and Samuelson (1988 and 1989), Phillips and Kirchhoff (1989), and Mahmood (1992).

most striking is that although there tend to be more entrepreneurial firms under what we have already defined in this book as the entrepreneurial regime, these firms actually account for less of the employment.

5.2 Measuring Entrepreneurship

Entrepreneurship is operationally defined to be new firms. But how long is a firm "new" and at which moment does an enterprise pass from being a new entrant to being an incumbent? Not only has this never been defined, it has only rarely been discussed. We are left with the feeling that a firm is considered to be new during the year of its entry. Subsequently it becomes an incumbent. But this clearly is a custom that has been dictated by measurement, in particular, where entry is measured at a single point in time, or more specifically, as occurring in a single year. After that year, the firm becomes like all other firms in the industry, in that it is no longer an entrant. Which is to say that a rather dichotomous view has emerged of the dynamic process of markets, where firms are either new entrants during the year or period that their entry is observed, and subsequently they are non-entrants, or what is more customarily referred to as incumbents. They are simply there.

As an alternative to this rather dichotomous view between entrants and incumbents, I wish to consider any firm younger than $T - t_0$ years, where T is defined as the year observed, and t_0 is defined as the earliest year that a startup will be considered to constitute a bona fide "new" firm. Thus firms younger than $T - t_0$ years are defined as entrepreneurial, and those older than $T - t_0$ years are considered to be incumbents.

The number of entrepreneurial startups, or firm births, B, in each year is measured by $\sum_{i=1}^{n} B_i$, where i indicates each new-firm startup. Thus the entire number of new-firm startups between t_0 and T can be measured by $\sum_{t=0}^{T} \sum_{i=1}^{n} B_{it}$. However, not all of entrepreneurial startups survive throughout this time period. The number of exits, or firm deaths, D, in each year is measured by $\sum_{i=1}^{d} D_i$. Over the entire period, the number of exits is represented by $\sum_{t=0}^{T} \sum_{i=1}^{d} D_{it}$. The number of entrepreneurial startups founded since year t_0 and still in existence in year T, E_T, is therefore captured by

$$E_T = \sum_{t=0}^{T} \sum_{i=1}^{n} B_{it} - \sum_{t=0}^{T} \sum_{i=1}^{n} D_{it}. \tag{5.1}$$

It should be noted that this is not the typical measure of net entry, which subtracts the number of exits in a given year from the number of entrants.

Rather, equation (5.1) measures the extent to which new-firm startups remain in the industry after $T - t_0$ years.

To measure the relative importance of entrepreneurship in each industry, the entrepreneurship rate calculated by dividing equation (5.1) by the sum of the entrepreneurial and incumbent enterprises, IE_T,

$$ER_T = \frac{\sum_{t=0}^{T} \sum_{i=1}^{n} B_{it} - \sum_{t=0}^{T} \sum_{i=1}^{d} D_{it}}{E_T + IE_T}. \tag{5.2}$$

Equations (5.1) and (5.2) are measures of entrepreneurial activity based on the number of new enterprises, but are unweighted by the extent of entrepreneurial economic activity relative to the amount of economic activity emanating from incumbent firms. That is, equation (5.2) will tend to overstate the relative importance of entrepreneurship, since, as Acs and Audretsch (1990) show, new firms are typically smaller than incumbents. Thus the extent of entrepreneurial activity can be weighted by the employment of each entrepreneurial startup in period T, EMP_T. Similarly, the entrepreneurial deaths can be weighted by their employment in the period prior to exit, EMP_{T^*}. Thus the number of employees accounted for by entrepreneurial firms in year T, $EEMP_T$, is given by

$$EEMP_T = \sum_{t=0}^{T} \sum_{i=1}^{n} (B_{it} * EMP_{it}) - \sum_{t=0}^{T} \sum_{i=1}^{d} (D_{it} * EMP_{T^*}). \tag{5.3}$$

Similarly, the share of employment accounted for by entrepreneurial activity, $EEMPR_T$, is calculated by dividing equation (5.3) by the sum of employment in entrepreneurial firms and employment in incumbent firms, $IEMP_T$, yielding,

$$EEMPR_T = \frac{\sum_{t=0}^{T} \sum_{i=1}^{n} (B_{it} * EMP_{it}) - \sum_{t=0}^{T} \sum_{i=1}^{d} (D_{it} * EMP_{T^*})}{EEMP_T + IEMP_T}. \tag{5.4}$$

That entrepreneurship should be conceptually defined as the presence of new firms in an industry is not entirely novel. Measurement is a different issue. Until recently, it was virtually impossible to implement such a definition, due to the lack of a longitudinal data base. That is, using an age criterion to measure entrepreneurship requires a data base that enables the identification of a new-firm startup, and then subsequently tracks its evolution over time. The SBDB longitudinal data base, described and documented in chapter 2, makes such measurement possible.

Although the availability of a longitudinal data base makes it possible to calculate the measures of entrepreneurial activity defined above, it does not help answer the question, "At which age does a startup evolve from being a new entrepreneurial firm to being an incumbent?" That is, what is the appropriate time span between T and t_0? No precise theory exists to answer this question, but at least some insight can be gleaned from chapter 4, where we found that the probability of a new firm surviving tends to stabilize six years subsequent to its startup. Thus there is at least some empirical evidence suggesting that $T - t_0$ should be no longer than six years. However, because of the vagueness involved in defining t_0, several alternative measures will be used in order to test for robustness.

Assuming $T - t_0 = 4$, where T is 1986 and t_0 therefore is 1982, those four-digit SIC industries with the greatest number of 1986 firms founded since 1982 still in existence as of 1986 are listed in descending order in table 5.1. The corresponding values of the share of firms accounted for by new enterprises, the amount of employment from new firms, and the share of 1986 employment accounted for by new firms, as well as the relative rankings of each of these measures (in parentheses) are identified. For example, the industry with the greatest number of 1986 firms classified as new was commercial printing (lithographic), where 10,141 of the 1986 firms had been established since 1982. This accounted for 38.18 percent of all enterprises in the industry. Similarly, the 66,059 employees in the industry working in firms opened since 1982 accounted for 17.70 percent of industry employment.

There are three important observations to be emphasized from table 5.1. First, just as the new firm and new-firm share measures yield quite different rankings, the rankings between the new-firm employment and new-firm employment share measures are also strikingly different. Second, the share of enterprises accounted for by new firms is always less than the new-firm share of employment. This is attributable to the smaller size of new firms compared to their more established counterparts. Thus the employment measure places less weight on the importance of entrepreneurial activity than does counting the number of new enterprises. In certain industries, such as electronic computing equipment (computers), radio and television communication equipment, and semiconductors, the relatively high shares of enterprises accounted for by young firms are accompanied by relatively low employment shares. That is, there tend to be a lot of new and young firms in the industry, relative to the number of incumbents, but they apparently do not contribute that much to overall economic activity. By contrast, in other industries, such as boat building, the difference between the new-firm shares of employment and enterprises is not particularly great.

The industries with the smallest number of 1986 firms founded since 1982 are ranked in table 5.2 according to ascending order. One major difference between tables 5.1 and 5.2 is that, on average, each young firm in the industries included in table 5.2 tends to account for a relatively high share of the total number of enterprises in the industry, whereas, in table 5.1 each young firm accounts for only a trivial share of the number of firms. This emphasizes the need to control for the total number of firms existing in the industry when comparing the extent of entrepreneurial activity across markets. Thus, in making such inter-industry comparisons, the young-firm enterprise and employment shares are preferable to the number of new firms and the amount of employment in new firms.

The number of entrepreneurial firms and their share of all enterprises for varying definitions of what constitutes a young firm are shown in table 5.3 for all of the major manufacturing sectors. If the broadest measure, six years old, is used, then entrepreneurial firms can be considered to constitute one-third of all manufacturing firms. However, the share of 1986 enterprises accounted for by entrepreneurial firms varies considerably across the major manufacturing sectors. For example, in certain sectors, such as office machinery and electronic components, over 40 percent of 1986 enterprises had been founded since 1980. In other sectors, such as stone, clay and glass, and nonferrous metals, only about one-quarter of the firms were less than six years old.

It should also be emphasized that this method of measuring the extent of entrepreneurship combines two major economic phenomena—the startup of a new firm with its survival over time. Thus the different measures of what constitutes an entrepreneurial firm places different weights on these two economic phenomena. If the number of new-firm startups was constant over time, the greater propensity of young firms to exit the industry than that of their more established counterparts would result in the share of enterprises accounted for by new firms to increase with the transition age used, but only at a decreasing rate. Even though the number of new-firm startups is anything but constant over time, as we found in chapter 3, the tendency for survival rates to be positively related to firm age, which was found in chapter 4, results in the six-year measure being less than one-third greater than the four-year measure, which in turn is less than one-half greater than the two-year measure.

These same observations apply to table 5.4, which disaggregates the amount of 1986 employment accounted for by entrepreneurial firms across

Table 5.1
The industries with the greatest number of 1986 firms founded since 1982 (relative ranking listed in parentheses)

Industry	Number of new firms	Share of 1986 firms	Employment from new firms	Employment share from new firms
Commercial printing (lithographic)	10,141	38.18 (90)	66,059 (1)	17.70 (50)
Non-electrical industrial machinery[a]	7,596	29.78 (252)	50,362 (3)	18.09 (46)
Miscellaneous plastic products	3,610	34.28 (167)	57,881 (2)	11.15 (142)
Commercial printing (letterpress)	3,311	32.27 (206)	21,471 (5)	15.13 (78)
Miscellaneous manufacturing	2,001	40.98 (55)	17,279 (8)	18.97 (39)
Special dies, tools, jigs, and fixtures	1,845	24.86 (354)	15,623 (12)	14.23 (87)
Wood kitchen cabinets	1,782	33.85 (174)	13,254 (20)	19.75 (32)
Electronic components[a]	1,639	41.49 (52)	34,152 (4)	11.23 (141)
Periodicals	1,580	38.62 (80)	13,651 (16)	7.99 (199)
Typesetting	1,452	41.99 (47)	7,775 (42)	21.95 (20)
Wood products[a]	1,421	37.29 (102)	11,502 (26)	18.23 (45)
Book publishing	1,384	37.68 (97)	7,900 (41)	5.55 (267)
Signs and advertising displays	1,349	30.42 (240)	10,764 (28)	14.63 (82)
Newspapers	1,320	21.69 (394)	16,694 (11)	3.17 (333)
Wood household furniture	1,311	40.02 (61)	14,159 (15)	10.74 (146)
Millwork	1,194	34.88 (147)	12,328 (22)	13.80 (95)
Sporting and athletic goods[a]	1,161	40.40 (60)	9,585 (33)	14.08 (91)
Electronic computing equipment	1,143	48.49 (13)	18,560 (7)	1.41 (403)
Sheet metal work	1,127	28.53 (285)	13,054 (21)	12.83 (112)
Radio and TV communication equipment	1,119	38.00 (93)	16,893 (9)	2.36 (364)
Jewelry and precious metal	1,064	29.21 (265)	7,610 (45)	9.30 (177)
Women's and misses' dresses	1,053	39.03 (72)	16,843 (10)	16.03 (61)

Fabricated structural metal	1,032	30.62 (234)	14,507 (14)	11.70 (131)
Women's and misses' outerwear[a]	982	44.41 (39)	18,933 (6)	16.29 (60)
Miscellaneous publishing	907	35.43 (138)	6,946 (52)	12.21 (118)
Plating and polishing	872	27.06 (313)	11,680 (24)	17.07 (54)
Motor vehicle parts	861	35.23 (141)	13,281 (19)	3.34 (324)
Semiconductors	740	48.88 (10)	13,455 (17)	4.74 (290)
Boat building	737	38.25 (88)	9,557 (34)	21.67 (22)
Women's and misses' blouses	733	43.30 (42)	14,740 (13)	15.79 (66)

a. Not elsewhere classified.

Table 5.2
The industries with the smallest number of 1986 firms founded since 1982 (relative ranking listed in parentheses)

Industry	Number of new firms	Share of 1986 firms	Employment from new firms	Employment share from new firms
Beet sugar	1	10.00 (446)	75 (433)	0.97 (418)
Chewing gum	1	12.50 (441)	8 (446)	0.10 (443)
Cane sugar refining	2	12.50 (442)	790 (302)	6.49 (240)
Malt	2	12.50 (440)	31 (441)	2.26 (368)
Household laundry equipment	2	14.29 (437)	72 (434)	0.16 (441)
Tanks and tank components	3	23.08 (380)	105 (427)	0.24 (439)
Primary zinc	3	23.08 (381)	36 (440)	3.15 (337)
Cigarettes	3	20.00 (408)	50 (438)	0.01 (446)
Crowns and closures	4	20.00 (407)	54 (437)	5.88 (258)
Cellulosic manmade fibers	4	17.39 (425)	997 (279)	1.79 (385)
Cigars	4	10.26 (445)	94 (428)	3.81 (311)
Hard surface floor coverings	4	28.57 (283)	19 (455)	0.26 (437)
Tire cord and fabric	4	30.77 (228)	21 (444)	3.36 (323)
Electron tubes, all types	5	35.71 (131)	22 (443)	13.17 (106)
Primary lead	5	29.41 (261)	24 (442)	10.67 (149)
Guided missiles and space vehicles	5	41.67 (50)	203 (412)	0.10 (444)
Particleboard	5	26.32 (329)	256 (400)	6.61 (238)
Creamery butter	6	10.71 (444)	210 (411)	2.13 (374)
Chewing and smoking tobacco	6	24.00 (366)	76 (432)	1.29 (408)
Household vacuum cleaners	6	21.43 (396)	239 (403)	0.50 (431)
Raw cane sugar	6	18.75 (417)	80 (431)	1.61 (393)
Lime	7	14.89 (434)	217 (410)	6.25 (250)

Electrotyping and stereotyping	8	44.44 (37)	39 (439)	8.92 (182)
Breakfast cereal	8	26.67 (320)	330 (384)	0.30 (436)
Typewriters	9	47.37 (23)	62 (436)	6.72 (237)
Fine earthenware food utensils	9	36.00 (123)	523 (341)	33.12 (12)
Measuring and dispensing pumps	9	19.57 (412)	64 (435)	0.79 (426)
House slippers	9	25.00 (350)	223 (407)	3.82 (310)
Space vehicle equipment[a]	10	38.64 (83)	172 (419)	65.57 (239)

a. Not elsewhere classified.

Table 5.3
Number (and share) of 1986 firms accounted for by entrepreneurial enterprises

Industry group	Period in which firm founded			Total 1986
	1980–1986	1982–1986	1984–1986	
Food	5,090 (29.37)	3,831 (22.10)	2,170 (12.52)	17,333
Textiles and apparel	11,024 (37.13)	8,147 (22.44)	4,466 (15.04)	29,693
Lumber and furniture	12,378 (31.24)	8,967 (22.63)	4,917 (12.41)	39,616
Paper	1,404 (29.10)	1,071 (22.20)	638 (13.22)	4,825
Chemicals	3,611 (30.54)	2,624 (22.20)	1,473 (12.46)	11,822
Industrial	877 (32.30)	616 (22.69)	352 (12.97)	2,715
Drugs and medicinals	503 (35.95)	370 (26.45)	217 (15.51)	1,399
Other	1,569 (28.66)	1,172 (21.41)	634 (11.58)	5,474
Petroleum	454 (31.27)	328 (22.59)	212 (14.60)	1,452
Rubber	4,104 (33.43)	3,043 (25.16)	1,743 (14.41)	12,094
Stone, clay, and glass	3,573 (25.76)	2,502 (18.04)	1,462 (10.54)	13,869
Primary metals	1,845 (29.82)	1,368 (22.11)	848 (13.71)	6,187
Ferrous metals	940 (32.51)	735 (25.42)	467 (16.15)	2,891
Nonferrous metals	905 (27.46)	633 (19.21)	381 (11.56)	3,296
Fabricated metal products	10,059 (28.96)	7,271 (20.93)	4,097 (11.79)	34,740
Machinery	17,838 (30.18)	12,181 (20.61)	6,712 (11.36)	59,096
Office	1,275 (46.41)	976 (35.53)	507 (18.46)	2,747
Nonelectrical	16,563 (29.39)	11,205 (19.89)	6,205 (11.01)	56,349
Electrical equipment	7,147 (37.90)	5,308 (28.15)	2,999 (15.90)	18,857
Radio and TV equipment	664 (36.99)	456 (25.40)	239 (13.31)	1,795
Communications equipment	1,386 (39.60)	1,060 (30.29)	607 (17.34)	3,500
Electronic components	2,541 (41.72)	1,891 (31.05)	1,091 (17.91)	6,090

Table 5.3 (cont.)

Industry group	Period in which firm founded			Total 1986
	1980–1986	1982–1986	1984–1986	
Other	2,556 (34.21)	1,901 (25.44)	1,062 (14.21)	7,472
Motor vehicles	1,687 (37.92)	1,309 (29.42)	781 (17.55)	4,449
Other transportation equipment	1,599 (37.68)	1,122 (26.44)	623 (14.68)	4,244 (2.99)
Aircraft	498 (31.80)	348 (22.22)	211 (13.47)	1,566
Instruments	4,219 (36.02)	3,042 (25.97)	1,634 (13.95)	11,713
Scientific and measuring	1,915 (36.99)	1,399 (27.02)	736 (14.22)	5,177
Optical, surgical, and photographic	2,304 (35.25)	1,643 (25.14)	898 (13.74)	6,536
Other manufacturing	30,199 (34.93)	21,458 (24.82)	11,553 (13.36)	86,451
Total manufacturing	116,729 (32.61)	83,920 (23.44)	46,539 (13.00)	358,007

Note: Entrepreneurial enterprises are defined as those firms established within the designated time period. The number in parentheses indicates the share of 1986 firms accounted for by young enterprises.

Table 5.4
1986 employment (and share) accounted for by entrepreneurial enterprises

Industry group	Period in which firm founded			Total 1986
	1980–1986	1982–1986	1984–1986	
Food	82,119 (3.37)	65,345 (3.00)	41,178 (1.89)	2,179,513
Textiles and apparel	183,044 (8.26)	135,328 (6.11)	77,222 (3.48)	2,216,567
Lumber and furniture	145,433 (11.79)	10,987 (8.87)	61,842 (5.01)	1,233,270
Paper	33,790 (3.59)	26,163 (2.78)	16,478 (1.75)	941,906
Chemicals	41,795 (2.00)	31,178 (1.49)	19,694 (0.94)	2,090,660
Industrial	15,158 (2.03)	11,614 (1.55)	7,919 (1.06)	747,801
Drugs and medicinals	7,826 (1.24)	5,600 (0.89)	3,724 (0.59)	632,042
Other	13,551 (2.28)	10,172 (1.71)	5,871 (0.99)	595,568

Table 5.4 (cont.)

Industry group	Period in which firm founded			Total 1986
	1980–1986	1982–1986	1984–1986	
Petroleum	7,144	5,957	4,494	284,907
	(2.51)	(2.09)	(1.58)	
Rubber	66,456	48,723	28,853	994,295
	(6.68)	(4.90)	(2.90)	
Stone, clay, and glass	44,393	31,828	19,326	809,526
	(5.48)	(3.93)	(2.39)	
Primary metals	46,323	37,709	26,018	834,698
	(5.55)	(4.52)	(3.12)	
Ferrous metals	29,651	24,915	17,778	527,479
	(5.62)	(4.72)	(3.37)	
Nonferrous metals	16,672	12,794	8,240	307,219
	(5.43)	(4.16)	(2.68)	
Fabricated metal products	138,585	102,835	60,771	1,718,035
	(8.07)	(5.99)	(3.54)	
Machinery	178,478	125,894	71,119	8,847,923
	(4.64)	(3.27)	(1.85)	
Office	20,888	15,927	8,194	1,392,676
	(1.50)	(1.14)	(0.59)	
Other nonelectrical	157,590	109,967	62,925	2,455,247
	(6.42)	(4.48)	(2.56)	
Electrical equipment	121,089	88,035	51,164	2,547,595
	(4.75)	(3.46)	(2.01)	
Radio and TV equipment	6,225	4,158	2,232	173,902
	(3.58)	(2.39)	(1.28)	
Communications equipment	22,676	16,866	10,638	785,582
	(2.89)	(2.15)	(1.35)	
Electronic components	51,377	36,444	20,384	709,650
	(7.24)	(5.14)	(2.87)	
Other	40,811	30,567	17,910	878,461
	(4.65)	(3.48)	(2.04)	
Motor vehicles	29,224	23,448	15,625	2,077,101
	(1.41)	(1.13)	(0.75)	
Other transportation equipment	21,853	14,857	8,335	234,191
	(9.33)	(6.34)	(3.56)	
Aircraft	8,683	6,059	4,070	1,182,919
	(0.73)	(0.51)	(0.34)	
Instruments	56,690	40,864	24,173	1,099,915
	(5.15)	(3.72)	(2.20)	
Scientific and measuring	29,388	22,093	13,957	538,745
	(5.45)	(4.10)	(2.59)	
Optical, surgical, and photographic	27,302	18,771	10,216	561,170
	(4.87)	(3.34)	(1.82)	
Other manufacturing	235,423	165,559	92,357	2,852,011
	(8.25)	(5.88)	(3.24)	
Total manufacturing	1,440,522	1,059,169	622,719	27,145,034
	(5.31)	(3.90)	(2.29)	

Note: Entrepreneurial enterprises are defined as those firms established within the designated time period. The number in parentheses indicates the share of 1986 firms accounted for by young enterprises.

major manufacturing sectors. For all of manufacturing, 5.31 percent of employment was in firms which were not older than six years, and 2.29 percent in firms not older than two years. Once again, it should be emphasized that the employment measures result in smaller estimates of the extent of entrepreneurial activity in manufacturing than do the enterprise count measures, regardless of the age definition used.

5.3   Innovation, Scale Economies, and Entrepreneurship

Why should the extent of entrepreneurial activity, or more precisely the shares of enterprises and employment accounted for by young firms, vary from industry to industry? The most obvious answer is that, as we found in chapter 3, the propensity for new firms to enter also varies across industries. But because the propensity for these new firms to survive not only varies across industries, but is also shaped in a different and sometimes contradictory way than the propensity to enter, as was found in chapter 4, the answer is considerably more complex.

The previous two chapters found that the entry of new firms and the likelihood of their survival are determined by many of the same factors, although the impact is sometimes quite different. In particular, the technological environment and degree of scale economies were found to be central to the entry of new firms and the likelihood of their survival. For example, in chapter 3 we found that new-firm startups tend to be deterred in an industry characterized by a high technological opportunity class, that is where the total innovation rate is high. At the same time, in industries characterized by the entrepreneurial technological regime, or where the innovative activity of small firms is high relative to that of the overall industry, startup activity tends to be higher. However, in chapter 4 we found that the likelihood of survival tends to be lower, not only in industries characterized by a high technological opportunity class, but also under the entrepreneurial technological regime. This raises a key empirical question: "Will the stimulative effect on new-firm startups under the entrepreneurial regime be more than offset by the lower likelihood of survival in shaping the role of entrepreneurial or young firms in industries characterized by the entrepreneurial regime? And will the overall net effect be more or fewer entrepreneurial firms, and will they account for relatively more or less economic activity?"

Similarly, we found in the third and fourth chapters that the presence of scale economies and capital intensity has no substantial deterrent impact on new-firm startups, but that the likelihood of those new firms surviving is in fact reduced. Does this mean that there will tend to be, on balance, less entrepreneurial activity in industries where scale economies and capital intensity play an important role?

New and young firms may not be immune from retaliatory strategies pursued by the incumbent enterprises to preserve their market dominance. That is, entrepreneurial activity is more likely to be impeded in industries where the incumbent firms can more easily detect the entrepreneurial firms and respond to their establishment through some type of retaliatory strategy. As Scherer and Ross (1990) point out, this is more likely to be the case in highly concentrated industries, where detection is facilitated. In addition, advertising provides a mechanism for retaliating against new entrants (Arndt and Simon, 1983; Boyer, 1974).[6] That is, industries where advertising plays a more important role may be less hospitable for entrepreneurial activity. Finally, market growth was found to have an important (positive) impact on the likelihood of new-firm survival, although the effect on start-up activity was considerably less.

To measure these industry-specific characteristics, I rely on the same measures of MES, capital intensity, small-firm innovation rate divided by the total innovation rate, company R & D/sales ratio, and market growth that were introduced in chapters 3 and 4. In addition, we include the 1977 four-firm concentration ratio and the 1977 advertising/sales ratio.

5.4 Empirical Results

The regression results for the employment share (first two equations) and enterprise shares (last equation) of 1986 firms founded since 1980 are shown in table 5.5. In equation (1) the negative and statistically significant coefficient suggests that entrepreneurial activity is lower in capital-intensive industries. Similarly, the negative coefficient of the R & D/sales ratio reflects a relatively low amount of economic activity accounted for by young firms in R & D-intensive industries. The share of employment accounted for by young firms also tends to be lower in industries better characterized by the entrepreneurial regime, where the small-firm innovation rate is high relative to the total innovation rate.

The negative and statistically significant coefficient of market concentration suggests that entrepreneurship tends to be deterred in highly con-

---

6. In addition, Comanor (1967) argues that advertising intensity can also pose a barrier to new firms. To the extent that scale economies exist in either production or advertising, the need to obtain funds for advertising will tend to raise the size disadvantage confronting young firms.

Table 5.5
Regression results for the shares of 1986 employment and firms emanating from enterprises founded since 1980 (t-statistics in parentheses)

	New-firm share of employment		New-firm share of enterprises
	(1)	(2)	(3)
Capital intensity	−0.6590 (−4.17)	—	−0.441 (−1.87)
Scale economies	—	−1.165 (−2.15)	—
Small-firm innovation rate/ total innovation rate	−0.248 (−2.01)	−0.138 (−1.04)	−0.306 (1.66)
R & D/sales	−4.651 (−1.78)	−2.355 (−0.85)	11.663 (2.98)
Concentration	−0.647 (−3.69)	−0.703 (−3.74)	0.358 (1.37)
Advertising/sales	−6.256 (−2.55)	−6.199 (−2.47)	1.481 (0.40)
Growth	−1.731 (−1.59)	−1.688 (−1.52)	−1.994 (−1.23)
Constant	0.135 (18.19)	0.127 (16.55)	0.291 (26.26)
Sample size	315	315	315
R^2	0.199	0.167	0.064
F	12.784	10.278	3.517

centrated industries. Similarly, in industries where advertising plays an important role, young firms account for significantly less of the industry employment. The negative and statistically insignificant coefficient of the industry growth rate suggests that the positive impact of high growth on the likelihood of survival does not prevail when entry and survival are combined into this measure of entrepreneurship. Apparently firms do not enter and subsequently survive, at least within the first six years, at any greater rate in high-growth industries than in low-growth markets. This may reflect the propensity of many of the newly established enterprises to exit from the industry within a short time interval subsequent to the startup year.

The MES measure is substituted for the capital-labor ratio in equation (2). Although the impact of scale economies on entrepreneurship remains negative, neither the measure of R & D intensity nor the measure of the technological regime can be considered statistically significant.

The alternative measure, the share of firms accounted for by young firms, is substituted as the dependent variable in equation (3). The regression results are quite different, which reflects the different measure of entrepreneurial activity. Although capital intensity is still found to exert a negative impact on entrepreneurship, the share of enterprises accounted for by young firms is found to be greater and not lower in industries characterized by a high technological opportunity class, or where the R & D intensity is high, as well as in industries characterized by the entrepreneurial technological regime, or where the small firms tend to have the innovative advantage.

Comparing the results for the two different measures of entrepreneurship would suggest that fundamental differences exist between the relative number of new firms in an industry and their impact or importance in the economic activity of the industry. That is, there tends to be a large number of young firms in R & D-intensive industries and under the entrepreneurial regime where the small-firm innovation rate is particularly high. However, these entrepreneurial firms apparently contribute less to overall industry employment than do new firms in other industries (that are not R & D intensive and where small firms are not particularly innovative).

In table 5.6 two alternative definitions of what constitutes an entrepreneurial or a young firm are used. In equations (1) and (3) enterprises that are no older than four years are considered, and in equations (2) and (4) only firms that are two years old or younger are considered. The major difference in the results is that for the shorter time periods the measure of the technological opportunity class, or R & D intensity, is no longer statistically significant. This suggests that the technological opportunity class of an industry may reduce the ability of new-firm startups to survive beyond four years, that is in the medium term, but not necessarily in the very short term.

5.5   Conclusions

The dynamic nature of U.S. manufacturing has been documented in this chapter. While nearly one-third of all manufacturing firms can be considered entrepreneurial, in the sense that they were started within the last six years, the impact on economic activity, as measured by employment, is substantially less. Only about 5 percent of all employment is accounted for by such entrepreneurial enterprises. However, the importance of entrepreneurship is found to vary considerably across industries. In particular, the existence of scale economies and capital intensity is found to diminish

Table 5.6
Regression results for the shares of 1986 employment and firms emanating from enterprises
founded since 1982 and 1984 (*t*-statistics in parentheses)

	New-firm share of employment		New-firm share of enterprises	
	1982–1986 (1)	1984–1986 (2)	1982–1986 (3)	1984–1986 (4)
Capital intensity	−0.432 (−3.59)	−0.193 (−2.94)	—	−0.042 (−0.32)
Scale economies	—	—	1.153 (2.65)	—
Small-firm innovation rate/ total innovation rate	−0.174 (−1.85)	−0.088 (−1.71)	−0.211 (1.98)	0.295 (2.87)
R & D/sales	−2.848 (−1.43)	−0.153 (−0.14)	1.953 (0.88)	3.519 (1.62)
Concentration	−0.513 (−3.85)	−0.350 (−4.82)	0.172 (1.14)	0.357 (2.46)
Advertising/sales	−4.464 (−2.39)	2.219 (−2.18)	0.461 (0.23)	0.045 (0.02)
Growth	−1.184 (−1.43)	−0.774 (−1.72)	−2.414 (−2.70)	−2.694 (−2.99)
Constant	0.981 (17.42)	0.055 (17.85)	0.118 (19.14)	0.115 (18.67)
Sample size	315	315	315	315
R^2	0.181	0.184	0.105	0.085
F	11.309	11.593	6.009	4.744

the role of entrepreneurship in an industry, a result that is not found when examining new-firm startups in the third chapter. Similarly, the role of young firms is clearly less important in concentrated industries and in markets where advertising plays an important role.

The role of innovative activity and technology is apparently more complicated. A high technological opportunity class, as measured by R & D intensity, promotes the number of entrepreneurial firms but not their overall contribution to economic activity. Similarly, in industries characterized by the entrepreneurial regime, or where the small firms have the innovative advantage, a greater share of the enterprises is accounted for by new firms. However, the impact that these entrepreneurial firms have on overall economic activity, as measured by employment, is actually less than in other industries. One explanation may be the greater product diversity in such industries, enabling entrepreneurial firms to survive by occupying distinct product niches. An alternative explanation is that these young firms have managed to gain a toehold in the industry but remain on the fringe without exerting any major impact on overall economic activity.

In any case, examining why the role of entrepreneurship—that is, the degree to which an industry is accounted for by young firms—varies from industry to industry provides an important insight into the dynamic process of industry evolution. As we learned in chapter 3, the startup of new firms tends to be greater under the entrepreneurial regime; but, at the same time, as was found in chapter 4, the likelihood of survival tends to be lower under the entrepreneurial regime. That is, although divergences in beliefs regarding (potential) innovations may induce a greater amount of startup activity, the likelihood of any new firm actually surviving and having a substantial impact on the industry is relatively low. Thus we observe a relatively high number of entrepreneurial or young firms, whose impact is, on average, relatively negligible. This suggests that at least some of the turbulent nature of U.S. markets is attributable to entrepreneurial activity, that is, to the attempt by individual agents to actualize a perceived idea to do something differently.

6   Compensating Strategies

6.1   Introduction

One of the more striking findings to emerge from chapter 4 is that not only are most new firms small, but they are so small as to preclude operating at anything approaching an efficient scale of output, at least for most industries. This finding that the bulk of enterprises are small applies to more than just new firms. Building on his 1964, 1976, and 1979 studies on the extent of suboptimal scale plants and firms in industrial markets, Leonard Weiss in 1991 concluded that, "In most industries the great majority of firms is suboptimal. In a typical industry there are, let's say, one hundred firms. Typically only about five to ten of them will be operating at the MES (miniumum efficient scale) level of output, or anything like it. So here is a subject that ought to be measured and critically analysed and evaluated."[1] Not only did Weiss (1976, p. 259) find that the MES level of output exceeds that of most firms (enterprises) and plants (establishments), but that, "On the average, about half of total shipments in the industries covered are from suboptimal plants. The majority of plants in most industries are suboptimal in scale, and a very large percentage of output is from suboptimal plants in some unconcentrated industries."[2]

Although the exact reason why the extent of suboptimal plants and firms should vary so much across industries has remained something of a controversy in the decades following to the pathbreaking studies by Weiss (1964 and 1976), Scherer (1973), and Pratten (1971), their actual existence

---

1. Quotation from p. xiv of the "editor's introduction" to Weiss (1991).
2. While Weiss (1964) concluded that suboptimal plants account for about 52.8 percent of industry value-of-shipments, Scherer (1973) found that 58.2 percent of value-of-shipments emanated from suboptimal plants in twelve industries, and Pratten (1971) identified the suboptimal scale establishments accounting for 47.9 percent of industry shipments.

has not.[3] The persistence of suboptimal plants to dominate industrial markets over time raises the question of not only why do suboptimal scale plants exist but how are they able to exist.[4] That is, while Weiss (1991, p. 403) assumed that "The term 'suboptimal capacity' describes a condition in which some plants are too small to be efficient," Caves and Barton (1990) systematically show that smaller establishments are less efficient than their larger counterparts.

How are such suboptimal scale establishments able to exist? The answer found in chapter 4 is that they cannot—at least not for an indefinite period of time. An important conclusion emerging from chapter 4 is that such small and suboptimal businesses are, at least to some extent, in a state of static disequilibrium (although they may not be in a state of dynamic disequilibrium), in that they must grow and approach an efficient scale of output to remain viable in the long run. They do, however, exist in the short run because they are incurring the risk that they possess the right endowments or qualities, in terms of both product being offered and management, to facilitate growth and ultimately survival. The purpose of this chapter is to offer a somewhat different, but complementary explanation for why suboptimal scale plants exist despite their inherent static efficiency disadvantages. We introduce a hypothesis suggesting that suboptimal scale plants compensate for their size disadvantage by deviating from the manner in which productive factors are deployed and remunerated by their larger counterparts which have attained the MES level of output. By engaging in a compensatory factor differential strategy, suboptimal scale plants are able to offset, at least to some extent, their size-induced scale disadvantages. This hypothesis is tested using both American and Japanese plants for 1982. Comparing the U.S. experience to that of the Japanese is presumably instructive, since Loveman and Sengenberger (1991) and Aoki (1988), among others, have emphasized that small plants and firms fulfill a somewhat different economic role in Japan than in the United States.

---

3. For example, Weiss (1991, p. 114) writes, "Mike Scherer had formulated a theory explaining the extent of suboptimal capacity. Firms make decisions about plant scale when they add to capacity, trading off increasing transport cost against falling production costs as additions to capacity are made. As a result, high concentration leads to larger scale plant and reduced suboptimal capacity."

4. Weiss (1991, p. 404) observes that, "The survival of smaller plants within any given industry may be due to their specialization in items with short production runs or to their service of small geographic markets within which their relatively small national market share is irrelevant. To the extent that such explanations hold, small plants are not necessarily suboptimal. However, such explanations seem unlikely to hold for a number of the industries where the percentage of suboptimal capacity is large."

In the following section the manner used to calculate the MES is explained, and the degree to which scale economies exist along with the prevalence of suboptimal sized firms is examined for both the United States and Japan. A model relating suboptimal scale firms to compensating factor differentials is introduced in the third section. Using a system of simultaneous equations, the hypothesis is then tested for U.S. manufacturing industries in the fourth section and a modified version for Japanese manufacturing in the fifth section. Finally, in the sixth section a summary and conclusions are provided. We find considerable evidence in both U.S. and Japanese manufacturing that a different deployment and remuneration of productive factors serves, at least to some extent, to compensate for the inherent scale disadvantages confronting suboptimal plants. The empirical results suggest that the degree to which such a strategy of compensatory factor differentials is implemented depends on the extent to which the MES level of output exceeds that of the suboptimal scale plant along with the extent to which efficiency declines along with plant size. Those factors identified as compensating for a size-induced efficiency disadvantage include employee compensation, length of the work week, and a strategy of product innovation.

6.2 Minimum Efficient Scale and Suboptimal Plant Share

As Caves, Khalilzadeh-Shirazi, and Porter (1975) and Scherer and Ross (1990, chapter 11) emphasize, estimating the extent of scale economies for plants is a rather hazardous and imprecise undertaking. Although a number of methodological approaches for estimating the industry MES have been introduced in the literature (see Scherer and Ross, 1990, chapters 4 and 11), here we follow our example from the previous chapters and adapt the method first introduced by Comanor and Wilson (1967), who approximated the MES by measuring the mean size of the plants accounting for the largest 50 percent of the industry value-of-shipments. Their measure, while used by numerous researchers, is a slight variation on the original method introduced by Weiss (1963), who proxied MES as the plant size accounting for one-half of the industry value-of-shipments. Thus the Comanor and Wilson measure is systematically larger than the Weiss measure. In any case, Scherer and Ross (1990, p. 424–425) report that the various estimates of MES derived from industry census statistics correlate reasonably well with the presumably more precise engineering estimates for a limited sample of industries.

Using the 1982 *Census of Manufactures* from the U.S. Bureau of the Census, the MES was calculated and is ranked for the industries exhibiting the largest MES in table 6.1. The first column shows the value of the output needed to be shipped from a plant in order to attain MES. Along with the obviously crude method used to approximate MES, there are several other weaknesses that should be emphasized. The MES will tend to be overstated in industries producing goods close to the final consumer and understated in industries producing goods that are predominantly used as intermediate inputs. That is, the level of the production process in the vertical chain is not controlled for in the value-of-shipments measure. To avoid this problem, and to facilitate comparisions within an international context by avoiding the exchange rate problem, the second column lists the number of employees associated with the MES plant. However, the employee measure is biased because it neglects the amount of capital input required to attain MES. Thus MES will tend to be understated in a highly capital-intensive industry and overstated in industries where the capital-labor ratio is relatively low. The limitations inherent in each of these measures explain why the rank order of industries according to the MES measured in terms of value-of-shipments does not exactly correspond to the rank order when the MES is measured in terms of employment.

Table 6.1 makes it clear that the industries exhibiting the largest MES tend to be concentrated within just several manufacturing sectors. That is, nine of the thirty industries with the largest MES are in the two-digit SIC (standard industrial class) sector 37, transportation equipment. Similarly, six are in the two-digit SIC sector 36, electrical equipment, and an additional five are in SIC sector 20, food and beverages. Thus nearly one-third of the thirty U.S. industries with the largest MES are contained in a single industrial sector, one-half can be found in just two sectors, and two-thirds fall within three sectors.

The last column indicates the share of plants in an industry accounted for by establishments that are at a suboptimal scale of production. For the largest MES industries, the share of suboptimal plants ranges from 58.62 percent in guided missiles to 99.25 percent in photographic equipment.

Using the data from the *Japanese Census of Manufactures*, the MES for Japanese industries can also be calculated. Table 6.2 shows the Japanese industries exhibiting the largest MES in 1982. As for the U.S. measures, the MES is expressed both in terms of value-of-shipments and employment. To facilitate comparisons between the two countries, the Japanese shipments have been converted from a yen denomination to a dollar denomination, using the 1982 mean exchange rate of $1 = 249.06 yen (from the 1989

Table 6.1
U.S. industries with the largest MES, 1982

Industry	MES Thousand$	Employees	Suboptimal plant share
Photographic equipment	1,975,017	12,200	99.25
Motor vehicles	1,393,362	4,732	88.73
Aircraft	1,156,223	11,000	86.67
Household laundry equipment	1,043,550	8,000	86.67
Aircraft engines	971,220	8,150	97.06
Guided missiles	775,617	7,258	58.62
Aluminum sheet	693,125	2,625	84.91
Railroad equipment	651,167	6,433	98.48
Tanks	640,667	4,600	92.68
Blast furnaces & steel mills	607,635	5,160	86.71
Space vehicle equipment	601,833	6,400	93.02
Telephone apparatus	587,717	5,572	94.30
Motor vehicle parts	572,179	4,169	98.37
Malt beverages	567,040	2,370	90.65
Household vacuum cleaners	536,900	6,400	96.55
Farm machinery	530,164	3,145	99.42
Roasted coffee	510,317	833	95.95
Canned seafoods	508,950	2,650	99.01
Aircraft equipment	503,364	5,891	98.86
Radio and TV receiving sets	461,522	2,900	98.03
Household refrigerators	455,675	3,975	91.67
Organic fibers	441,847	3,320	75.81
Semiconductors	402,253	4,871	97.78
Meat packing plants	382,127	1,133	96.63
Turbines	378,283	3,133	93.18
Industrial organic chemicals	365,763	1,335	92.15
Chocolate	346,875	1,775	95.29
Pharmaceutical preparations	336,239	2,352	95.46
Automotive and apparel trimmings	333,025	3,025	99.51
Agricultural chemicals	320,860	940	96.94
Primary nonferrous metals	319,680	1,140	94.32
Vehicular lighting equipment	303,900	3,450	97.59
Electronic computing equipment	303,479	2,638	95.63
Breakfast cereal	298,350	1,080	80.39
Engine electrical equipment	295,583	2,883	98.61
Ship building	292,005	4,836	96.81
Internal combustion engines	271,658	2,300	90.51
Cellulosic manmade fibers	267,075	3,075	76.47
Tires	259,838	1,910	81.87

Note: The petroleum refining industry has been omitted from this list due to data unreliability.

Table 6.2
Japanese industries with the largest MES, 1982

Industry	MES Thousand$	MES Employees	Suboptimal plant share
Motor vehicles	1,433,690	5,312	31.37
Stem engines	559,154	5,312	95.77
Tractors	459,889	3,040	98.63
Computers	446,014	2,475	98.74
Petroleum chemicals	419,174	693	57.14
Motor vehicle bodies	399,826	2,363	94.50
Copper smelting and refining	373,434	652	55.56
Aliphatic intermediates	354,987	1,153	89.71
Synthetic rubber	343,259	1,520	78.57
Radio and TV receivers	341,669	2,141	94.02
Integrated circuits	294,823	2,663	89.37
Newspaper printing	255,754	1,963	89.93
Internal combustion engines	251,551	1,934	97.77
Malt liquors	251,275	498	48.57
Communication equipment	227,091	2,119	95.36
Cyclic intermediates	223,871	925	91.49
Aircraft	214,353	2,640	66.67
Foreign style paper mills	199,847	924	94.61
Tires and tubes	193,634	1,542	72.50
Railroad cars	192,023	2,049	86.21
Precious metal smelting	186,876	—	—
Electron tubes	177,963	2,145	85.71
Chemical machinery	169,531	1,402	98.74
Flat glass	163,572	—	—
Office machinery	162,926	1,279	98.36
Electrical control equipment	159,255	1,659	99.14
Combustion engines equipment	138,246	1,677	98.88
Medical preparations	137,136	880	94.89
Construction machinery	134,864	909	98.84
Refrigerators	133,866	1,071	98.83
Motor vehicle parts	130,746	1,154	98.41
Aircraft engines	123,662	1,441	90.32
Aluminum smelting	116,523	500	30.77
Watches and clocks	110,972	1,067	97.39
Camers	105,988	1,143	78.79
Pumps	105,566	1,010	98.26
Ball bearings	104,879	1,256	97.80
Engines and turbines (misc.)	101,120	—	—
Sewing machines	99,406	1,019	98.69

Note: The Japanese MES has been converted from a yen to a dollar denomination using the 1982 exchange rate of 1$ = 249.06 yen.

Economic Report of the President). Thus, in the Japanese industry with the greatest extent of scale economies, motor vehicles, a plant had to ship $1,433 million of output in order to exhaust scale economies. This corresponds to a plant workforce of 5,312 employees.

As is the case for the United States, high-MES industries in Japan tend to be concentrated within just several manufacturing sectors. Seven of the thirty Japanese industries exhibiting the highest MES are contained in the electrical equipment sector and an additional seven are in the non-electrical machinery sector. Similarly, five of the industries are in the chemical sector and four are in the transportation equipment sector. Thus nearly one-half of the thirty largest Japanese MES industries included in table 6.2 are contained in just two sectors, while almost two-thirds fall within three sectors, and over three-fourths can be found in four sectors. However, it should be noted that industries from the food and beverage sector, which appears with high frequency in table 6.1 for the United States, does not contain many high-MES industries in Japan. By contrast, the industries in the non-electrical machinery sector and in the chemical sector do not rank among the highest MES industries as frequently in the United States as they do in Japan.

Different systems of industrial classification at the disaggregated industry level do not permit a systematic comparison of the MES between the United States and Japan. However, certain industries, where the classification is consistent for both countries, provide at least some insight into the extent to which MES varies between the two nations. For example, measured in terms of shipments, the MES for the motor vehicles industry is quite similar in the United States and Japan. By contrast, measured in terms of employees, the MES is substantially smaller in the United States than in Japan. This disparity between the measures based on value-of-shipments and employees may reflect a higher labor productivity in the United States. It could also reflect differences in the degree of vertical integration between Japanese and American plants. By contrast, in the radio and television receiving sets industry, the MES in the American industry is clearly greater than that in Japan, measured both in terms of shipments and employees.

In fact, the examples of the motor vehicles and radio and television receiving sets industries raise a perplexing question at the heart of measuring the industry MES on an internationally comparative basis: "Are differences in the computed national MES attributable to disparities in efficiency emanating from scale differences or do they reflect similar levels of efficiency which are attained using different methods of production?" Particularly striking is that despite the American superiority in MES in both of these industries, Audretsch and Yamawaki (1988) pointed out that of all the U.S. manufacturing industries, Japanese imports were the greatest in the motor vehicles industry and third greatest in the radio and television receiving sets industry.

There are at least four major reasons why the MES for any given industry should vary between nations. First, not all countries may be at the technological, management, and production frontier. Although historically it was a convenient and perhaps not all too inaccurate assumption that this frontier was defined by American manufacturing industries, as Dertouzos et al. (1989) make clear, this assumption is becoming increasingly less accurate, particularly vis-à-vis the other most developed nations, such as Japan. In any case, there are likely to be a number of industries where either country, or perhaps neither country, is on this technological frontier. Second, even if both nations are at the technological frontier, variation in relative factor input prices will result in differences in the observed MES. That is, there is more than one way to skin a cat, even most efficiently. Third, the aggregation of various productive activities under the umbrella of an encompassing industry classification will result in differences in the measured MES between the two countries, if the composition of various productive activities included in the industry varies between nations.

Finally, differences in domestic vertical and horizontal relationships as well as managerial techniques may result in variations in the MES between countries. For example, as Loveman and Sengenberger (1991) and Aoki (1988) point out, formal and informal subcontracting relationships are much more prevalent in Japanese manufacturing than in the United States. To the extent that Japanese plants tend to be less vertically integrated, the computed MES for a given Japanese industry will be less than that for its American counterpart.

These four factors probably account for a considerable amount of the differentials in the aggregated mean MES for broad industrial sectors between the United States and Japan as shown in table 6.3. In comparing the MES's for broadly aggregated industrial sectors between the United States and Japan, several points should be emphasized. First, the same sectors exhibit a relatively high MES in both Japan and the United States, just as those branches where scale economies tend to be less important also are the same in the two countries. That is, the sectors with the greatest mean MES are transportation equipment, primary metals, electrical equipment, and chemicals. Low-MES sectors are lumber, leather, apparel, and furniture.

Second, the MES tends to be greater in each U.S. sector than in its Japanese counterpart. There are, however, important exceptions, such as in

Table 6.3
Mean MES in U.S. and Japanese manufacturing sectors, 1982

Sector	United States			Japan		
	MES		Suboptimal plant share	MES		Suboptimal plant share
	Thousand$	Employees		Thousand$	Employees	
Food	54,785	295	83.33	15,728	130	91.54
Tobacco	885,679	3,071	87.16	—	—	—
Textiles	38,151	579	86.37	4,905	85	90.08
Apparel	10,852	251	83.22	1,840	70	87.54
Lumber	4,136	51	79.60	3,088	43	86.88
Furniture	17,291	309	90.89	4,678	74	92.74
Paper	160,480	1,025	94.28	39,810	253	96.69
Printing	30,229	392	96.64	29,982	280	98.09
Chemicals	156,423	798	92.16	151,517	741	94.95
Rubber	23,289	271	86.58	72,824	786	98.56
Leather	21,829	449	84.22	2,456	45	86.04
Stone, clay, and glass	25,054	284	89.77	11,383	136	92.58
Primary metals	206,757	1,555	95.19	462,123	2,320	98.33
Fabricated metal products	24,962	280	74.29	10,790	126	95.56
Machinery (non-electric)	77,627	764	96.31	68,724	634	98.35
Electrical equipment	121,198	1,432	93.21	154,649	1,317	98.58
Transportation equipment	937,049	6,547	98.08	571,658	3,057	99.11
Instruments	104,673	1,454	97.36	58,814	728	98.29
Miscellaneous	18,885	249	90.50	6,105	756	90.60

Note: The Japanese MES has been converted from a yen to a dollar denomination using the 1982 exchange rate of $1 = 249.06 yen.

electrical equipment, rubber, chemicals, and printing. Third, there is a distinct tendency for the suboptimal plant share to be directly related to MES size for both the United States and Japan. That is, in the sector with the lowest MES in both countries, lumber, the share of suboptimal plants is the lowest in Japan, 86.88 percent, and the second lowest in the United States, 79.60 percent. Conversely, in the transportation sector, which has the highest MES in both the United States and Japan, the suboptimal plant share is the largest.

Finally, despite the tendency for the measured MES in the United States to exceed that in Japan, the share of establishments accounted for by suboptimal plants in Japan exceeds the U.S. suboptimal plant share in every major industrial sector. This is somewhat surprising, since, as observed above, within each nation, a higher extent of suboptimal capacity is associated with a larger MES. However, the higher propensity for plants to be of a suboptimal size in Japan than in the United States is consistent with the observation by Loveman and Sengenberger (1991) that small businesses account for a considerably greater extent of manufacturing activity in Japan than in the United States.

6.3   Suboptimal Plants and Compensating Factor Differentials

The final observation made from table 6.3 raises a question that has never been answered in the industrial organization literature: "How is the vast bulk of plants, not only in the U.S. but even more so in Japan, able to survive if they are operating at a scale that is suboptimal, in that their level of production is less than the MES level of output?" The question arises because, as Weiss (1963 and 1964) makes clear, suboptimal scale plants are confronted with a cost disadvantage vis-à-vis their counterparts that have attained the MES level of output. As figure 6.1 shows, the long-run average cost of a plant operating at a suboptimal scale of Q_{so} exceeds that of an optimal plant by $AC_{so} - AC_o$.

One answer to the question of how the suboptimal plants manage to survive is that they do not, at least, as we found in chapter 4, not to the same extent that optimal-sized plants are able to survive. In chapter 4 we identified a positive relationship between the likelihood of survival and plant and/or firm size. And, those suboptimal plants surviving in the long run undoubtedly do so through growing, so that presumably more than a few of them attain the MES level of output. That is, small plants tend also to be young plants, and the results from chapter 4 clearly show that, although the probability of a young small plant surviving is lower than that

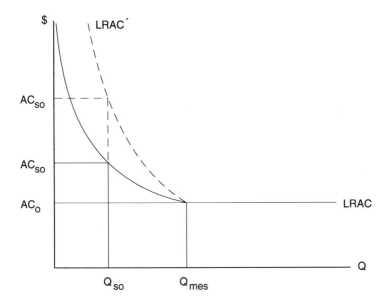

Figure 6.1
Suboptimal plant size and compensating factor differentials

of a larger and more experienced establishment, the growth rate of those young small plants that do survive tends to be greater than that of older and larger plants (see also Acs and Audretsch, 1990, chapter 7).

Still, until suboptimal plants grow sufficiently to attain the MES level of output, the question of how they manage to stay viable remains. Here the observation made by Brown and Medoff (1989) and Brown, Hamilton, and Medoff (1990) that employee compensation tends to be systematically lower in small plants than in large plants provides at least one explanation. Through providing a lower level of employee compensation than that provided by their larger counterparts, suboptimal plants can effectively offset their inherent cost disadvantage.[5] To the degree that suboptimal

5. An example of compensating factor differentials is provided by the *Wall Street Journal* (1991, p. 1), which reports that "Wall Street has been in love with Nucor Corp.," which has become the seventh largest U.S. steel company through its fifteen "mini-mill" plants. Nucor has pursued a strategy not only of "... declaring war on corporate hierarchy," but also by being "... terribly efficient, aggressively non-union and quite profitable. Most of its 15 mini-mills and steel fabrication operations are situated in small towns, where they have trained all sorts of people who never thought they'd make so much money. And Nucor has developed a revolutionary new plant that spins gleaming sheet steel out of scrapped cars and refrigerators." In the case of Nucor, compensating factor differentials also apparently includes the health and safety of the employees: "Its worker death rate since 1980 is the

plants are able to reduce the level of employee compensation below that paid by optimal-sized plants, the average cost will be reduced from AC_{so} and approach AC_o. Should the suboptimal plant succeed in reducing employee compensation to a sufficient degree, it can actually lower its average cost to AC_o, at which point it will be viable and can survive indefinitely in the long run.

Table 6.4 shows that suboptimal scale plants do, in fact, experience a considerable productivity disadvantage. Productivity is measured here as value added divided by employment. The productivity differential tends to be the greatest in those industrial sectors exhibiting the largest MES in table 6.3. That is, in the American tobacco industry, which is characterized by one of the largest estimated MES's, productivity in the suboptimal plants was only 27.6 percent as great at that in the optimal plants. By contrast, in the textile and apparel sectors, where scale economies do not play an important role, there is virtually no difference in the productivity levels between the suboptimal and optimal plants in the United States, and only a slight difference in Japan. Not only are the suboptimal plants at a greater productivity disadvantage in Japanese manufacturing than in American manufacturing, but this relationship holds in every major industrial sector.

Table 6.5 confirms that employee compensation is lower in suboptimal plants than in optimal plants for both the United States and Japan. The differential in employee compensation generally reflects the differentials in productivity shown in table 6.4. Thus, in the American industry exhibiting the greatest differential in productivity, tobacco, the compensation differential is also the greatest. By contrast, in the two sectors where there is virtually no difference in productivity between suboptimal and optimal plants—textiles and apparel—there is also no difference in employee compensation. The greater differential in employee compensation in Japanese plants than in their American counterparts presumably reflects the greater productivity differential in Japan observed in table 6.4. Thus, for the entire manufacturing sector, employees in suboptimal plants were compensated at a level of about 80 percent of that in optimal plants in the United States, whereas in Japan the suboptimal plant compensation level was at a level of about 72 percent of that in optimal plants.

---

highest in the steel industry.... Nucor is a highly decentralized company with little corporate structure. It doesn't have a corporate safety director or uniform training programs, leaving safety up to plant managers." One employee reports, "If something's not right, and you can fix it in a half hour the wrong way and two hours the right way, you take the shorter way."

Table 6.4
Productivity ($) in optimal and suboptimal plants for U.S. and Japanese manufacturing sectors, 1982

Industry	U.S. plants			Japanese plants[a]		
	Optimal	Suboptimal	Suboptimal / Optimal	Optimal	Suboptimal	Suboptimal / Optimal
Food	62,456	51,239	0.820	34,455	18,152	0.527
Tobacco	190,402	52,527	0.276	—	—	—
Textiles	25,700	26,133	1.017	19,400	16,193	0.835
Apparel	21,659	22,909	1.058	11,439	11,185	0.978
Lumber	27,807	23,408	0.842	20,980	15,740	0.750
Furniture	30,102	28,238	0.938	24,396	16,173	0.663
Paper	67,797	42,639	0.629	39,267	22,816	0.581
Printing	49,286	33,721	0.684	57,868	23,061	0.399
Chemicals	94,278	78,827	0.836	73,411	56,390	0.768
Rubber	43,311	34,082	0.787	35,361	19,620	0.555
Leather	24,337	22,297	0.916	18,547	16,418	0.885
Stone, clay, and glass	47,430	37,536	0.791	36,847	24,005	0.652
Primary metals	40,987	36,631	0.894	51,172	32,112	0.638
Fabricated metal products	44,434	34,662	0.780	32,337	20,903	0.646
Machinery (non-electric)	53,921	38,261	0.710	42,966	25,408	0.591
Electrical equipment	49,253	37,344	0.758	45,477	18,394	0.405
Transportation equipment	58,783	45,965	0.782	46,052	23,654	0.514
Instruments	64,681	43,400	0.671	28,606	18,870	0.660
Miscellaneous	40,491	28,965	0.715	27,387	18,577	0.678
Total	54,585	37,831	0.693	35,889	22,093	0.616

Note: Productivity is measured as value added per employee (dollars).
a. The Japanese productivity measures have been converted from a yen to a dollar denomination using the 1982 exchange rate of $1 = 249.06 yen.

Table 6.5
Employee compensation ($) in optimal and suboptimal plants for U.S. and Japanese manufacturing sectors, 1982

Industry	U.S. plants			Japanese plants		
	Optimal	Suboptimal	Suboptimal/Optimal	Optimal	Suboptimal	Suboptimal/Optimal
Food	18,335	15,366	0.838	10,415	7,900	0.691
Tobacco	25,840	14,351	0.555	—	—	—
Textiles	12,618	14,351	0.998	9,374	6,886	0.735
Apparel	10,135	10,455	1.032	6,315	5,572	0.882
Lumber	15,894	11,383	0.716	9,958	7,742	0.777
Furniture	14,262	13,414	0.941	10,355	8,375	0.809
Paper	24,331	18,473	0.759	15,102	9,902	0.656
Printing	19,329	15,521	0.803	20,585	11,405	0.554
Chemicals	25,842	20,494	0.793	17,452	14,317	0.820
Rubber	18,333	14,728	0.803	15,118	9,521	0.630
Leather	11,149	10,927	0.930	8,977	7,396	0.824
Stone, clay, and glass	20,659	16,567	0.802	13,362	9,457	0.708
Primary metals	27,978	19,617	0.701	17,877	13,486	0.754
Fabricated metal products	20,931	17,191	0.821	13,190	10,196	0.773
Machinery (non-electric)	23,356	19,172	0.821	16,625	12,115	0.729
Electrical equipment	22,570	16,675	0.739	14,530	8,885	0.612
Transportation equipment	28,642	21,572	0.753	16,929	12,022	0.710
Instruments	23,261	18,052	0.776	13,720	9,680	0.706
Miscellaneous	15,328	13,575	0.886	11,024	8,325	0.775
Total	19,940	16,059	0.805	13,385	9,582	0.716

Note: The Japanese employee compensation have been converted from a yen to a dollar denomination using the 1982 exchange rate of $1 = 249.06 yen.

As table 6.5 indicates, there is considerable evidence suggesting that a suboptimal plant can exist by compensating for its inherent size disadvantages through deviating from the manner in which factor inputs are paid, or from the manner in which they are deployed. As Brown, Hamilton, and Medoff (1990) point out, smaller plants may be able to avoid labor rigidities imposed by unions and therefore subject employees to longer working hours. Similarly, compensating differentials may be reflected in differing managerial organizations and methods of production. For example, as a result of their small size, suboptimal plants may require less of a vertical management hierarchy than their larger optimal counterparts, thereby reducing the amount of "white-collar" overhead cost. Carlsson (1989) and Dosi (1988) have argued that small establishments are more adept at implementing flexible methods of production than are larger plants, which are more likely to be burdened with rigid work rules. And Caves and Pugel (1980) found evidence that small firms can offset their inherent size disadvantage through pursuing a strategy of product innovation and deploying inputs differently than their larger counterparts.

An important insight of Caves, Khalilzadeh-Shirazi, and Porter (1975) was that the extent to which suboptimal-sized plants are encumbered with an inherent cost disadvantage is determined not only by the extent to which the MES level of output is in excess of a suboptimal plant output level, but also by the slope of the long-run average cost curve over the suboptimal scale range. In fact, they introduced what they termed as the "cost disadvantage ratio," which they defined as average value-added per employee in establishments providing the lowest 50 percent of industry value-added divided by the mean value-added per employee in establishments supplying the top half. The greater their computed cost disadvantage ratio, the greater would be the (negative) slope of the long-run average cost function in figure 6.1. Thus $LRAC^1$ represents a larger cost disadvantage ratio than $LRAC$. As the cost disadvantage ratio rises, the long-run average cost of a suboptimal plant of a given size, Q_{so}, rises correspondingly, from AC_{so} to AC'_{so}. This suggests that for a suboptimal plant to be viable, for any given size, the compensating differentials in the salary and wages paid, hours per employee, and other factors must be sufficiently greater to offset the greater cost disadvantage.

Thus the extent to which a suboptimal plant shipping an output with a value of $VSHIP_{so}$ falls short of the equivalent value-of-shipments corresponding to Q_{MES}, $VSHIP_o$, will determine the degree to which the plant must compensate for its productivity disadvantage, by reducing its labor costs and deploying its resources differently from that practiced in optimal-sized plants, so that

$$VSHIP_{so} - VSHIP_o = \beta_0 + \beta_1(W_{so} - W_o) + \sum_{j=i}^{m} \beta_{2i}(F_{so} - F_o)_i$$

(6.1)

$$+ \beta_3(VA_{so} - VA_o) + \sum_{j=i}^{n} \beta_{4j}K_j + u,$$

where W_{so} and W_o represent the employee compensation in suboptimal and optimal plants, F_{so} and F_o represent the deployment of factor and managerial practices i in suboptimal and optimal plants, VA_{so} and VA_o refer to the value-added per employee in suboptimal and optimal plants. Finally, K refers to the j industry-specific characteristics that influence the extent to which suboptimal plants must compensate for the cost disadvantage in order to be viable.

Equation (6.1) can be most easily interpreted as identifying the extent to which wages must be lowered and factors deployed differently, such as hours per employee raised, in order for a suboptimal plant of a given size to compensate for its size-induced productivity disadvantage. Three different phenomena determine the extent to which the payment to factors and their deployment must compensate for the inherent plant size disadvantage. The first is the degree to which the MES level of output exceeds that of the suboptimal plant. The greater this difference becomes, the more wages must be reduced, and the more hours each employee must work, etc., to offset the size disadvantage, ceteris paribus. That is, as $Q_{SO} - Q_{MES}$ becomes (negatively) greater in figure 6.1, the more the plant must compensate for its size-induced cost disadvantage.

Second, for a given extent to which the MES level of output exceeds that of a suboptimal plant, a greater slope of the long-run average cost function over the suboptimal range, that is as $VA_{so} - VA_o$ (negatively) increases holding the size difference constant, the greater must be the compensating differentials. Finally, certain industry-specific characteristics will presumably reduce or increase the extent to which a suboptimal plant must compensate for a disadvantage of a given magnitude. For example, to the extent that the market price is elevated above $LRAC$ in figure 6.1, the need for a suboptimal plant which has already entered and exists in the industry to compensate will be that much less. As Weiss (1976, p. 127) argues, to the degree that a certain market structure "... results in prices above minimum long-run average cost, suboptimal plants would be protected in the long run, especially if their cost disadvantage were mild."

More specifically, Weiss (1979 and 1989) and others have found that industry-specific characteristics such as advertising intensity in concentrated markets tend to be associated with an elevated price. And, as Bradburd and Caves (1982) showed, high unexpected industry growth is associated with higher industry profitability, and therefore presumably prices.

Caves and Pugel (1980) argued and found evidence that pursuing a strategy of product innovation is one mechanism that small and presumably suboptimal business can deploy to compensate for size-induced disadvantages. Similarly, Pratten (1991) found that small firms tend to occupy product niches that differ from those of their large counterparts. However, an important theme emerging from Acs and Audretsch's 1987, 1988, and 1990 studies (and running throughout every chapter of this book), is that the relative innovative advantage of small firms vis-à-vis their larger and more established counterparts is anything but constant across industries. In fact, what has been termed throughout this volume as the entrepreneurial technological regime is characterized as a high innovative advantage bestowed upon small and new enterprises. Thus the extent to which suboptimal plants need to compensate for their size disadvantages may be reduced somewhat in industries best characterized by the entrepreneurial regime, where small enterprises tend to have the innovative advantage.

A particular econometric challenge posed in estimating equation (6.1) is that, as Brown and Medoff's (1989) work makes clear, the gap in employee compensation between suboptimal and optimal plants is largely determined by the size difference between the suboptimal plant and the MES level of output. Similarly, differentials in value-added per employee between plants within an industry are determined, to a considerable extent, by differences in plant size. This suggests that, in fact, equation (6.1) must be estimated within the context of a simultaneous equations model, where the differences in value-added per employee and employee compensation between suboptimal and optimal plants, as well as the size differential, are endogenous variables. Thus the gap between optimal plant and suboptimal plant employee compensation is estimated as being determined by the differentials in plant size and value added, along with the extent of unionization in the industry. Since small plants have a lower propensity to be unionized (Brown, Hamilton, and Medoff, 1990), and wages tend to be elevated in highly unionized industries (Brown and Medoff, 1989), the wage differential between suboptimal and optimal plants would be expected to be positively related to the extent of unionization in an industry.

The differential in value-added per employee between optimal and suboptimal plants is estimated as being determined not only by the differential in plant size, but also by the degree of capital intensity in an industry. That is, a difference in plant size of a given amount will presumably result in a greater difference in value-added per employee in highly capital-intensive industries than in industries where the capital-labor ratio is relatively low.

6.4 Empirical Results for the United States

To empirically estimate equation (6.1) and test the hypothesis that sub-optimal scale plants offset, at least to some extent, their size-induced dis-advantages by deviating from the manner that optimal-sized plants deploy and compensate labor and other productive factors, the 1982 *United States Census of Manufactures*, published by the U.S. Bureau of Census, was used. Each (usable) four-digit industry yielded as many observations as sub-optimal size classes exist, as determined by the computed MES size class. Thus the dependent variable in equation (6.1) is measured as the mean value-of-shipments (millions of dollars) in each suboptimal size class (the total value-of-shipments in the size class divided by the number of estab-lishments) minus the value-of-shipments (millions of dollars) corresponding to the MES level of output. An industry with, say, four suboptimal plant size classes, will in principle yield four observations.

The difference in employee compensation—measured as employee pay-roll (millions of dollars) divided by the number of employees (thousands)—between suboptimal and optimal plants is also constructed in an analogous manner. A positive coefficient is expected, which would indicate that a suboptimal scale plant can compensate, at least partially, for its size-induced disadvantages by reducing workers wages and salaries below that paid by optimal-sized plants.

Similarly, the employee utilization is measured by dividing the hours (millions) worked by production workers by the number of production workers (thousands). The difference in employee utilization is then com-puted by subtracting the hours per employee in optimal plants from those in suboptimal-sized plants. A negative coefficient would imply that sub-optimal plants can offset their inherent size disadvantages by utilizing their employees more intensively vis-à-vis their larger counterparts.

The difference in the share of the workforce accounted for by production workers, measured as the number (thousands) of production workers di-vided by the total number (thousands) of employees, is also included as an explanatory variable. A negative coefficient is expected, which would indi-cate that suboptimal plants take advantage of a less hierarchical managerial structure as a compensatory strategy.

In addition, differences in investment activity and inventory behavior between suboptimal and optimal plants are also included as possible strategies for compensating for size disadvantages. Plant capital expenditures per employee is measured as new capital expenditures (millions of dollars) divided by the number (thousands) of employees. Inventory strategy is measured as the end-of-year inventories (millions of dollars) divided by value-of-shipments (millions of dollars). Whereas a negative coefficient of the differential between capital expenditures would suggest that suboptimal plants can resort to a strategy of higher capital investment to offset their scale disadvantages, a positive coefficient of the inventory differential variable would indicate that inventory policy serves as a compensating mechanism.

Finally, the productivity differential between suboptimal scale plants and plants having attained the MES level of output is measured as the difference in the value added per employee, defined as manufacturing value-added (millions of dollars) divided by the number (thousands) of employees. A negative coefficient is expected and would reflect the need for differential strategies to be deployed by suboptimal scale plants to compensate for a productivity disadvantage. That is, as the productivity disadvantage increases for a given suboptimal plant size, a negative coefficient of this variable will contribute to determining the extent to which wages must be reduced or the number of hours which much be extracted from each employee, etc.

As explained in the previous section, in addition to the above variables, which are specific to each size class within an industry, several industry-specific characteristics are also hypothesized to influence the extent to which suboptimal scale plants engage in compensatory strategies to offset their size-induced disadvantages. Industry growth is measured as the percentage change in value-of-shipments between 1976 and 1982. It is expected that compensatory differentials are less important in industries experiencing high growth than in those growing more slowly. Because market price tends to be elevated in industries that are concentrated and advertising intensive, the multiplicative variable of advertising expenditures divided by value-of-shipments, 1977, times the four-firm concentration rate is included as an explanatory variable. To the extent that the market price is positively related to the interaction between advertising intensity and concentration, a negative estimated coefficient for this variable will reflect less of a need to engage in compensatory strategies on the part of suboptimal plants.

Finally, the degree to which small firms have the innovative advantage over their larger counterparts, or the extent to which an industry conforms alternatively to the entrepreneurial or routinized technological regime, is represented by the small-firm innovation rate divided by the total innovation rate. The small-firm innovation rate is measured as the number of 1982 innovations from enterprises with fewer than 500 employees divided by small-firm employment (thousands). The total innovation rate is correspondingly measured as the total number of 1982 innovations divided by industry employment (thousands). A negative coefficient of the small-firm innovative advantage would indicate that in industries where the small firms tend to have the relative innovative advantage, less of a compensatory strategy is needed by suboptimal plants to offset any given size disadvantage.

Based on the 1,620 establishment size classes for which full records and compatible industry-specific variables are available, the regression was estimated first using the method of ordinary least squares (OLS). The results are shown in the first two equations in table 6.6. The positive and statistically significant (at the 95 percent level of confidence for a two-tailed test) coefficient of the employee compensation differential suggests that a suboptimal scale plant of a given size can offset, at least to some extent, size-induced disadvantages by reducing employee compensation from that paid by its counterparts which have attained the MES level of output.

The coefficient of the differential in the share of employees accounted for by production workers is negative as expected. However, the t-ratio is sufficiently small that the composition of the work force between production and nonproduction workers cannot be considered to be a compensatory strategy available to suboptimal plants. The negative and statistically significant coefficient of the differential in the number of hours worked by each production employee suggests that the utilization of the labor force is, in fact, a mechanism used by suboptimal plants to offset their inherent size disadvantages.

The negative and statistically significant coefficient of the differential between suboptimal and optimal plant capital expenditures implies that capital investment can serve as a compensatory strategy available to a suboptimal establishment. However, as the low t-ratio for the inventory differential implies, this is apparently not the case for inventory policy.

The difference in value-added per employee between suboptimal- and optimal-sized plants is clearly statistically significant, but the sign of the coefficient contradicts the theoretical prediction. A positive coefficient reflects the simple statistical association observed between smaller plants and

Table 6.6
Regression results for U.S. differences between suboptimal and optimal plant size (t-statistics in parentheses)

	OLS		2SLS	
	(1)	(2)	(3)	(4)
Compensation difference	12.976	13.136	38.690	38.458
	(13.08)	(13.26)	(7.60)	(7.75)
Production worker difference	−0.254	−0.612	−0.580	−0.562
	(−0.07)	(−0.17)	(−1.06)	(−1.04)
Hours per worker difference	−0.523	−0.527	−0.677	−0.671
	(−6.14)	(−6.18)	(−3.04)	(−2.99)
Capital expenditure difference	−0.234	—	0.096	—
	(−2.50)		(0.65)	
Inventory difference	−0.053	—	−2.705	—
	(−0.03)		(−0.99)	
Productivity difference	0.734	0.678	−7.886	−7.854
	(3.10)	(2.87)	(−3.65)	(−3.70)
Growth	−6.592	−6.411	−3.460	−3.631
	(−1.54)	(−1.50)	(−0.59)	(−0.62)
AD*CON	−1.240	−1.247	−10.064	−10.074
	(−1.89)	(−1.90)	(−4.04)	(−4.06)
Small-firm innovation rate/	−1.445	−1.442	−2.120	−2.140
total innovation rate	(−1.93)	(−1.92)	(−1.86)	(−1.88)
Intercept	−23.233	−25.942	−3.788	−3.577
	(−2.36)	(−2.39)	(−0.19)	(−0.18)
Sample size	1,620	1,620	1,620	1,620
R^2	0.199	0.195	—	—
F	44.321	55.943	—	—
Standard error	184.00	184.25	249.15	248.77

Note: The coefficients of the production worker difference and invertory difference have been multiplied by 100 for presentation purposes.

a lower value-added per employee, but it also implies that the compensating mechanism for this disadvantage is to raise (not lower) wages in the suboptimal plant—a result that clearly contradicts common sense.

The negative coefficients of the industry-specific variables, market growth, and the advertising-concentration interactive term suggest that, presumably due to the elevation of price, less of a compensating strategy is required of suboptimal plants in industries experiencing high growth as well as in markets that are concentrated and where advertising plays an important role. Similarly, as indicated by the negative coefficient of the final industry-specific variable, innovative activity serves as a compensating strategy for a suboptimal plant size in industries where the small firms tend to have the relative innovative advantage.

Not only does the high t-ratio of the coefficient for the employee compensation differential suggest the presence of simultaneity, but the incorrect sign of the productivity differential also implies that OLS may not be the most appropriate method of estimation. Thus, in equations (6.3) and (6.4) the two-stage least squares (2SLS) method is used to estimate the system of equations where the differences in the employee compensation and the value-added per employee, as well as the difference in plant size, are endogenous variables. As explained in the previous section, the percentage of the industry employment belonging to a union (using data from Freeman and Medoff, 1979), along with the productivity and size differentials, are used to estimate the differential in wages between suboptimal- and optimal-sized plants. The productivity differential between suboptimal and optimal plants is estimated by the 1977 capital-labor ratio (from the *Census of Manufactures*) and the extent to which the MES output exceeds that of the suboptimal size class. That is, a given output differential would be expected to result in a greater productivity differential as the industry capital intensity increases.[6]

Two major differences emerge when the method of 2SLS instead of OLS is used to estimate the model. First, the t-ratios of the coefficients of the compensation differential are considerably smaller in equations (3) and (4). This would suggest that at least some of the bias due to simultaneity has been eliminated. Second, the sign of the coefficients of the productivity differential reverses from positive under the OLS estimation shown in equations (1) and (2) to negative when the 2SLS method of estimation is used in the last two equations. Because of the endogeneity problem that

---

6. The two-stage least squares estimation for equation (3) in table 6.6 resulted in (t-statistics in parentheses):

Compensation difference = 1.433   −0.002 Size difference
                                       (3.30)   (−0.35)

                          +0.214   Productivity difference
                          (14.78)

                          −0.083 Union
                          (−5.41)

and

Productivity difference = −4.285   +0.084 Size difference
                                        (−2.88)   (6.88)

                          −0.165   Capital/labor
                          (−4.99)

exists in the OLS estimation, it can be inferred that the negative coefficients of the productivity differential in equations (6.3) and (6.4) are unbiased. They can be interpreted as identifying the extent to which a strategy of compensating factor differentials must be pursued for a suboptimal plant of a given size to be viable.

6.5   Empirical Results for Japan

Due to data constraints, a somewhat modified version of the model introduced in section 6.3 has to be implemented for Japan. Besides the differentials in compensation and productivity between suboptimal- and optimal-sized plants, the extent to which subcontracting relationships prevail within the industry is considered to promote the viability of small plants. As Sato (1989) argues, suboptimal scale plants may effectively be the recipients of cross-subsidization from their larger partners, since it has been long been a practice of established Japanese companies to maintain a network of multiple suppliers. The relative importance of subcontracting in an industry is measured as the share of total material costs accounted for by consigned production costs. This measure, like all of the variables used for Japan, is derived from the 1982 *Japanese Census of Manufactures*. Although it is possible to measure the growth rate of industry value-of-shipments (1977–1982), no measures comparable to the small-firm innovative advantage and the multiplicative variable of advertising intensity times concentration used in the previous section are available for Japanese manufacturing.

The first two equations in table 6.7 provide the results based on OLS estimation. The positive and statistically significant coefficient of the compensation differential suggests that reducing wages in suboptimal plants is an effective strategy for compensating for size disadvantages. The coefficient of the productivity differential cannot be considered statistically significant. However, the degree of industry growth apparently facilitates the viability of suboptimal plants. This result is apparently stronger in Japan than in the United States. The coefficient of the subcontracting measure is positive. This may suggest the tendency for suboptimal plants to be larger and therefore more efficient in industries characterized by a high degree of subcontracting. In any case, contrary to the conventional impression, there is no support suggesting that suboptimal plants are the beneficiaries of cross-subsidization from their larger partners.

Equations (3) and (4) are based on 2SLS estimation for a system of equations where the compensation and productivity differentials are endogenously estimated along with the size differential. In the 2SLS estimation,

Table 6.7
Regression results for Japan differences between suboptimal and optimal plant size
(*t*-statistics in parentheses)

	OLS		2SLS	
	(1)	(2)	(3)	(4)
Compensation difference	17.721	17.732	46.522	49.855
	(13.18)	(13.18)	(7.10)	(6.79)
Productivity difference	0.246	0.567	−19.166	−21.110
	(0.13)	(0.30)	(−3.95)	(−3.93)
Growth	−10.483	−10.425	−58.279	−52.364
	(−5.81)	(−5.25)	(−2.22)	(−1.89)
Subcontracting	15.669	—	14.611	—
	(1.58)		(1.21)	
Intercept	12.664	14.624	28.350	31.927
	(3.81)	(4.74)	(5.33)	(5.82)
Sample size	944	944	944	944
R^2	0.240	0.283	—	—
F	74.153	97.884	—	—
Standard error	33,082	33,108	40,254	41,870

Note: The coefficients of the compensation difference have been divided by 10, and the
coefficients of subcontracting and the inventory multiplied by 100 for presentation purposes.

the compensation differential is estimated by the size and productivity
differentials and the share of employment accounted for by production
workers. The productivity differential is estimated by the size differential
and capital expenditures per employee. Two major differences emerge
when 2SLS rather than OLS estimation is used. First, the *t*-ratio for the
coefficients of the compensation differentials in equations (6.3) and (6.4) is
considerably smaller. Second, the coefficient of the productivity differential
becomes negative and statistically significant.

There are several striking similarities that should be emphasized between
the U.S. and Japanese results. First, using the 2SLS estimates, the coefficients of the productivity differentials are negative, suggesting that, as the
productivity disadvantage increases for a suboptimal scale plant of a given
size, a greater compensating strategy is required for that plant to be viable.
Second, a reduced level of employee compensation is apparently one such
compensating strategy pursued by suboptimal scale plants in both the
United States and Japan. Third, less of a compensating strategy is required
in high-growth markets.

A closer inspection of the results however, reveals several important
distinctions between the American and Japanese plants. The estimated elas-

ticity of the size differential with respect to the compensation differential
(at the means) is 1.846 for the U.S. plants (based on equation [3] in table
6.6) and 2.558 for the Japanese plants (based on Equation [3] in table 6.7).
Reversing the usual elasticity concept suggests that the (percentage) reduction in employee compensation resulting from a (percentage) reduction in
(suboptimal) plant size is greater in the United States than in Japan. That is,
a given extent of suboptimal size requires a greater reduction in employee
compensation in the United States than in Japan. The reason for this difference is at least partially explained by the difference in the estimated elas-
ticities of the size differential with respect to the productivity differential
(at the means), which is -1.129 for U.S. plants and -0.404 for Japanese
plants. This implies that a (percentage) increase in the size differential results in a substantially greater increase in the productivity differential in the
United States than in Japan. Consequently, less of a compensatory strategy
is required of Japanese plants than of their American counterparts for any
given extent of suboptimal scale. This is consistent with the finding above
that the reduction in employee compensation corresponding to any particular degree of suboptimal scale is greater in U.S. plants than in Japanese
plants.

6.6   Conclusions

As Leonard Weiss (1976, p. 126) observed nearly two decades ago, "In
purely competitive long-run equilibrium, no suboptimal capacity should
exist at all." However, just as Weiss (1964) and Scherer (1973 and 1976)
made it clear in their earlier work, suboptimal scale plants not only do exist
but actually comprise the overwhelming majority of establishments in virtually every manufacturing industry. And, as is shown in the second section of this chapter, the presence of suboptimal scale plants is even greater
in Japan than in the United States.

    Although a line of research in industrial organization has attempted to
identify why the extent of suboptimal firms and plants should vary so
much across markets, we have addressed a more fundamental question:
"How are suboptimal scale plants able to exist at all?" The answer apparently is that suboptimal plants exist by doing things differently from their
larger counterparts. They compensate, at least to some extent, for their
inherent size disadvantages not only by deploying labor differently but
also by remunerating it differently. The empirical evidence from both U.S.
and Japanese manufacturing suggests that the degree to which a strategy
of compensatory factor differentials is implemented depends not only on

the extent of the size disadvantage confronting a suboptimal plant, but also on the productivity differential associated with the size disadvantage. That is, either a decrease in plant size or an increase in the productivity differential confronting an establishment of a given size will result in the need for a greater reliance on a strategy of compensating factor differentials for the plant to remain viable.

Throughout his work, Weiss assumed that the existence of suboptimal capacity within an industry represented a (potential) loss in economic efficiency. Weiss (1979, p. 1137) advocated any public policy that "... creates social gains in the form of less suboptimal capacity." However, the empirical findings here suggest that in compensating for their inherent size disadvantages, suboptimal plants, at least in certain industries, pursue a strategy of product innovation. To the extent that at least some of these suboptimal plants are able to successfully innovate and subsequently grow to attain the MES level of output, these establishments—although inefficient in a static sense—are certainly efficient in a dynamic context. That is, at least some of the suboptimal plants of today will become the optimal plants of tomorrow as a consequence of having done something different to preserve viability. In fact, this is precisely the result we found in chapter 4. Taken together these two chapters suggest two mechanisms explaining the prevalence of small enterprises. The first is the dynamic selection process of markets, exerting a pressure on new and small firms to grow, either through innovative activity or some other similar mechanism. But to the extent that such suboptimal scale enterprises can engage in a strategy of compensating factor differentials, the pressure exerted by the cost differential is reduced. Thus the ability of new and small enterprises to reduce costs below those of their larger and more established counterparts is a key mechanism in the selection process of the market. Pursuing a strategy of compensating factor differentials essentially buys the time needed for new firms to launch their new ideas and to learn, in both the discovery and adaptive senses. However, as the results from chapter 4 suggest, the time won from pursuing a strategy of compensating factor differentials appears to be limited. In this sense, new firms may be living on borrowed time.

7   Who Exits and Why

7.1   Introduction

Three key stylized facts have emerged from the recent wave of studies examining entry and exit.[1] The first is that entry and exit rates tend to be surprisingly high within a relatively short period of time.[2] Second, there is a high degree of (positive) correlation between entry and exit rates across industries—that is, where entry rates tend to be high, exit rates also tend to be high and vice versa.[3] A third stylized fact sheds at least some light on the question regarding the type of firm exiting from the industry. The likelihood of a firm exiting apparently declines with both age and size.[4] This result is not only consistent with the evidence found in chapter 4, but it also suggests that the bulk of firms exiting from the industry tend to be new and small enterprises.

There is reason however, to suspect that the process of firm selection is not constant across industries. For example, Klepper and Graddy (1990) and Gort and Klepper (1982) found that the type of firm that exits out of an industry—that is, a new entrant or an established incumbent—is closely

---

1. Examples of this burgeoning literature include, but are not limited to, the country studies contained in Geroski and Schwalbach (1991), Geroski (1989a, 1991b, and 1992), Dunne, Roberts, and Samuelson (1988 and 1989), Audretsch (1991 and 1994), Audretsch and Mahmood (1993, 1994, and 1995), Siegfried and Evans (1992), Mahmood (1992), Schary (1991), Baden-Fuller (1989), and Acs and Audretsch (1989a, 1989b, and 1990, chapter 4).
2. Dunne, Roberts, and Samuelson (1988) found four-year entry rates to range from an average of 0.205 in tobacco to 0.603 in instruments.
3. A high correlation between entry and exit rates has been found in a number of studies, including most of the country studies contained in Geroski and Schwalbach (1991) which are summarized in Cable and Schwalbach (1991), Dunne, Roberts, and Samuelson (1988), and Siegfried and Evans (1992).
4. These results have been found in Evans (1987a and 1987b), Hall (1987), Dunne, Roberts, and Samuelson (1988 and 1989), Audretsch (1991 and 1994), Audretsch and Mahmood (1993, 1994, and 1995), and Mahmood (1992).

linked to the stage of the industry life cycle. Generalizing from a wide range of empirical evidence,[5] Klepper (1992, p. 20) proposes a model of the industry life cycle where, "... initially entry is positive and exceeds the rate of exit but eventually there is a shakeout of producers and the rate of entry approaches zero." Since the stage of the life cycle varies considerably across industries, the extent to which exiting firms consist of new entrants or established incumbents is also likely to vary from industry to industry. This is certainly consistent with the findings in chapter 4 that not only does the likelihood of new-firm survival vary considerably across industries, but that it is strongly influenced by the technological conditions underlying the industry. That is, the propensity for new entrants to exit was found to depend on a number of industry-specific characteristics, most notably the technological regime.

The purpose of this chapter is to explicitly identify the type of establishment exiting and why it varies from industry to industry. In particular, I focus on the age characteristics of establishments to distinguish between new entrants and established incumbents. In the second section, I introduce two metaphors of industry evolution that may shape the types of firms exiting—the metaphor of displacement of incumbent enterprises by new firms and the metaphor of the revolving door, where the bulk of exiting firms tends to be comprised of new entrants. Measurement issues are discussed in the third section. In the fourth section a logit model for the shares of exiting establishments accounted for alternatively by new and old establishments is estimated. Finally, a summary and conclusions are provided in the last section. In particular, I find that the type of establishment exiting depends considerably on the technological and demand characteristics of the industry. The evidence suggests that the process of firm selection may be better characterized by the revolving-door metaphor in markets where scale economies play an important role and where innovative activity is dominated by larger enterprises. By contrast, the forest metaphor of the new saplings overtaking the old large trees may be more applicable in industries where the underlying conditions closely conform to the entrepreneurial regime.

7.2 Displacement and the Revolving Door

The relationship between new and incumbent enterprises is anything but clear. As table 7.1 shows, between 1980 and 1986 there were 205,000 new establishments started in manufacturing. This represents a gross entry rate

---

5. This evidence is summarized in Klepper (1992).

Table 7.1
Change in number of establishments by size of firm (thousands), 1980–1986

	Aggregate			Manufacturing			Services			Finance		
	Small	Large	Total	Small	Large	Total	Small	Large	Total	Small	Large	Total
1980	4,093	386	4,180	379	69	448	856	67	924	301	37	338
1986	4,485	480	4,965	413	68	480	1,052	92	1,144	350	62	412
Births	2,273	239	2,513	177	29	205	589	52	641	198	36	234
Deaths	−1,881	−146	−2,027	−143	−30	−173	−392	−28	−421	−150	−11	−160
Net change	393	93	486	33	−1	32	196	24	220	49	25	74
Birth rate	0.555	0.619	0.561	0.467	0.420	0.458	0.688	0.776	0.694	0.658	0.973	0.692
Death rate	0.460	0.378	0.452	0.377	0.435	0.386	0.458	0.418	0.456	0.498	0.297	0.473
Net birth rate	0.096	0.241	0.108	0.087	−0.014	0.071	0.229	0.358	0.238	0.163	0.676	0.219

Source: U.S. Small Business Administration, Small Business Data Base.
Note: The birth (death) rate is defined as births (deaths) divided by the number of establishments in 1980. The net birth rate is defined as the net change (births minus deaths) in the number of establishments between 1980 and 1986 divided by the number of establishments in 1980. A small firm is defined as an enterprise with fewer than 500 employees. A large firm is defined as an enterprise with at least 500 employees.

of over 45 percent. But at the same time, the 173,000 establishments exiting from the manufacturing sector represent an exit rate of just under 39 percent. But were those establishments exiting generally the same ones entering? That is, can the evolutionary process of markets be better characterized by the model of a revolving door, where the bulk of new entrants subsequently exit from the industry within a relatively short period, or are these new entrants displacing incumbent enterprises and driving them out of the market?

The model of dynamic industry evolution characterized by new enterprises displacing older incumbents dates back at least to 1920, when Alfred Marshall (p. 263) described the evolutionary market process where one can observe, "... the young trees of the forest as the struggle upwards through the benumbing shade of their older rivals." And even before Marshall, Joseph Schumpeter (1911) argued that a process of "creative destruction," where new firms with the entrepreneurial spirit displace the tired old incumbents, ultimately leading to higher economic growth.

Why should established incumbent enterprises be unable to fend off new entrants, especially given their inherent advantage both in available resources and leverage? To some extent this question was answered in the third chapter of this book—because of information asymmetries, principal-agent problems, and the difficulties involved in monitoring and setting incentives. That is, one important tradition of the organization literature has focused on ways that large organizations can learn and change. This view is characterized by James March (1982, p. 563), who argues that, "Organizations are continually changing, routinely, easily, and responsibly, but change within organizations cannot be arbitrarily controlled ... What most reports on implementation indicate is not that organizations are rigid and inflexible, but that they are impressively imaginative."

On the other hand is the view characterized by Michael T. Hannan and John Freeman (1989, p. 69), "We think that it is a reasonable first approximation to think of organizations as possessing relatively fixed repertoires of highly reproducible routines ... Our argument is that resistance to structural change is a likely by-product of the ability to reproduce a structure with high fidelity; high levels of reproducibility of structure imply strong inertial pressures." This view is consistent with Arrow's (1974) observation that there is a cost to acquiring new information. Personnel within a vertical hierarchy tend to specialize in using certain information channels even when other, perhaps newer channels would provide superior information. That is, such personnel involved in information acquisition represent a sunk cost of the accumulation of specific human capital: "Such specialization limits the range of information about the environment that an organization can obtain and process."[6] According to Arrow (1974, p. 49), "the combination of uncertainty, indivisibility, and capital intensity associated with information channels and their use imply (a) that the actual structure and behavior of an organization may depend heavily upon random events, in other words history, and (b) the very pursuit of efficiency may lead to rigidity and unresponsiveness to further change."

On the other hand is the metaphor of the selection process of markets resulting in something like a conical revolving door. According to this view, the bulk of new entrants will not survive past the very short run. They enter the industry based on the expectation that their (potential) innovation or new ideas would prove to be viable in the market. This view is generally consistent with the model of the life cycle. Thus, according to this view, the industrial organization of virtually every manufacturing industry, in a dynamic sense, can be represented by a conical revolving door, where the top part—representing the largest enterprises in the industry—revolves much more slowly than the lower part—representing the small firms in the industry. This view is consistent with the findings in chapter 4 that (1) the likelihood of survival is positively related to firm size and age, and (2) firm growth tends to be negatively related to firm size.[7]

Oliver Williamson (1975, pp. 215–16) has depicted three stages in the industry life cycle:

an early exploratory stage, an intermediate development stage, and a mature stage. The first or early formative stage involves the supply of a new product of relatively primitive design, manufactured on comparatively unspecialized machinery, and marketed through a variety of exploratory techniques. Volume is typically low. A high degree of uncertainty characterizes business experience at this stage. The second stage is the intermediate development stage in which manufacturing techniques are more refined and market definition is sharpened; output grows rapidly in responses to newly recognized applications and unsatisfied market demands. A high but somewhat lesser degree of uncertainty characterizes market outcomes at this stage. The third stage is that of a mature industry. Management, manufacturing, and marketing techniques all reach a relatively advanced degree of refinement. Markets may continue to grow, but do so at a more regular and predictable rate ... established connections with customers and suppliers (including

---

6. Quoted from Hannan and Freeman (1989, p. 68).

7. More generally, see the studies by Mansfield (1962), Dunne, Roberts, and Samuelson (1988 and 1989), Evans (1987a and 1987b), Phillips and Kirchhoff (1989), Audretsch (1991 and 1994), Audretsch and Mahmood (1993, 1994, and 1995), Mahmood (1992), Hall (1987), Mata (1993), and Wagner (1992 and 1994).

capital market access) all operate to buffer changes and thereby to limit large shifts in market shares. Significant innovations tend to be fewer and are mainly of an improvement variety.[8]

As Klepper (1992) points out, one of the most heavily studied aspects of the life cycle is the evolution of the number of firms in the market.[9] These studies typically find that the entry of new firms is the greatest during the formation stage of a new industry, and then levels off and begins to decline, even before the industry has attained the mature phase. Klepper (1992) terms this as the "shakeout phase," where the greatest number of exits from the industry occurs, and which typically take place well after the number of new entrants into the industry has declined. As illustrated in figure 7.1, which is derived from the patterns of industry evolution empirically observed in the Gort and Klepper (1982) and Klepper and Graddy (1990) studies, it is the combination of the drop in new entrants along with the high number of exiting firms during the shakeout period that leads to a decline in the total number of firms during the mature and declining stage of the life cycle.[10]

There is in fact substantial evidence from chapter 3 supporting the hypothesis that the startup of new firms is more prevalent in industries characterized by a greater extent of information asymmetries, as measured by the entrepreneurial regime, where small firms have a decided innovative advantage over their larger counterparts. That is, where the probability of innovating is greater, more entrepreneurs apparently incur the risk that they will succeed by growing into a viably sized enterprise. In such industries, entry is apparently higher while the likelihood of survival is lower.[11] At the same time, in chapter 4 it was found not only that the likelihood of new firms surviving is not particularly high, but even more striking, the

---

8. For an empirical study linking market-specific characteristics to the industry life cycle, see Audretsch (1987).

9. For example, Gort and Klepper (1982) and Klepper and Graddy (1990) examine forty-six new products introduced during the previous century and find that following an initial period of substantial growth in the number of independent producers, a sharp drop, or what they refer to as a "shakeout" occurs. Klepper and Graddy (1990) found that on average the number of firms was reduced by slightly more than one-half during the shakeout phase.

10. For detailed industry studies on the patterns of entry and exit over the life cycle in mechanical typewriters, automobiles, televisions, cathode ray tubes, transistors, integrated circuits, electronic calculators, and supercomputers, see Utterback and Suarez (1992).

11. Along similar lines, Acs and Audretsch (1990, chapter 7 and 1993) find that the extent of turbulence is actually greater in industries where small firms tend to have the innovative advantage.

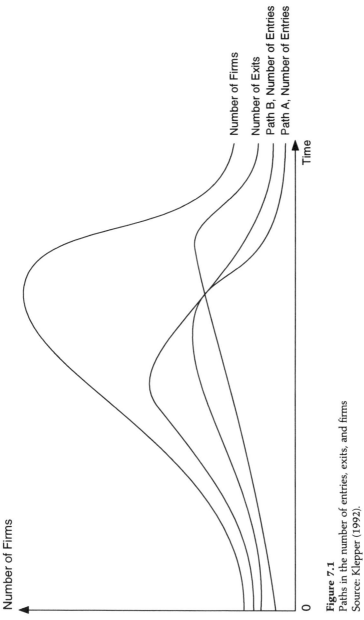

Figure 7.1
Paths in the number of entries, exits, and firms
Source: Klepper (1992).

chances of a new firm surviving are even lower in industries characterized by the entrepreneurial regime. In addition, we found that new firms do not appear to be significantly deterred from entering industries where scale economies play an important role. Rather, firms may begin at a small and even suboptimal scale of output and then, if merited by subsequent performance, grow. Apparently those firms that are successful grow, whereas those that are not successful remain small and may be forced to exit out of the industry if they remain at a suboptimal scale of output.

Taken together, the results already found in this book suggest that the greater the degree of technological change and extent of scale economies in the industry, the faster this conical door will revolve. That is, as was found in chapter 3, firms will continue to enter the industry regardless of the degree of scale economies in the industry. Rather, it is what could best be termed as "barriers to survival" that determine the speed of the door, at least at the small end of the firm-size distribution. In an industry with, say, no or only negligible scale economies, the results from chapter 4 suggest that new and small firms are not really in any sense suboptimal, and thus they will not be forced to exit the industry based on size-induced cost disadvantages alone. However, in an industry with substantial scale economies, new firms must grow relatively fast to become viable. Presumably in industries characterized by a high degree of scale economies the conical door is revolving relatively rapidly.

Thus the relevant question may be less, "Which metaphor, that of displacement, where the new saplings in a forest overtake the old trees, or of the revolving door, where there is considerable exit but very little permanent penetration is correct?" than, "Under which circumstances is the metaphor of displacement more applicable and when is that of the revolving door more applicable?" The model of firm selection and industry evolution applied throughout this book provides a useful framework for answering this second question. In particular, industries characterized by substantial scale economies should tend to be better represented by the model of the revolving door. Rather than displacing existing incumbents, most of the new entrants will not become large enough to be viable in the long run; and therefore will be forced to exit. And after controlling for the degree to which new firms are entering, the model of displacement should be more appropriate in industries where small firms tend to have the innovative advantage. It is in such industries where new entrants will tend to introduce the new products inducing demand to shift away from the incumbents and toward the new entrants.

7.3   Measurement

Virtually every study investigating exit rates has focused on the number of enterprises or establishments exiting relative to the stock of existing businesses. In fact, this is exactly what is done in chapter 4, where the propensity for firms to exit out of the industry is analyzed with respect to the reference group of firms deciding not to exit. Such an implicit (or explicit in the case of rates of exit) reference group is conducive to identifying why exit tends to be relatively low or high across various industries; it but sheds virtually no light on the type of firm exiting or why the type of firm exiting tends to vary from industry to industry. Thus, to gain some insight as to who exits and why, I introduce a new measure of relative exit, XR, defined as

$$XR_j = \sum_{t=t_1}^{t_2} X_t^e \Bigg/ \sum_{t=0}^{T} X_t^e, \tag{7.1}$$

where X_t^e refers to the number of exiting establishments in industry j between the ages of t_1 and t_2. The total number of exiting establishments is given in the denominator of equation (7.1). Thus XR_j measures the share of exiting establishments accounted for by establishments between the ages of t_1 and t_2.

The greatest impediment to measuring the shares of exiting establishments alternatively accounted for by new entrants and by incumbents has been the lack of longitudinal data bases that identify the actual startup and closure dates of businesses.[12] The U.S. Small Business Administration's Small Business Data Base (SBDB) documented and described in chapter 2 identifies both the year in which new establishments were started as well as their subsequent performance over time, and thus is well suited for such a longitudinal study.[13]

Using the SBDB, table 7.2 shows the age cohort, measured in terms of years, of manufacturing establishments exiting in 1978. There are two important trends exhibited among exiting establishments. The first is that the number of exiting establishments tends to decrease as the age of the cohort increases. That is, establishments less than two years old accounted for nearly one-fifth of the 61,034 manufacturing establishments exiting in 1978. Of course, as the surprisingly high startup and entry rates observed

---

12. The census data base used by Dunne, Roberts, and Samuelson (1988 and 1989) provides observations only at five-year intervals.
13. This is possible using the USELM file, but not the USEEM file of the SBDB.

Table 7.2
Age cohort (years) of exiting establishments (percentage listed in parentheses)

Age cohort	Number of establishments	Employment
1–2	11,597 (19.0)	165,749 (11.6)
3–4	8,664 (14.2)	115,011 (8.0)
5–6	6,592 (10.8)	110,111 (7.7)
7–8	4,664 (7.6)	105,354 (7.4)
9–10	3,207 (5.3)	66,924 (4.7)
11–12	3,004 (4.9)	65,069 (4.5)
13–14	2,740 (4.5)	61,782 (4.3)
15–16	2,455 (4.0)	42,472 (4.4)
17–18	2,231 (3.7)	52,714 (3.7)
19–20	1,947 (3.2)	48,647 (3.4)
All ages	61,034	1,432,473

in chapter 3, as well as those observed by Dunne, Roberts, and Samuelson (1988 and 1989) suggest, along with the observation by Evans (1987a and 1987b), Hall (1987), Audretsch (1991 and 1994), and Audretsch and Mahmood (1994 and 1995) that survival rates tend to be positively related to age, the skewed distribution of exits no doubt mirrors the age distribution of establishments. The second point is that, while the distribution of employees in exiting establishments is also skewed toward new businesses, the degree is somewhat less. For example, only about 12 percent of employment in exiting establishments is accounted for by the youngest cohort, yet that same cohort accounts for 19 percent of the number of establishments exiting.

According to the discussion in section 7.2, the age distribution of exiting establishments would be expected to vary across manufacturing industries. For presentation purposes, the four-digit SIC industries have been aggregated to two-digit industrial sectors in table 7.3. However, despite this high level of aggregation, several important trends regarding variations in the age distribution of exiting establishments can be observed. First, the sectors with the highest shares of exiting establishments accounted for by the youngest businesses are transportation equipment, electrical equipment, and petroleum. As can be seen in chapter 6, all three of these sectors are comprised of industries characterized by a relatively high MES. By contrast, the youngest establishments accounted for the smallest shares of exiting establishments in the food, lumber, and printing sectors. In chapter 6 it was similarly found that these three sectors are generally comprised of industries characterized by the lowest MES level in U.S. manufacturing.

Table 7.3
Age cohort (years) of exiting establishments according to industrial sector (percentage listed in parentheses)

Sector	All ages	1–2	3–4	5–6	7–8	9–10
Food	4,234	560 (13.2)	415 (9.8)	326 (7.7)	258 (6.1)	209 (4.9)
Textiles	2,008	381 (19.0)	237 (11.8)	182 (9.1)	110 (5.5)	82 (4.1)
Apparel	5,301	1,133 (21.4)	683 (12.9)	551 (10.4)	368 (6.9)	276 (5.2)
Lumber	5,682	869 (15.3)	712 (12.5)	495 (8.7)	392 (6.9)	274 (4.8)
Furniture	2,496	510 (20.4)	322 (12.9)	257 (10.3)	152 (6.1)	107 (4.2)
Paper	681	123 (18.1)	87 (12.8)	85 (12.5)	49 (7.2)	25 (3.7)
Printing	9,626	1,443 (15.0)	1,338 (13.9)	1,038 (10.8)	725 (7.5)	530 (5.5)
Chemical	2,239	417 (18.6)	294 (13.1)	244 (10.8)	275 (7.8)	209 (4.9)
Petroleum	278	76 (27.3)	47 (16.9)	25 (9.0)	21 (7.6)	15 (5.4)
Rubber and plastics	1,630	387 (23.7)	345 (21.2)	214 (13.1)	143 (8.8)	85 (5.2)
Leather	701	150 (21.4)	98 (14.0)	80 (11.4)	49 (7.0)	26 (3.7)
Stone, clay, and glass	2,877	515 (17.9)	404 (14.0)	305 (10.6)	216 (7.5)	120 (4.2)
Primary metals	812	195 (24.0)	127 (15.6)	103 (12.7)	44 (5.4)	38 (4.7)
Fabricated metal products	4,674	951 (20.4)	676 (14.5)	506 (10.8)	373 (8.0)	257 (5.5)
Machinery (non-electrical)	7,266	1,351 (18.6)	1,043 (14.4)	768 (10.6)	648 (8.9)	481 (6.6)
Electrical equipment	2,687	731 (27.2)	520 (19.0)	394 (14.7)	243 (9.0)	155 (5.8)
Transportation equipment	1,970	529 (26.9)	379 (19.2)	282 (14.3)	181 (9.2)	202 (5.2)
Instruments	1,460	321 (22.0)	263 (18.0)	181 (12.4)	122 (8.4)	80 (5.5)

Second, the variation in the shares of exiting establishments across industrial sectors tends to decrease as the cohort ages. That is, the variation in shares of exiting establishments accounted for by the oldest cohort in table 7.3, establishments between nine and ten years old, is considerably smaller than that for the youngest cohort. Still, the share of exiting establishments accounted for by older establishments is relatively high in the non-electrical machinery, instruments, printing, electrical equipment, and fabricated metal products sectors. By contrast, in the leather, paper, and textiles sectors the share of exiting establishments accounted for by older establishments is relatively small.

In certain of the industrial sectors, such as non-electrical machinery, instruments, and printing, a pattern conforming to the forest metaphor where the new businesses are displacing their more established counterparts can be observed. That is, the youngest establishments account for only a relatively small share of exiting businesses, and the older ones account for a relatively high share. By contrast, a pattern better characterized by the metaphor of the revolving door can be observed in primary metals, where a relatively high share of exiting establishments is accounted for by new businesses, and more mature businesses account for only a small share of exiting establishments. Thus a preliminary answer to the question, "Who exits?" is "It depends—on the specific industry considered." Apparently in certain industries, such as those in the primary metals sector, new entrants are much more likely to exit, suggesting that the model of the revolving door is more applicable. In still other industries, such as those comprising the printing and instruments sectors, exiting businesses are more likely to be established incumbents. In these industries, there is apparently a greater propensity for incumbent businesses to be displaced by new entrants.

7.4   The Age Cohort of Exiting Firms

To test the hypotheses that the type of business exiting is shaped by characteristics of technology and demand, particularly the underlying technological regime and the extent of scale economies, the shares of exiting establishments accounted for by new entrants and older incumbents, as measured in equation (7.1), are estimated for 340 four-digit SIC industries. As was pointed out in chapter 5, the concepts of "new" and "incumbent" establishments do not lend themselves to obvious measurement. Therefore, several specifications of what constitutes a new and an incumbent establishment are used. For example, a new establishment is defined alternatively as an establishment younger than two years old or younger than four years old. By contrast, incumbent establishments are defined as those establishments more than ten or alternetively, more than fifteen years old. These definitions of what constitutes a new entrant and established incumbent are certainly arbitrary, and providing alternative measurement criteria is important in ascertaining the degree to which the results are sensitive to measurement.

As the discussion in section 7.2 emphasizes, two elements of technology should be especially important in shaping the age distribution of exiting establishments. The first is the extent of scale economies. Here we follow the practice used throughout this book and adapt the standard Comanor-Wilson (1967) proxy for measuring the MES, which is defined as the mean size of the largest plants in each industry accounting for one-half of the industry value-of-shipments, 1977. As the MES level of output increases, the more likely an establishment of any given suboptimal level of capacity will be to exit. As already found in chapters 3, 4, and 5, new establishments tend to be substantially smaller than their mature counterparts. This means that they should be more vulnerable to the cost disadvantages imposed by high scale economies.[14] That is, the (negative) consequences of small-scale production in an industry with extensive scale economies are certainly greater than in an industry where only negligible economies of scale exist. Thus the model of the revolving door—that is, where a relatively large share of the exiting businesses is accounted for by new entrants—should be more applicable to industries where economies of scale play an important role than in those markets where scale economies are negligible.

The second aspect of technology influencing the type of firm exiting from the industry involves the technological regime. Where new and small firms tend to have the innovative advantage, the displacement of incumbent firms will presumably be greater. The measure of the technological regime, where the entrepreneurial regime is distinguished from the routinized regime, is adapted here. Because small-firm innovative activity is greater under the entrepreneurial regime, where the ratio of the small-firm innovation rate to the total innovation rate is particularly high, the share of exiting establishments accounted for by new businesses should be lower, but the share accounted for by incumbent businesses should be higher.

While industry growth may depress the propensity to exit for business of all ages, the impact may not be neutral with respect to age. The

---

14. It should be pointed out that in chapter 6 it was found that at least some of the size-induced cost disadvantages can be offset to the extent a strategy of compensating factor differentials is deployed.

consequences of negative or inadequate growth are presumably greater on new and smaller businesses than on their more established and larger counterparts. That is, as we found in chapter 3, in the absence of high growth the likelihood of failure becomes greater for new firms. Given their size and degree to which resources have been sunk, at least short-term fluctuations in growth are not likely to cause large incumbent enterprises to exit from the market. They may reduce their levels of employment as a result of low or negative market growth, or engage in what has recently become known as "corporate downsizing," but they need not necessarily exit from the market. By contrast, the problem confronting new firms inherent in a low- or no-growth market is that, given their very low startup size (in chapter 3 we found it was on average fewer than eight employees), there is not a long way to go down. That is, "downsizing" for a small firm can quickly come to mean exit. The hypothesis that new firms will tend to be more adversely affected by low growth (and therefore more positively affected by high growth) is consistent with the findings of Mills and Schumann (1985) that small firms account for a greater share of economic activity during economic expansions and a reduced share during contractions. Thus high industry growth rates should lead to a relatively lower share of new establishments exiting from the industry, whereas low growth rates would be expected to raise the share of exiting establishments accounted for by new entrants.

The degree of industry concentration has been hypothesized by Harrigan (1980), Baden-Fuller (1989), and Cossutta and Grillo (1986) to influence the type of firm exiting from an industry. In modeling the process of exit as a strategic game between competitors, Harrigan (1980) obtained the result that not only do firms have an incentive to encourage incumbent rivals to exit from the industry, but as Cossutta and Grillo (1986) showed, the incentive rises along with industry concentration. This would suggest that incumbent establishments should account for a greater share of exiting businesses in more highly concentrated industries.

An important qualification in addressing the question of which type of business tends to exit from various types of industries is that who exits—that is, the type of exiting establishment—is certainly not independent of who is already in the industry—that is, the type of establishment already inhabiting the market. Thus the 1977 share of establishments accounted for by small businesses, or those having fewer than 500 employees, is included to control for the existing establishment size distribution. Similarly, the extent to which exiting establishments are accounted for by new entrants may be influenced by the degree to which new businesses are entering the

Table 7.4
Logit regression results for share of exiting establishments accounted for by age cohort (*t*-statistic in parentheses)

	Age cohort (years) of exiting establishments			
	1–2	1–4	10+	15+
Gross entry	−4.331	−2.647	3.518	4.311
	(−5.43)	(−4.38)	(3.30)	(3.66)
Scale economies	7.632	7.048	−11.832	−1.693
	(2.00)	(2.43)	(−3.01)	(−3.91)
Small-firm innovation rate/	−0.218	−0.724	0.551	0.542
total innovation rate	(−0.41)	(−1.79)	(0.97)	(0.87)
Growth	−6.976	−6.340	−2.543	−5.525
	(−2.12)	(−2.55)	(−0.80)	(−0.16)
Concentration	0.124	−0.107	3.727	4.429
	(0.65)	(−0.07)	(1.75)	(1.88)
Small-firm share	−0.385	−0.297	0.193	0.140
	(−2.47)	(−2.52)	(1.19)	(0.78)
Constant	−2.960	−1.834	2.684	3.057
	(−23.32)	(−19.07)	(−19.19)	(−20.63)
Log-likelihood	−359.04	−243.28	−300.56	−336.67

industry. For example, an industry with no, or only inconsequential entry could not conform to the model of the revolving door, where the bulk of exiting businesses are new entrants. Thus we include the 1976 gross entry rate, measured as the number of new establishments in 1976 divided by the total number of establishments in the industry in 1976.[15]

Table 7.4 shows the regression results estimating the share of exiting establishments accounted for by four different age cohorts, of which two reflect new entrants and two reflect established incumbent businesses. Because the dependent variable can vary only between zero and one by definition, ordinary least squares estimation would produce inefficient variances of the estimated coefficients, rendering the appropriate hypothesis tests unreliable. Following the procedure recommended by Judge et al. (1980), this statistical inefficiency is corrected by using the logit estimation.[16]

---

15. The type of business exiting from an industry might be expected to influence the gross entry rates, giving rise to a simultaneous relationship between gross entry rates and the measure of relative exit. While this is certainly a topic for future research, this potential econometric problem is perhaps somewhat diffused by considering the gross exit rate of the previous period to be a predetermined variable.

16. The transformed dependent variable, Y^*, is defined as $Y^* = (Y/1 - Y)$.

The regression results indicate that new entrants apparently account for a greater share of exiting establishments in industries characterized by high scale economies and a lower share in industries where only negligible economies of scale exist. By contrast, incumbent enterprises account for a lower share of exiting establishments in industries where scale economies play an important role. This would suggest that the extent of scale economies determine, at least to some extent, who exits and why. The model of the revolving door is apparently more applicable in industries where scale economies play an important role, in that new entrants are particularly vulnerable and constitute a significantly greater share of the exiting businesses. In those industries exhibiting negligible scale economies the model of the revolving door is less applicable. In fact, in the absence of scale economies, the metaphor of the forest, where new entrants displace the existing incumbents, may be more appropriate.

The evidence with respect to the underlying technological regime is somewhat more ambiguous. Industries where large firms tend to have the innovative advantage, which are best characterized by the routinized regime, also tend to exhibit a relatively high share of exiting establishments accounted for by new entrants. However, only the coefficient for the cohort of establishments younger than four years old can be considered statistically significant. Still, this provides at least some evidence that the model of the revolving door is more applicable under the routinized regime, while the displacement of incumbent businesses by new entrants is more characteristic of the entrepreneurial regime.

The industry growth rate apparently exerts an asymmetric effect on the type of firm exiting. Just as lower growth rates tend to elevate the propensity to exit of new entrants more than that of incumbent businesses, a higher rate of growth tends to shift the type of establishment exiting away from new entrants and toward incumbent businesses. Consistent with the models of Harrigan (1980), Cossutta and Grillo (1986), and Baden-Fuller (1989), incumbent businesses apparently account for a greater share of exiting establishments in highly concentrated markets.

Perhaps one might have thought that new entrants tend to comprise the largest share of exiting establishments where they are most pervasive—that is, in industries where new and small businesses play the greatest role. However, as the negative coefficients of the small-firm establishment share and gross entry rate indicate, even after controlling for a number of the most important factors of demand and technology, this is clearly not the case.

7.5   Conclusions

The answer to the question, "Who exits and why?" sheds considerable light on the process of firm selection and market evolution. Some industries can be best characterized by the metaphor of the conical revolving door, where new businesses enter, but where there is a high propensity to subsequently exit from the market. Other industries may be better characterized by the metaphor of the forest, where incumbent establishments are displaced by new entrants.

Whether the revolving door or forest metaphor better applies to any given industry is apparently determined by the conditions of market demand and underlying technology. There appear to be two key elements of technology—the importance of scale economies and the underlying technological regime. Where scale economies play an important role, the model of the revolving door seems to be more applicable. While the rather startling result in chapter 3 that the startup and entry of new businesses is apparently not deterred by the presence of high scale economies, a process of firm selection analogous to a revolving door ensures that only those establishments successful enough to grow will be able to survive beyond more than a few years. Thus the bulk of new entrants that are not so successful ultimately exit within a few years subsequent to entry.

There is at least some evidence suggesting that the underlying technological regime influences the process of firm selection and therefore the type of firm with a higher propensity to exit. Under the entrepreneurial regime new entrants have a greater likelihood of making an innovation. Thus they are less likely to decide to exit from the industry, even in the face of negative profits. By contrast, under the routinized regime the incumbent businesses tend to have the innovative advantage, so that a higher portion of exiting businesses tend to be new entrants. Thus the model of the revolving door is more applicable under technological conditions consistent with the routinized regime, and the metaphor of the forest—where the new entrants displace the incumbents—is more applicable to the entrepreneurial regime.

8   Conclusions

8.1   Major Findings

Each of the preceding five chapters has provided a snapshot of an important aspect of the process of industry evolution and, in particular, the role that innovation plays in shaping that process. These dynamic aspects involve the startup of new firms (chapter 3), survival (chapter 4), growth (chapter 4), entrepreneurship (chapter 5), the deployment of a strategy of compensating factor differentials (chapter 6), and a discussion of whether the evolutionary process of an industry is better characterized by the metaphor of the revolving door or displacement (chapter 7). Taken together the conclusions from each of these chapters constitute a broad picture of the process of industry evolution.

The fundamental theory common to all of these chapters is that the dynamic process through which industries evolve is shaped, at least to some extent, by three major factors—technology, scale economies, and demand. While most studies link technology to industrial organization on a dichotomous scale, typically high technology versus low technology, we focus here not just on the technological opportunity class within which firms in any given industry operate, but also on how the underlying technological conditions influence the cost of transmitting new economic knowledge, that is, the type of technological regime.

The major conclusion of the studies by Acs and Audretsch (1987, 1988, and 1990) was that there is, in fact, substantial empirical evidence supporting the notion of distinct technological regimes. An inference I make from these findings is that under the routinized regime there tends to be convergence regarding the expected value of new ideas, or potential innovations, across agents and decisionmaking hierarchies within the industry. By contrast, under the entrepreneurial regime there tends to be much more divergence regarding the expected value of new ideas, or

potential innovations across agents. And it is differences in the extent
to which new economic knowledge tends to converge or diverge across
agents that, to a considerable degree, shapes the evolution of industries.
The contribution of the preceding five chapters is therefore less to point
out that industries evolve over time than to categorically explain why the
patterns of market evolution vary from industry to industry. And that one
of the principal factors driving variations in the evolutionary process across
industries is indeed the underlying technological conditions.

The impact of six different measures reflecting some aspect of the underlying technological conditions (entrepreneurial regime and routinized regime), extent of scale economies (scale economies, capital intensity, and
firm size), or market demand (market growth) on the eight aspects of
industry evolution identified above is summarized in table 8.1. Taken
together, these findings suggest not only how the pattern of industry
evolution varies from industry to industry but why such variations across
industries emerge in a consistent pattern.

As was shown in chapter 3, the propensity for people to start new firms
is not constant across industries. The finding that new-firm startups tend to
be more prevalent under the entrepreneurial regime than under the routinized regime is consistent with the view that differences in beliefs about
the expected value of new ideas, or potential innovations, lead people, at
least in some cases, to start a new firm. Such divergences across agents
about the expected value of new ideas are not constant over industries but
rather depend on the underlying technological regime. A rather startling
result in chapter 3 is that new-firm startups are apparently not deterred
in capital-intensive industries or where scale economies play an important
role.

At least some resolution to this apparent paradox is provided in chapter
4, which examines the post-entry performance of new firms. An important
finding is that although entry may still occur in industries characterized by
a high degree of scale economies, the likelihood of survival is considerably
less. People will start new firms in an attempt to appropriate the expected
value of their new ideas, or potential innovations, particularly under the
entrepreneurial regime. As entrepreneurs gain experience in the market
they learn in at least two ways. First, they discover whether they possess
"the right stuff," in terms of producing a product for which sufficient demand exists, as well as whether they can produce that product more efficiently than their rivals. Second, they learn whether they can adapt to market
conditions as well as to strategies engaged in by rival firms. In terms of the
first type of learning, entrepreneurs who discover that they have a viable

Table 8.1
Summary of findings

	New-firm startups	Survival	Growth	Entrepre-neurship	Compensating factor differentials	Revolving door	Displacement
Scale economies	0	−	+	−	+	+	−
Capital intensity	+	+	−	−	NA	NA	NA
Market growth	+	+	+	0	−	−	0
Entrepreneurial regime	+	−	+	+	−	−	+
Routinized regime	−	+	−	−	+	+	−
Firm size	NA	+	−	NA	−	NA	NA

Note: + refers to the statistical findings of a positive relationship.
− refers to the statistical findings of a negative relationship.
0 refers to the statistical findings of a nonsignificant relationship.

firm will tend to expand and ultimately survive. But what about those entrepreneurs who discover that they do not possess the "right stuff?" The answer is, "It depends—on the extent of scale economies as well as on conditions of demand." The consequences of not being able to grow will depend, to a large degree, on the extent of scale economies. Thus, in markets with only negligible scale economies, firms have a considerably greater likelihood of survival. However, where scale economies play an important role the consequences of not growing are substantially more severe, as evidenced by a lower likelihood of survival.

The process of firm selection in markets apparently revolves around two driving selection mechanisms. The first is the gap between the startup size of a firm and the MES level of output. The greater this gap is, the greater the growth rates of surviving firms tend to be; but at the same time, the lower the likelihood of firm survival is. Since the variance of new-firm startup sizes is low relative to the variance in the MES levels of output across industries, it is essentially the degree of scale economies that determines the extent of this gap and therefore the severity of this selection mechanism.

The second selection mechanism in markets is the degree of uncertainty inherent in the nature of the product being sold and in how to produce it. In industries characterized by divergent beliefs about new economic knowledge, the likelihood of any particular agent being wrong in her beliefs is greater. Thus, under the entrepreneurial regime there is a greater likelihood that any particular new firm will be producing a product that is not viable on the market. On the other hand, those entrepreneurs whose beliefs are ultimately borne out in the market tend to experience greater growth.

This selection process of firms is also apparent in chapter 5, which focuses on entrepreneurship, or the relative role that new and young firms play in a market. Although nearly one-third of all manufacturing firms are less than six years old, their impact on employment is substantially less than older firms, accounting for only 5 percent of total manufacturing employment. It is because these new firms typically operate at a suboptimal scale level of output and may be producing a product that is not viable that forces many of them out of the market. At the same time, in any given time period, there will be a large number of new firms entering to offset the exiting firms.

How are these new firms, many of which operate at a suboptimal scale of output, able to exist? The answer in chapter 4 was that they cannot—at least not indefinitely. Rather, they must grow to at least approach the MES level of output. An alternative answer is provided in chapter 6. By deploying a strategy of compensating factor differentials, where factor inputs are both deployed and remunerated differently than they are by the larger incumbent enterprises, suboptimal scale enterprises are to some extent able to offset their size-related cost disadvantages. Just as it was found in chapter 4 that the gap between the MES and firm size lowers the likelihood of survival, in chapter 6 there is evidence suggesting that factors of production, and in particular labor, tend to be used more intensively (that is, in terms of hours worked) and remunerated less generously (in terms of employee compensation). Taken together, these two chapters suggest how it is that small, suboptimal scale enterprises are able to exist in the short run. In the initial period of learning, during which time the entrepreneur discovers whether she has the "right stuff" and whether she is able to adapt to market conditions, new firms are apparently able to suppress the cost of production in order to compensate for their small scale of production.

What emerges from chapters 3 through 6 is that markets are in motion, with a lot of firms coming into the industry and a lot of firms exiting out of the industry. But is this motion horizontal, in that the bulk of firms exiting are comprised of firms that had entered relatively recently, or vertical, in that a significant share of the exiting firms had been established incumbents that were displaced by younger firms? In trying to shed some light on this question, chapter 7 asks, "Who exits and why?" The answer is, "It depends." In industries where scale economies play an important role, new firms tend to comprise a greater share of exiting firms. And under the routinized regime, where the incumbent firms have the relative innovative advantage, incumbent enterprises account for a relatively low share of exiting firms.

Two views on the evolutionary process of industries emerge from these five chapters—the metaphor of the revolving door and the metaphor of the forest, or the displacement of incumbents by new entrants. Which view is more applicable apparently depends on the three major factors discussed throughout this volume—the underlying technological conditions, scale economies, and demand.

Why is the general shape of the firm-size distribution not only strikingly similar across virtually every industry—that is, skewed with only a few large enterprises and numerous small ones—but has persisted with tenacity not only across developed countries but even over a long period of time? The dynamic view of the process of industry evolution is that new firms typically start at a very small scale of output. They are motivated by the desire to appropriate the expected value of new economic knowledge. But, depending on the extent of scale economies in the industry, the firm may not be able to remain viable indefinitely at its startup size. Rather, if scale economies are anything other than negligible, the new firm is likely to have to grow to survive. The temporary survival of new firms, is presumably supported through the deployment of a strategy of compensating factor differentials that enables the firm to determine if it has the "right stuff."

The empirical evidence presented in the preceding chapters supports such a dynamic view of the role of new firms in manufacturing, because the post-entry growth of firms that survive tends to be spurred by the extent to which there is a gap between the MES level of output and the size of the firm. However, the likelihood of any particular new firm surviving tends to decrease as this gap increases. Such new suboptimal scale firms are apparently engaged in the selection process. Only those firms offering a viable product that can be produced efficiently will grow and ultimately approach or attain the MES level of output. The remainder will stagnate, and depending on the severity of the other selection mechanism—the extent of scale economies—may ultimately be forced to exit out of the industry. Thus the persistence of an asymmetric firm-size distribution biased toward small-scale enterprises reflects the continuing process of the entry of new firms into industries and not necessarily the permanence of such small and suboptimal enterprises over the long run. Although the skewed size distribution of firms persists with remarkable stability over long periods of time, a constant set of small and suboptimal scale firms does not appear to be responsible for this skewed distribution.

8.2   Broader Implications

As Knight (1921, p. 199) pointed out, uncertainty is the result of possessing only partial or bounded knowledge: "The essence of the situation is action according to *opinion*, of greater or less foundation and value, neither entire ignorance nor complete and perfect information, but partial knowledge." In fact, it is the fundamental condition of incomplete knowledge that leads Arrow (1974 and 1985) to focus on the firm as an organization whose main distinction is processing information. As March and Simon (1993a, p. 299) argue, "Organizations process and channel information." But as, Arrow (1985, p. 303) emphasizes, "The elements of a firm are *agents* among whom both decision making and knowledge dispersed ... Each agent observes a random variable, sometimes termed a *signal* ... Each agent has a set of actions from which choice is to be made ... We may call the assignment of signals to agents the *information structure* and the choice of decision rules the *decision structure."* Arrow goes on to note, as do Sah and Stiglitz (1986), that the cost of acquiring that signal or information is nontrivial.

How will economic agents, and ultimately hierarchical organizations, respond when confronted by incomplete knowledge? Knight's answer was "differently," because agents differ "in their capacity by perception and inference to form correct judgements as to the future course of events in the environment" (Knight, 1921, p. 241). In addition, there are differences in "men's capacities to judge means and discern and plan the steps and adjustments necessary to meet the anticipated future situation." Which is to say that different economic agents confronted by the same signal, in Arrow's terms (1985), or simply incomplete information, in Knight's terms, will respond differently because they have a different set of experiences from which to evaluate that incomplete information.

March and Simon (1993a and 1993b) argue that one of the main functions of an organization is to filter both the signal, or information, and the response in a way that is not only efficient, but also unique to that organization. They do this by shaping the goals and loyalties of those agents participating in the organization; for example, "They create shared stories—an organization ethos that includes common beliefs and standard practices" (March and Simon, 1993a, p. 300). And they offer incentives for conduct that is consistent with the organizational goals.

Like Nelson and Winter (1982), March and Simon (1993a, p. 309) emphasize the role of established routines in the functioning of organizations:

> The process of gaining individual expertise by coding experience into recognition/action pairs is parallelled by organizational processes for developing pairings between rules and situations ... Organizations are collections of roles and identities, assemblages of rules by which appropriate behavior is paired with recognized situations ... (these) are developed in an organization through collective experience and stored in the organizational memory as standard procedures ... Organizations turn their own experience as well as the experience and knowledge of others into rules that are maintained and implemented despite turnover in personnel and without necessary comprehension of their bases. As a result, the processes for generating, changing, evoking, and forgetting rules become essential in analysing and understanding organizations.

As long as new information is consistent with the routines established in an organization, it will be processed by economic agents and a decision-making hierarchy in a manner that is familiar. New information under the routinized regime is familiar turf for organizations. A more fundamental problem arises, however, when the nature of that new information is such that it can no longer be processed by the familiar routines. Under these circumstances the organizational routines for searching out new relevant information and making (correct) decisions on the basis of that information break down. And it is under such information conditions that divergences tend to arise not only among economic agents in evaluating that information, but between agents and organizational hierarchies.

If each economic agent were identical, such divergences in beliefs would not arise. The greater the degree of heterogeneity among agents, the greater the tendency will be for beliefs in evaluating uncertain information to converge. But individuals are not homogeneous. Rather, agents have varied personal characteristics and different experiences that shape the lens through which each agent evaluates where to get new information and how to assess it. That is, reasonable people confronted by the same information may evaluate it very differently, not just because they have different abilities, but because each has had a different set of life experiences which shapes the decisionmaking process. Perhaps this helps to explain why IBM, for all its collective knowledge, not to mention resources, was proven wrong about its early rejections of the minicomputer. Steve Jobs, a college dropout, was able to see something that the decisionmaking hierarchy at IBM did not. After all, Jobs emerged from the milieu of computer "hackers" and "freaks" in Northern California that provided him with experience and knowledge that must have seemed invisible to the IBM decisionmakers who generally populated upper-middle-class East Coast residential areas, such as White Plains.

Thus, to some extent, the phenomenon of a new firm being established represents not just imperfect information, but a diverse population of economic agents. That is, diversity in the population of economic agents may ultimately lead to diversity in the types of firms populating the enterprise structure. And to some extent, these diverse firms represent experiments, based on differing visions about the product and how to produce it. As Albach (1994) points out, one of the distinct advantages the United States has in generating innovative activity may reside in the rich and diverse backgrounds of its population. And, as he also points out, this innovative activity may be more closely related to new and small firms in the United States than in most other leading developed nations.

Diversity, however, may also be the source of the high degree of *turbulence* that is also apparently experienced in at least the United States, if not in all leading developed nations.[1] That is, industrial markets are character-

---

1. For a direct analysis of the degree of turbulence in industrial markets, see Audretsch and Acs (1990 and 1993) for the United States, Invernizzi and Revelli (1993) for Italy, and Beesley and Hamilton (1984) for Great Britain.

ized by a high degree of churning. But is this industrial turbulence desirable or undesirable? What are the welfare implications? The notion that a turbulent market is more conducive to economic growth than a stable one dates back at least to 1920, when Alfred Marshall (p. 263) described the dynamic process of markets where one can observe, "... the young trees of the forest as they struggle upwards through the benumbing shade of their older rivals." Building on Marshall's analogy, Brown et al. (1990, p. 270) observe that, "The health of a forest fluctuates from year to year, depending upon rainfall, temperature, etc. and their effect on the rates of birth, death, growth, and decline. In the long run, the forest will get larger or smaller and more or less dense depending upon how these rates react to the ecological environment, the richness of the soil, disease, management practices, and so forth. And, over extended periods, a forest may (will) need new varieties of trees or new strains of existing vegetation in order to adapt to changing circumstances." And even before Marshall, Joseph Schumpeter (1911) argued that a process of "creative destruction" takes place, where new firms with entrepreneurial spirit displace the tired old incumbents, leading to higher economic growth.

Thus, while the public is generally alarmed by the news of firm closings, layoffs, and "corporate downsizing," Brown et al. (1990, p. 271) warn that,

The concern for policy makers and economic observers should be the rates of birth and long-term job growth and the types of firms experiencing decline and failure. What we may be observing is the regeneration of the economic forest. In manufacturing, these losses are likely the result of large, older firms losing their competitiveness in the world economy. In some instances these firms may be simply going out of business or dramatically reducing their activity. These declining firms are being replaced by a large number of new, small firms. Over the past decade, these new firms have shown a higher rate of employment growth that has led to net long-term job creation. This is the process one hopes to find in a mature forest with a large number of large, older trees.

On the other side are two arguments weighing against the benefits that restructuring economic activity may have on a society. The first revolves around longer-term innovative capacity, productivity growth, and ultimately international competitiveness. Ferguson (1988), for example, argues that all of these tend to be promoted when companies and agents have more incentives to invest in long-term commitments, or what is sometimes referred to as "relationship" capital. Ferguson, writing in 1988 (p. 61), goes on to argue that the

subsequent market selection process. Ultimately it is through this selection process that industries evolve by incorporating those new ideas of economic agents that survive the selection process, either within incumbent organizations or through the alternative—by starting a new firm. This again evokes the metaphor provided by Albert O. Hirschman; if "voice" proves to be ineffective within incumbent organizations, and "loyalty" weakens, economic agents will resort to "exit," in the form of taking their ideas elsewhere.

This dynamic and potentially innovative role of new firms in industrial markets would seem to contradict one of the most prevalent models of technological change, the knowledge production function. As formalized by Zvi Griliches (1979), the knowledge production function links inputs in the innovation process to innovative outputs.[6] Cohen and Klepper (1991 and 1992a), among others, point out that the most decisive innovative input is new economic knowledge, and the greatest source generating new economic knowledge is generally considered to be R & D. And, as Scherer (1991) observes, the bulk of industrial R & D is undertaken in the largest corporations; and small enterprises—especially new firms—account only for a minor share of R & D inputs. Thus the knowledge production function seemingly implies that, as the Schumpeterian hypothesis predicts, innovative activity favors those organizations with access to knowledge-producing inputs—the incumbent large corporations.

That a recent wave of studies has revealed small enterprises to be the engine of innovative activity in certain industries, despite an obvious lack of formal R & D activities, raises the question, "Where do new and small firms get the innovation producing inputs, that is the knowledge?" One answer, consistent with the findings throughout this book, is that, although the model of the knowledge production function may still be valid, the implicitly assumed unit of observation—at the level of the firm—may be less valid. Krugman (1991) is among the most recent to argue that the relevant unit of observation may actually be a constellation of complementary firms within a geographic unit, so that knowledge can "spill over" from one firm within the region to another.[7]

An important finding of Jaffe (1989), Acs, Audretsch, and Feldman (1992), and Feldman (1994a and 1994b) was that investment in R & D by private corporations and universities "spills over" for economic exploita-

---

6. Examples of the innovation production function at the firm level can be found in Acs and Audretsch (1991), Audretsch and Acs (1991), Scherer (1965, 1983, and 1984), and Soete (1979).

7. This argument can be traced back to Alfred Marshall (1920).

tion by third-party firms. In these studies the knowledge production function was modified where the innovative activity within a geographical unit—a state—was related to the private corporate expenditures on R & D within that state as well as the research expenditures undertaken at universities.

Not only was innovative activity found to increase in the presence of high private corporate expenditures on R & D, but also as a result of research expenditures undertaken by universities within the states. In order to explicitly identify the recipients of R & D spillovers, Acs, Audretsch, and Feldman (1994) estimated separate knowledge production functions for large and small firms. Their results suggested that the innovative output of all firms rises along with an increase in the amount of R & D inputs, in both private corporations and university laboratories. However, R & D expenditures made by private companies play a particularly important role in providing inputs to the innovative activity of large firms; and expenditures on research made by universities serve as an especially key input for generating innovative activity in small enterprises.

These findings provide at least some insight into the puzzle posed by the recent wave of studies identifying a vigorous amount of innovative activity emanating from small firms in certain industries. How are these small and frequently new firms able to generate innovative output when undertaking a generally negligible amount of investment into knowledge-generating inputs, such as R & D? One answer is apparently through exploiting knowledge created by expenditures on research in universities and on R & D in large corporations.[8] The findings regarding the importance of knowledge spillovers are consistent with the correlation of 0.74 between R & D inputs and innovative output at the level of aggregated industries (Acs and Audretsch, 1990) but only 0.38 at the level of individual firms (Audretsch and Acs, 1991).

The findings in this book also challenge an assumption implicit to the knowledge production function—that firms exist *exogenously* and then *endogenously* seek out and apply (knowledge) inputs to generate innovative output. Although this may be valid some, if not most of the time, this book suggests that, at least in some cases, it is the knowledge in the possession

---

8. Link and Rees (1990) surveyed 209 innovating firms and found that large firms tend to be more activity in university-based research. However, small-and medium-sized enterprises are apparently better able to exploit their university-based associations to generate innovations. Link and Rees (1990, p. 25) conclude that there are diseconomies of scale in the production of innovations, due to the "inherent bureaucratization process which inhibits both innovative activity and the speed with which new innovations move through the corporate system towards the market."

of economic agents that is *exogenous*, and in an effort to appropriate the returns from that knowledge, the spillover of knowledge from its producing entity involves *endogenously* creating a new firm. In any case, the view knowledge being exogenous and the new firms being endogenous is consistent with the findings of Audretsch and Stephan (1994) and Kenney (1986a and 1986b) that virtually all new firms in the U.S. biotechnology industry are formed around, and typically by, scientists at universities and research institutions.[9]

The importance of university research, as well as private corporate R & D, to the generation of new economic knowledge and the dynamic process of markets suggests an important role for public policy. It is the unequivocal task of governments to ensure that funding of such knowledge-creating institutions is as strong as possible. In addition, it is the task of governments to facilitate the transmission of that knowledge by promoting dissemination and accessibility. It also seems clear that highly trained graduates are a crucial source for new economic knowledge and disseminating research out of university laboratories and into firms.

In a survey of nearly 1,000 corporate executives in America's sixty largest metropolitan areas, Raleigh/Durham was ranked as the best city for knowledge workers and for innovative activity.[10] *Fortune* magazine reports, "A lot of brainy types who made their way to Raleigh/Durham were drawn by three top research universities ... U.S. businesses, especially those whose success depends on staying atop new technologies and processes, increasingly want to be where hot new ideas are percolating.[11] A presence in brain-power centers like Raleigh/Durham pays off in new products and new ways of doing business ... Dozens of small biotechnology and software operations are starting up each year and growing like *kudzu* in the fertile business climate."

Location clearly matters in generating knowledge spillovers.[12] Not only have Jaffe, Trajtenberg, and Henderson (1993) found that patent citations

---

9. See also Dorfman (1983).

10. The survey was carried out in 1993 by the management consulting firm, Moran, Stahl & Boyer (New York City), on behalf of *Fortune* magazine. The results of the survey are reported in "The Best Cities for Knowledge Workers," *Fortune*, 15 November 1993, pp. 44–57.

11. *Fortune* magazine reports, "What makes the (triangle) park work so well is a unique nexus of the business community, area universities, and state and local governments ... It is home to more than 34,000 scientists and researchers and over 50 corporate, academic and government tenants specializing in microelectronics, telecommunications, chemicals, biotechnology, pharmaceuticals, and environmental health sciences," ibid., p. 46.

12. *Fortune* magazine notes that, "Business is a social activity, and you have to be where important work is taking place," ibid., p. 46.

tend to occur more frequently within the state in which they were patented than outside of that state, but Audretsch and Feldman (1994) found that the propensity of innovative activity to cluster geographically tends to be greater in industries where new economic knowledge plays a more important role. In studying the networks in California's Silicon Valley, Saxenian (1990, pp. 96–97) emphasized that communication between individuals facilitates the transmission of knowledge across agents, firms, and even industries; and it is the high endowment of workers' knowledge, that has promoted the high degree of innovative activity:

It is not simply the concentration of skilled labor, suppliers and information that distinguish the region. A variety of regional institutions—including Stanford University, several trade associations and local business organizations, and a myriad of specialized consulting, market research, public relations and venture capital firms—provide technical, financial, and networking services which the region's enterprises often cannot afford individually. These networks defy sectoral barriers: individuals move easily from semiconductor to disk drive firms or from computer to network makers. They move from established firms to startups (or vice versa) and even to market research or consulting firms, and from consulting firms back into startups. And they continue to meet at trade shows, industry conferences, and the scores of seminars, talks, and social activities organized by local business organizations and trade associations. In these forums, relationships are easily formed and maintained, technical and market information is exchanged, business contacts are established, and new enterprises are conceived ... This decentralized and fluid environment also promotes the diffusion of intangible technological capabilities and understandings.[13]

Several major studies (Acs and Audretsch, 1993; and Loveman and Sengenberger, 1991) recently identified that since the mid-1970s a shift has taken place in economic activity away from large corporations and toward smaller firms. Although this might seemingly be confused with a similar shift that has occurred from manufacturing to services, in fact careful analysis found that the shift toward smaller enterprises is even greater in manufacturing than in the service sector. Perhaps even more compelling, this shift has left virtually no major industrialized nation unaffected. For example, the share of employment accounted for by small firms (with fewer than 500 employees) increased in the United Kingdom from 30.1 percent in 1979 to 39.9 percent by 1986. And in northern Italy, the small-firm (with fewer than 200 employees) share of employment increased from 44.3 percent of in 1981 to 55.2 percent by 1987.

---

13. Saxenian (1990, pp. 97–98) claims that even the language and vocabulary used by technical specialists is specific to a region, "... a distinct language has evolved in the region and certain technical terms used by semiconductor production engineers in Silicon Valley would not even be understood by their counterparts in Boston's Route 128."

What accounts for this shift toward an increased role for smaller firms in manufacturing? One answer, consistent with the view in this book, is that new economic knowledge is playing a more important role in the leading developed economies, especially in the United States. When the comparative advantage of the United States was based on scale economies and mass production in the 1950s and 1960s, the major inputs in the production function, land, capital, and labor, were more or less known commodities. While there have always been varying gradients of human capital, and even land and physical capital, these variations were identifiable. But there is something inherently different about new economic knowledge as an input in the production function. As Arrow (1962) pointed out, along with new economic knowledge comes inherent uncertainty. And as the United States, and other leading industrialized nations, are increasingly forced to shift into new high technology industries, and as new and high technology methods are introduced into relatively mature industries, a more fluid and turbulent industrial structure may be replacing a more static and stable one in an increasing number of industries. In terms of this book, this would suggest a shift away from industries being characterized by the routinized regime toward industries characterized by the entrepreneurial regime. The United States may be finding it increasingly difficult to maintain a comparative advantage in industries characterized by the routinized regime. As *The Economist* points out, "The great renewing forces in American business have been its ability to create small firms and the country's openness not only to competition but also to people from overseas."[14]

Another way to ask that question, is "Will Dell Computer and AST and Gateway achieve the same size as Digital and Wang and IBM?" Is a new wave of new firms being developed that will displace the old generation? The amount of time that it takes for one-third of the Fortune 500 to be replaced has not been constant, rather it has been diminishing. It took two decades for one-third of the Fortune 500 to be displaced by new firms in the 1950s and 1960s. In the 1970s it took around eleven years. And in the 1980s it took just five years. Gateway, Dell, AST, and Apple are all Fortune 500 companies. But none of them existed in 1970 and two of them did not exist as of 1980. This would suggest that industrial turbulence, as characterized by the entrepreneurial technological regime, is becoming characteristic of more industries and the routinized technological regime is becoming characteristic of fewer industries. But at this point such speculations remain exactly that. Until a long enough time series panel data base is established, it is difficult to make comparisons over long periods of time.

---

14. "Ready to Take on the World," *The Economist*, 15 January 1994, pp. 65–66.

Brown, Hamilton, and Medoff (1990) draw a number of economic welfare conclusions regarding the recent shift away from large corporations toward smaller enterprises. After documenting the systematically lower wages and poor working conditions associated with smaller enterprises, in terms of hours worked and the safety and health environments, they conclude that there is a net economic welfare loss associated with such a shift in economic activity. But seen through the more dynamic lens of this book, these conclusions may not hold. To the extent that workers, especially highly skilled employees, also have differing evaluations about new economic knowledge, they will align themselves with enterprises accordingly. That is, asymmetric information would influence economic agents to work for those companies that they believe will do well. If the new firm does, in fact, grow and become viable, those employees will tend to grow with the company, both in terms of salary and position.[15] Of course, in the startup phase of the company, the employees, like the founders, are incurring a risk (either willingly or unwillingly). But rather than being compensated for incurring a greater risk through a higher level of income and better working conditions, in the case of new firms the employees are actually subjected to lower wages and inferior working conditions. The trick is that the compensation occurs in the future, if the expectations hold and the firm prospers. Thus employees are willing to sacrifice short-term wages, working conditions, and even job security, for the possibility of a longer-term gain. In a static model, Brown, Hamilton, and Medoff's economic welfare implications seem justifiable. But when viewed through the dynamic lens suggested in this book, not only does the new and small firm of today become, in some cases, the viable firm of tomorrow, but an ancillary point may be that the low wage and undesirable working conditions of today will, in some cases, become the higher wages of tomorrow. In fact, it is the ability of new firms to do something different from their incumbent counterparts, not only in terms of the product but of how the factor inputs are used and the manner in which they are remunerated, that induces change and enables them to be viable.

As F. M. Scherer (1988 and 1992) points out, the vision of the link between industrial organization and technological change, and ultimately

---

15. Cringley (1993) reports that one of the mythologies of Silicon Valley involves a man who walked into the front door of Apple Computer asking to buy a Porsche. Upon driving by and observing the cars in the parking lot, he had naturally assumed that it must be a Porsche dealership. Cringley (1993) similarly reports that there was a point in the mid-1980s when most of the employees at Apple Computer were millionaires. As part of their employee compensation they had received stock options, which when the company prospered, made them all rich.

international competitiveness, typically shapes public policy and especially industrial policy. The findings of this book strongly argue for a vision of the American industrial structure as one that is dynamic, fluid, and turbulent. Change is more the rule and stability the exception. But Scherer (1992) also notes that the

> findings from economic research on Schumpeter's 1942 conjectures seem strangely at odds with recent developments in national policy. Theory and empirical evidence suggest that *Capitalism, Socialism and Democracy* provided faulty guidance concerning the industrial structures most conducive to technological innovation. Yet especially in the United States, it has been argued with increasing frequency that domestic enterprises are too small to maintain technological leadership in an increasingly global marketplace, and that antitrust policies aimed at maintaining competitive *domestic* market structures discourage innovation.

For example, in 1986 the U.S. Secretary of Commerce, Malcolm Baldridge (1986), asserted, "We are simply living in a different world today. Because of larger markets, the cost of research and developments, new product innovation, marketing, and so forth ... it takes larger companies to compete successfully." Baldridge pointed out that the American share of the largest corporations in the world fell considerably between 1960 and 1984. He warned that programs promoting large scale enterprise must "not be stopped by those who are preoccupied with outdated notions about firm size."[16] Acting on this vision of the industrial structure, the Reagan administration proposed emasculating the antitrust statutes, particularly those in the areas of mergers, collusion, joint ventures, and cooperative agreements, and promoting horizontal mergers as a means of enhancing the international competitiveness of U.S. firms.[17] It was argued that American corporations needed to "combine and restructure ... to meet new competition from aboard" (U.S. House of Representatives, 1986, pp. 5–42), because "... if our industries are going to survive there have to be additional consolidations to achieve the needed economies of scale."[18]

This static view of the industrial structure has at least as great a following among policymakers in Europe.[19] More than two and a half decades ago, Servan-Schreiber warned European to beware the "American chal-

---

16. Statement of the Honorable Malcolm Baldridge, Secretary, Department of Commerce, in Merger Law Reform: Hearings on S.2022 and S.2160 before the Senate Committee on the Judiciary, 99th Congress, 2nd Session 1986.
17. For a more academic pleas for these proposals, see Jorde and Teece (1991).
18. "Making Mergers Even Easier," *New York Times*, 10 November 1985.
19. See David B. Audretsch, "America's Challenge to Europe," *The Wall Street Journal*, 31 July 1989, p. 6, and Adams and Brock (1987 and 1988).

lenge" in the form of the "dynamism, organisation, innovation, and bold-ness that characterize the giant American corporations" (1968, p. 153). Because giant corporations are needed to amass the requisite resources for innovation, Servan-Schreiber advocated the "creation of large industrial units which are able both in size and management to compete with the American giants" (1968, p. 159). According to Servan-Schreiber (1968, p. 159), "The first problem of an industrial policy for Europe consists in choosing 50 to 100 firms which, once they are large enough, would be the most likely to become world leaders of modern technology in their fields. At the moment we are simply letting industry be gradually destroyed by the superior power of American corporations." Ironically, with the Euro-pean integration currently taking place, Servan-Schreiber's policy perscrip-tions are now more than ever likely to be followed, as is clearly docu-mented in the *Cecchini Report* (1988).

With Servan-Schreiber's (1968) prescriptions in mind, one has to wonder what would have happened to the U.S. computer and semiconductor indus-tries had IBM been selected as "a national interest" say around 1980 and promoted through favorable treatment as well as protected from threats like Apple Computer, Microsoft, and Intel. Would the United States now have the world lead in the computer, semiconductor, and software indus-tries? While Robert McNamara's proclamation "What is good for General Motors is good for America" may have sounded sensible for the 1950s, the analogy may not hold into the 1990s. It may be that the industrial structure has shifted sufficiently from being better characterized as static and stable to dynamic and turbulent.

It should, however, be emphasized that this is not a book prescribing industrial policy or how the appropriate industrial policy shifts over time. Nor is the main argument of the book that the industrial structure is becoming more turbulent over time, even if that may be more true. With-out undertaking the painstaking statistical research to compare the degree to which the structure of industries is characterized by turbulence has changed over long periods of time, such conjectures remain just that—conjectures. After all, the observation that the structure of industries in America tends to be remarkably fluid and turbulent is not new. Before the country was even half a century old, Alexis de Tocqueville, in 1835, re-ported, "What astonishes me in the United States is not so much the marvellous grandeur of some undertakings as the innumerable multitude of small ones."[20]

---

20. Quoted from *Business Week*, Bonus Issue, 1993, p. 12.

Thus the main message of this book is that, with respect to the dynamic patterns of firms over time, there is, in fact, no tendency that can be generalized. Rather, the dynamic nature in which firms and industries tend to evolve over time varies substantially from industry to industry. And there is at least some evidence that it is differences in the knowledge conditions and technology underlying the specific industry, that is the nature of innovative activity, that account for variations in industry evolution across markets.

References

Acs, Zoltan J., and David B. Audretsch, eds. 1993. *Small Firms and Entrepreneurship: An East-West Perspective*. Cambridge: Cambridge University Press.

Acs, Zoltan J., and David B. Audretsch. 1991. "R & D, Firm Size and Innovative Activity." In Z. J. Acs and D. B. Audretsch, eds. *Innovation and Technological Change: An International Comparison*. Ann Arbor: University of Michigan Press, pp. 39–59.

Acs, Zoltan J., and David B. Audretsch. 1990. *Innovation and Small Firms*. Cambridge, MA: MIT Press.

Acs, Zoltan J., and David B. Audretsch. 1989a. "Small-Firm Entry in U.S. Manufacturing." *Economica* 56(2): 255–265.

Acs, Zoltan J., and David B. Audretsch. 1989b. "Births and Firm Size." *Southern Economic Journal* 56(2): 467–475.

Acs, Zoltan J., and David B. Audretsch. 1989c. "Patents as a Measure of Innovative Activity." *Kyklos* 42(2): 171–180.

Acs, Zoltan J., and David B. Audretsch. 1988. "Innovation in Large and Small Firms: An Empirical Analysis." *American Economic Review* 78(4): 678–690.

Acs, Zoltan J., and David B. Audretsch. 1987. "Innovation, Market Structure and Firm Size." *Review of Economics and Statistics* 69(4): 567–575.

Acs, Zoltan J., David B. Audretsch, and Maryann P. Feldman. 1994. R & D Spillovers and Recipient Firm Size." *Review of Economics and Statistics* 100(2): 336–340.

Acs, Zoltan J., David B. Audretsch, and Maryann P. Feldman. 1992. "Real Effects of Academic Research." *American Economic Review* 82(1): 363–367.

Adams, Walter, and James W. Brock. 1988. "The Bigness Mystique and the Merger Policy Debate: An International Perspective." *Northwestern Journal of International Law and Business* 9(1): 1–48.

Adams, Walter, and James W. Brock. 1987. *The Bigness Complex*. New York: Pantheon.

Albach, Horst. 1994. *Culture and Technical Innovation: A Cross-Cultural Analysis and Policy Recommendations*. Berlin: Walter de Guyter.

Albach, Horst. 1984. "Die Rolle des Schumpeter Unternehmers Heute. Mit besonderer Berücksichtigung der Innovationsdynamik in der mittelständischen Industrie in Deutschland." In D. Bös and H. D. Stolper, eds. *Schumpeter oder Keynes? Zur Wirtschaftspolitik der neunziger Jahre.* Berlin: Springer Verlag, pp. 125–146.

Albach, Horst, Kurt Bock, and Thomas Warnke. 1984. "Wachstumskrisen von Unternehmen." *Schmalenbachs Zeitschrift für betriebswirtschaftliche Forschung* 36(10): 779–793.

Alchian, Almerin. 1950. "Uncertainty, Evolution, and Economic Theory." *Journal of Political Economy* 58: 211–21.

Alchian, Almerin, and H. Demsetz. 1972. "Production, Information Costs, and Economic Organization." *American Economic Review* 62: 777–795.

Aoki, M. 1988. *Information, Incentives and Bargaining in the Japanese Economy.* Cambridge: Cambridge University Press.

Armington, Catherine, Candee Harris, and Marjorie Odle. 1984. "Formation and Growth in High-Technology Firms: A Regional Assessment." Prepared for the National Science Foundation under Grant No. ISI 8212970 and the U.S. Small Business Administration under SBA Contract No. 2641-OA-79 and reprinted in Office of Technology Assessment, U.S. Congress, *Technology, Innovation, and Regional Economic Development*, Washington, DC, July.

Armington, Catherine, and Marjorie Odle. 1983. "Weighting the USEEM Files for Longitudinal Analysis of Employment Growth." Working Paper No. 12, Business Microdata Project, The Brookings Institution, Washington, DC April.

Armington, Catherine, and Marjorie Odle. 1982. "Small Business—How Many Jobs?" *The Brookings Review* 1 (Winter): 14–17.

Arndt, Johan, and Julian L. Simon. 1983. "Advertising and Economies of Scale: Critical Comments on the Evidence." *Journal of Industrial Economics* 32(2): 229–243.

Arrighetti, Alessandro. 1994. "Entry, Growth and Survival of Manufacturing Firms." *Small Business Economics* 6(2): 127–138.

Arrow, Kenneth J. 1985. "Informational Structure of the Firm." *American Economic Review* 75(2): 303–307.

Arrow, Kenneth J. 1983. "Innovation in Large and Small Firms." In J. Ronen, ed. *Entrepreneurship.* Lexington, MA: Lexington Books, pp. 15–28.

Arrow, Kenneth J. 1974. *The Limits of Organizations.* New York: Norton.

Arrow, Kenneth J. 1962. "Economic Welfare and the Allocation of Resources for Invention." In R. R. Nelson, ed. *The Rate and Direction of Inventive Activity.* Princeton, NJ: Princeton University Press, pp. 609–626.

Audretsch, David B. 1994. "Business Survival and the Decision to Exit." *Journal of Business Economics* 1(1): 125–138.

Audretsch, David B. 1993. "Industrial Policy and International Competitiveness: The Case of Eastern Europe." In K. Hughes, ed. *European Competitiveness.* Cambridge: Cambridge University Press, pp. 259–290.

Audretsch, David B. 1991. "New Firm Survival and the Technological Regime." *Review of Economics and Statistics* 73(3): 441–450.

Audretsch, David B., and Zoltan J. Acs. 1992. "Technological Regimes, Learning, and Industry Turbulence." In F. M. Scherer and M. Perlman, eds. *Entrepreneurship and Innovation: A Schumpeterian Perspective.* Ann Arbor: University of Michigan Press, pp. 305–320.

Audretsch, David B., and Zoltan J. Acs. 1991. "Innovation and Size at the Firm Level." *Southern Economic Journal* 57(3): 739–744.

Audretsch, David B., and Maryann P. Feldman. 1994. "Knowledge Spillovers and the Geography of Innovation and Production." Discussion Paper FSIV 94-2, Wissenschaftszentrum Berlin für Sozialforschung.

Audretsch, David B., and Talat Mahmood. 1995. "New-Firm Survival: New Results Using a Hazard Function." *Review of Economics and Statistics* (forthcoming).

Audretsch, David B., and Talat Mahmood. 1994. "The Rate of Hazard Confronting New Firms and Plants in U.S. Manufacturing." *Review of Industrial Organization* 9(1): 41–56.

Audretsch, David B., and Talat Mahmood. 1993. "Entry, Growth, and Survival: The New Learning on Firm Selection and Industry Evolution." *Empirica* 20(1): 25–33.

Audretsch, David B., and Paula E. Stephan. 1994. "How Localized Are Networks in Biotechnology?" Discussion Paper FSIV 94-9. Wissenschaftszentrum Berlin für Sozialforschung.

Audretsch, David B., and Hideki Yamawaki. 1988. "R & D Rivalry, Industrial Policy, and U.S.-Japanese Trade." *Review of Economics and Statistics* 70(3): 438–447.

Austin, John S., and David I. Rosenbaum. 1990. "The Determinants of Entry and Exit Rates into U.S. Manufacturing Industries." *Review of Industrial Organization* 5(2): 211–223.

Baden-Fuller, C. W. F. 1989. "Exit from Declining Industries and the Case of Steel Castings." *Economic Journal* 99(4): 949–961.

Bain, Joe. 1956. *Barriers to New Competition*. Cambridge, MA: Harvard University Press.

Baldridge, Malcolm. 1986. "The Administration's Legislative Proposal and Its Ramifications." *Antitrust Law Journal* 29(1): 112–139.

Baldwin, John R., and Paul K. Gorecki. 1991. "Entry, Exit and Productivity Growth." In P. Geroski and J. Schwalbach, eds. *Entry and Market Contestability: An International Comparison.* Oxford: Basil Blackwell, pp. 244–256.

Baldwin, John R., and Paul K. Gorecki. 1989. "Firm Entry and Exit in the Canadian Manufacturing Sector." Mimeo.

Baldwin, John R., and Paul K. Gorecki. 1987. "Plant Creation versus Plant Acquisition: The Entry Process in Canadian Manufacturing." *International Journal of Industrial Organization* 5(1): 27–42.

Baldwin, John R., and Paul K. Gorecki. 1985. "The Determinants of Small Plant Market Share in Canadian Manufacturing Industries in the 1970s." *Review of Economics and Statistics* 67(1): 156–161.

Baldwin, William L., and John T. Scott. 1987. *Market Structure and Technological Change.* London and New York: Harwood Academic Publishers.

Baumol, William J. 1990. "Entrepreneurship: Productive, Unproductive, and Destructive." *Journal of Political Economy* 98(5): 893–921.

Beesley, M. E., and R. T. Hamilton. 1984. "Small Firms' Seedbed Role and the Concept of Turbulence." *Journal of Industrial Economics* 33(4): 217–232.

Birch, David L. 1981. "Who Creates Jobs?" *The Public Interest* 65 (Fall) 3–14.

Blair, John M. 1948. "Technology and Size." *American Economic Review* 38(2): 121–152.

Blanchflower, D., and B. Meyer. 1994. "A Longitudinal Analysis of Young Entrepreneurs in Australia and the United States. *Small Business Economics* 6(1): 1–20.

Blanchflower, D., and A. Oswald. 1990. "What Makes an Entrepreneur?" National Bureau of Economic Research Working Paper 3252. Cambridge, MA: National Bureau of Economic Research, September.

Boden, Richard, and Bruce D. Phillips. 1985. "Uses and Limitations of USEEM/USELM Data." Office of Advocacy, U.S. Small Business Administration, Washington, DC, November.

Bolton Report. 1971. *Committee of Inquiry on Small Firms*, Cmnd 4811. London: HMSO.

Boyer, Kenneth D. 1974. "Informative and Goodwill Advertising." *Review of Economics and Statistics* 56(4): 541–548.

Bradburd, Ralph, and Richard E. Caves. 1982. "A Closer Look at the Effect of Market Growth on Industries' Profits." *Review of Economics and Statistics* 64(4): 635–645.

Breslow, N. 1974. "Covariance Analysis of Censored Survival Data." *Biometrics* 30(1): 88–99.

Brock, William A., and David S. Evans. 1989. "Small Business Economics." *Small Business Economics* 1(1): 7–20.

Brown, Charles, Judith Connor, Steven Heeringa, and John Jackson. 1990. "Studying (Small) Business with the Michigan Employment Security Commission Longitudinal Data Base." *Small Business Economics* 2(4): 261–278.

Brown, Charles, James Hamilton, and James Medoff. 1990. *Employers Large and Small*. Cambridge, MA: Harvard University Press.

Brown, Charles, and James Medoff. 1989. "The Employer Size Wage Effect." *Journal of Political Economy* 97(4): 1027–1059.

Brown, H. Shelton, and Bruce D. Phillips. 1989. "Comparison Between Small Business Data Base (USEEM) and Bureau of Labor Statistics (BLS) Employment Data: 1978–1986." *Small Business Economics* 1(4): 273–284.

Burns, Tom, and George M. Stalker. 1961, *The Management of Innovation*. London: Tavistock.

Cable, John, and Joachim Schwalbach. 1991. "International Comparisons of Entry and Exit." In P. Geroski and J. Schwalbach, eds. *Entry and Market Contestability: An International Comparison*. Oxford: Basil Blackwell, pp. 257–281.

Cantillon, Richard. 1931. *Essai sur la Nature du Commerce en Général*. Edited and translated by H. Higgs. London: Macmillan.

Carlsson, Bo. 1989. "The Evolution of Manufacturing Technology and its Impact on Industrial Structure: An International Study." *Small Business Economics* 1(1): 21–38.

Carrol, Paul. 1993. *Big Blues: The Unmaking of IBM*. New York: Crown Publishers.

Case, John. 1992. *From the Ground Up: The Resurgence of American Entrepreneurship*. New York: Simon & Schuster.

Caves, Richard E., and David Barton. 1990. *Efficiency in U.S. Manufacturing Industries.* Cambridge, MA: MIT Press.

Caves, Richard E., J. Khalilzadeh-Shirazi, and M. E. Porter. 1975. "Scale Economies in Statistical Analyses of Market Power." *Review of Economics and Statistics* 57(2): 133–140.

Caves, Richard E., and Michael E. Porter. 1977. "From Entry to Mobility Barriers." *Quarterly Journal of Economics* 91: 241–261.

Caves, Richard E., and Michael E. Porter. 1976. "Barriers to Exit." In R. T. Masson and P. D. Qualls, eds. *Essays on Industrial Organization in Honor of Joe S. Bain.* Cambridge, MA: Ballinger, pp. 39–69.

Caves, Richard E., and T. A. Pugel. 1980. *Intraindustry Differences in Conduct and Performance: Viable Strategies in U.S. Manufacturing Industries.* New York: New York University Press.

Cecchini, P. 1988. *1992 The European Challenge.* London: Gower.

Chandler, Alfred D. Jr. 1977. *The Visible Hand: The Managerial Revolution in American Business.* Cambridge, MA: Harvard University Press.

Coase, R. H. 1937. "The Nature of the Firm." *Economica* 4(4): 386–405. Reprinted in Oliver E. Williamson and Sidney G. Winter, eds. *The Nature of the Firm: Origins, Evolution, and Development.* New York: Oxford University Press, pp. 18–33.

Cohen, Wesley M., and Steven Klepper. 1992a. "The Tradeoff between Firm Size and Diversity in the Pursuit of Technological Progress." *Small Business Economics* 4(1): 1–14.

Cohen, Wesley M., and Steven Klepper. 1992b. "The Anatomy of Industry R & D Intensity Distributions." *American Economic Review* 82(4): 773–799.

Cohen, Wesley M., and Steven Klepper. 1991. "Firm Size Versus Diversity in the Achievement of Technological Advance." In Z. J. Acs and D. B. Audretsch, eds. *Innovation and Technological Change: An International Comparison.* Ann Arbor: University of Michigan Press, pp. 183–203.

Cohen, Wesley M., and Richard C. Levin. 1989. "Empirical Studies of Innovation and Market Structure." In R. Schmalensee and R. Willig, eds. *Handbook of Industrial Organization,* Vol. 2, Amsterdam: North-Holland, 1059–1107.

Comanor, William S. 1967. "Market Structure, Product Differentiation and Industrial Research." *Quarterly Journal of Economics* 81 November: 639–657.

Comanor, William S., and Thomas A. Wilson. 1967. "Advertising, Market Structure, and Performance." *Review of Economics and Statistics* 49(4): 423–440.

Cossutta, D., and M. Grillo. 1986. "Excess Capacity, Sunk Costs and Collusion: A Non-Cooperative Bargaining Game." *International Journal of Industrial Organization* 4(3): 251–270.

Cox, David R. 1975. "Partial Likelihood." *Biometrics* 62(3): 269–275.

Cox, David R. 1972. "Regression Models and Life Tables." *Journal of the Royal Statistical Society* 34 (May/August): 187–220.

Cringley, Robert X. 1993. *Accidental Empires: How the Boys of Silicon Valley Make Their Millions, Battle Foreign Competition, and Still Can't Get a Date.* New York: Harper Business.

Cyert, Richard M., and James G. March. 1963. *A Behavioral Theory of the Firm.* Englewood Cliffs, NJ: Prentice Hall.

Davis, Steven J., John Haltiwanger, and Scott Schuh. 1993. "Small Business and Job Creation: Dissecting the Myth and Reassessing the Facts." National Bureau of Economic Research Working Paper 4492. Cambridge, MA: National Bureau of Economic Research.

Dertouzos, Michael L., Richard K. Lester, Robert M. Solow, and the MIT Commission on Industrial Productivity. 1989. *Made in America: Regaining the Productive Edge*. Cambridge, MA: MIT Press.

Dorfman, Nancy S. 1983. "Route 128: The Development of a Regional High Technology Economy." *Research Policy* 12 (December): 299–316.

Dosi, Giovanni. 1988. "Sources, Procedures, and Microeconomic Effects of Innovation." *Journal of Economic Literature* 26(3): 1120–1171.

Dosi, Giovanni. 1982. "Technological Paradigms and Technological Trajectories: A Suggested Interpretation of the Determinants and Directions of Technical Change." *Research Policy* 13(1): 3–20.

Droucopoulos, Vassilis, and Stavros Thomadakis. 1993. "The Share of Small and Medium-sized Enterprises in Greek Manufacturing." *Small Business Economics* 5(3): 187–196.

Duetsch, Larry L. 1984. "Entry and the Extent of Multiplant Operations." *Journal of Industrial Economics* 32 (June): 477–487.

Duetsch, Larry L. 1975. "Structure, Performance, and the Net Rate of Entry into Manufacturing Industries." *Southern Economic Journal* 41: 450–456.

Dunkelberg, William C., and Arnold C. Cooper. 1990. "Investment and Capital Diversity in the Small Enterprise." In Z. J. Acs and D. B. Audretsch, eds. *The Economics of Small Firms: A European Challenge*. Boston: Kluwer Academic Publishers, pp. 119–134.

Dunne, Timothy, Mark J. Roberts, and Larry Samuelson. 1989. "The Growth and Failure of U.S. Manufacturing Plants." *Quarterly Journal of Economics* 104(4): 671–698.

Dunne, Timothy, Mark J. Roberts, and Larry Samuelson. 1988. "Patterns of Firm Entry and Exit in U.S. Manufacturing Industries." *Rand Journal of Economics* 19(4): 495–515.

Economic Report of the President. 1989. Washington, D.C.: United States Government Printing Office.

Edwards, Keith L., and Theodore J. Gordon. 1984. "Characterization of Innovations Introduced on the U.S. Market in 1982." The Futures Group, prepared for the U.S. Small Business Administration under Contract No. SBA-6050-0A-82, March.

Evans, David S. 1987a. "The Relationship Between Firm Growth, Size, and Age: Estimates for 100 Manufacturing Industries." *Journal of Industrial Economics* 35(2): 567–581.

Evans, David S. 1987b. "Tests of Alternative Theories of Firm Growth." *Journal of Political Economy* 95(4): 657–674.

Evans, David, and Boyan Jovanovic. 1989. "Estimates of a Model of Entrepreneurial Choice under Liquidity Constraints." *Journal of Political Economy* 97(3): 808–827.

Evans, David, and Linda S. Leighton. 1990a. "Small Business Formation by Unemployed and Employed Workers." *Small Business Economics* 2(4): 319–330.

Evans, David S., and Linda S. Leighton. 1990b. "Some Empirical Aspects of Entrepreneurship." In Z. J. Acs and D. B. Audretsch, eds. *The Economics of Small Firms: A European Challenge*. Boston: Kluwer Academic Publishers, pp. 79–97.

Evans, David S., and Linda S. Leighton. 1989. "The Determinants of Changes in U.S. Self-Employment. 1968–1987." *Small Business Economics* 1(2): 111–120.

Feldman, Maryann P. 1994a. "Knowledge Complementarity and Innovation." *Small Business Economics* 6(5).

Feldman, Maryann P. 1994b, *The Geography of Innovation*. Boston: Kluwer Academic Publishers.

Ferguson, Charles H. 1988. "From the People Who Brought You Voodoo Economics." *Harvard Business Review* 87 (May/June): 55–62.

FitzRoy, Felix R. 1989. "Firm Size, Efficiency and Employment: A Review Article." *Small Business Economics* 1(1): 75–80.

Foti, Alessandro, and Marco Vivarelli. 1994. "An Econometric Test of the Self-Employment Model: The Case of Italy." *Small Business Economics* 6(2): 81–94.

Freeman, Richard B., and James L. Medoff. 1979. "New Estimates of Private Sector Unionism in the United States." *Industrial and Labor Relations Review* 32 (January): 143–174.

Galbraith, John K. 1956. *American Capitalism: The New Industrial State*. Rev. ed. Boston: Houghton Mifflin.

Geroski, Paul A. 1992. *Market Dynamics and Entry*. Oxford: Basil Blackwell.

Geroski, Paul A. 1991a. "Domestic and Foreign Entry in the United Kingdom: 1983–1984." In P. Geroski and J. Schwalbach, eds. *Entry and Market Contestability: An International Comparison*. Oxford: Basil Blackwell, pp. 63–88.

Geroski, Paul A. 1991b. "Entry and the Rate of Innovation." *Economics of Innovation and New Technology* 1(1): 203–214.

Geroski, Paul A. 1991c. "Some Data-Driven Reflections on the Entry Process." In P. Geroski and J. Schwalbach, eds. *Entry and Market Contestability: An International Comparison*. Oxford: Basil Blackwell, pp. 282–286.

Geroski, Paul A. 1990. "Innovation and the Evolution of Market Structure." *Journal of Industrial Economics* 38(3): 299–314.

Geroski, Paul A. 1989a. "Entry, Innovation and Productivity Growth." *Review of Economics and Statistics* 71(4): 572–578.

Geroski, Paul A. 1989b. "The Interaction Between Domestic and Foreign Based Entrants." In D. B. Audretsch, L. Sleuwaegen, and H. Yamawaki, eds. *The Convergence of International and Domestic Markets*. Amsterdam: North-Holland, pp. 59–83.

Geroski, Paul, and Joachim Schwalbach, eds. 1991. *Entry and Market Contestability: An International Comparison*. Oxford: Basil Blackwell.

Ghemawat, Pankaj, and Barry Nalebuff. 1990. "The Devolution of Declining Industries." *Quarterly Journal of Economics* 105(1): 167–186.

Gilder, George. 1989, *Microcosm*. New York: Touchstone.

Gort, Michael, and Steven Klepper. 1982. "Time Paths in the Diffusion of Product Innovations." *Economic Journal* 92(3): 630–653.

Graf, J. de V. 1957. *Theoretical Welfare Economics*. Cambridge: Cambridge University Press.

Griliches, Zvi. 1990. "Patent Statistics as Economic Indicators: A Survey." *Journal of Economic Literature* 28(4): 1661–1707.

Griliches, Zvi, ed. 1984. *R & D, Patents, and Productivity*. Chicago and London: University of Chicago Press.

Griliches, Zvi. 1979. "Issues in Assessing the Contribution of R & D to Productivity Growth." *Bell Journal of Economics* 10 (Spring): 92–116.

Hall, Bronwyn H. 1987. "The Relationship Between Firm Size and Firm Growth in the U.S. Manufacturing Sector." *Journal of Industrial Economics* 35 (June): 583–605.

Hall, Bronwyn H., Zvi Griliches, and Jerry A. Hausman. 1986. "Patents and R & D: Is There a Lag?" *International Economic Review* 27: 265–302.

Hannan, Michael T., and John Freeman. 1989. *Organizational Ecology*. Cambridge, MA: Harvard University Press.

Harrigan, K. R. 1980. *Strategies for Declining Business*. Lexington, MA: Lexington Books.

Harris, Candee S. 1983. *U.S. Establishment and Enterprise Microdata (USEEM): A Data Base Description*, Business Microdata Project, The Brookings Institution, Washington, DC, June.

Hayek, Friedrich von. 1949. "The Use of Knowledge in Society." *American Economic Review* 35: 519–530.

Hébert, Robert F., and Albert N. Link. 1989. "In Search of the Meaning of Entrepreneurship." *Small Business Economics* 1(1): 39–49.

Highfield, Richard, and Robert Smiley. 1987. "New Business Starts and Economic Activity: An Empirical Investigation." *International Journal of Industrial Organization* 5(1): 51–66.

Hirschman, Albert O. 1970. *Exit, Voice, and Loyalty*. Cambridge, MA: Harvard University Press.

Holmes, Thomas J., and James A. Schmitz Jr. 1990. "A Theory of Entrepreneurship and its Application to the Study of Business Transfers." *Journal of Political Economy* 98(4): 265–294.

Holmstrom, Bengt. 1989. "Agency Costs and Innovation." *Journal of Economic Behavior and Organization* 12: 305–327.

Holmstrom, Bengt, and Paul Milgrom. 1987. "Aggregation and Linearity in the Provision of Intertemporal Incentives." *Econometrica* 55(2): 303–328.

Holmstrom, Bengt, and Jean Tirole. 1989. "The Theory of the Firm." In R. Schmalensee and R. Willig, eds. *Handbook for Industrial Organization*. Amsterdam: Elsevier.

Ichbiah, Daniel, and Susan I. Knepper. 1993. *The Making of Microsoft: How Bill Gates and His Team Created the World's Most Successful Software Company*. Rocklin, CA: Prima.

Ijiri, Yuji, and Herbert A. Simon. 1977. *Skew Distributions and Sizes of Business Firms*. Amsterdam: North-Holland.

Invernizzi, B., and Revelli, R. 1993. "Small Firms in the Italian Economy: Structural Changes and Evidence of Turbulence." In Z. J. Acs and D. B. Audretsch, eds. *Small Firms and Entrepreneurship: An East-West Perspective*. Cambridge: Cambridge University Press.

Jacobson, Louis. 1985. *Analysis of the Accuracy of SBA'S Small Business Data Base*. Alexandria, VA: Center of Naval Analysis.

Jaffe, Adam B. 1989. "Real Effects of Academic Research." *American Economic Review* 79(5): 957–970.

Jaffe, Adam B. 1986. "Technological Opportunity and Spillovers of R & D: Evidence from Firms' Patents, Profits and Market Value." *American Economic Review* 76(5): 984–1001.

Jaffe, Adam B., Manuel Trajtenberg, and Rebecca Henderson. 1993. "Geographic Localization of Knowledge Spillovers as Evidenced by Patent Citations." *Quarterly Journal of Economics* 63(3): 577–598.

Jensen, Michael C., and William H. Meckling. 1976. "Theory of the Firm: Management Behavior, Agency Costs and Ownership Structure." *Journal of Financial Economics* 3: 305–360.

Jorde, Thomas M., and David J. Teece. 1991. "Antitrust Policy and Innovation: Taking Account of Performance Competition and Competitor Cooperation." *Journal of Institutional and Theoretical Economics* 147(1): 118–144.

Jovanovic, Boyan. 1994. "Entrepreneurial Choice When People Differ in Their Management and Labor Skills." *Small Business Economics* 6(3): 185–192.

Jovanovic, Boyan. 1982. "Selection and Evolution of Industry." *Econometrica* 50(2): 649–670.

Judge, George G., E. Griffiths, R. Carter-Hill and Tsoung-Chao-Lee. 1980. *The Theory and Practice of Econometrics.* New York: John Wiley & Sons.

Kenney, M. 1986a. "Schumpeterian Innovation and Entrepreneurs in Capitalism: The Case of the U.S. Biotechnology Industry." *Research Policy* 15(1): 21–31.

Kenney, M. 1986b. *Biotechnology: The University-Industry Complex.* New Haven: Yale University Press.

Khemani, R. S., and Daniel M. Shapiro. 1986. "The Determinants of New Plant Entry in Canada." *Applied Economics* 18 (November): 1243–1257.

Kiefer, Nicholas M. 1988. "Economic Duration Data and Hazard Functions." *Journal of Economic Literature* 26(2): 646–679.

Kihlstrom, Richard E., and Jean-Jacques Laffont. 1979. "A General Equilibrium Entrepreneurial Theory of Firm Formation Based on Risk Aversion." *Journal of Political Economy* 87(4): 719–748.

Kirzner, Israel M. 1985. *Discovery and the Capitalist Process.* Chicago: University of Chicago Press.

Kirzner, Israel M. 1979. *Perception, Opportunity, and Profit: Studies in the Theory of Entrepreneurship.* Chicago: University of Chicago Press.

Klein, Burton H. 1977. *Dynamic Economics.* Cambridge, MA: Harvard University Press.

Kleinknecht, Alfred. 1989. "Firm Size and Innovation: Observations in Dutch Manufacturing Industry." *Small Business Economics* 1(1): 215–222.

Kleinknecht, Alfred. 1987. "Measuring R & D in Small Firms: How Much Are We Missing?" *Journal of Industrial Economics* 34(4): 253–256.

Kleinknecht, Alfred, Tom P. Poot, and Jeroen O. N. Reijnen. 1991. "Technical Performance and Firm Size: Survey Results from the Netherlands." In Z. J. Acs and D. B. Audretsch, eds., *Innovation and Technological Change: An International Comparison*. Ann Arbor: University of Michigan Press, pp. 84–108.

Kleinknecht, Alfred, and Bart Verspagen. 1989. "R & D and Market Structure: The Impact of Measurement and Aggregation Problems." *Small Business Economics* 1(4): 297–302.

Klepper, Steven. 1992. "Entry, Exit, Growth, and Innovation over the Product Life Cycle." Paper presented at the Conference on Market Processes and Corporate Networks, Wissenschaftszentrum Berlin, November.

Klepper, Steven, and Elizabeth Graddy. 1990. "The Evolution of New Industries and the Determinants of Market Structure." *Rand Journal of Economics* 21(1): 27–44.

Knight, Frank H. 1921. *Risk, Uncertainty and Profit*. New York: Houghton Mifflin.

Kreps, David. 1991. "Corporate Culture and Economic Theory." In J. Alt and K. Shepsle, eds., *Positive Perspectives on Political Economy*. Cambridge: Cambridge University Press.

Krugman, Paul. 1991. *Geography and Trade*. Cambridge, MA: MIT Press.

Kuznets, Simon. 1962. "Inventive Activity: Problems of Definition and Measurement." In R. R. Nelson, ed. *The Rate and Direction of Inventive Activity*. National Bureau of Economic Research Conference Report, Princeton, NJ. pp. 19–43.

Lawless, Jerald F. 1982. *Statistical Models and Methods for Lifetime Data*. New York: John Wiley & Sons.

Lawrence, Paul, and Jay Lorsch. 1967. *Organization and Environment*. Cambridge, MA: Harvard University Press.

Link, Albert N., and John Rees. 1990. "Firm Size, University Based Research, and the Returns to R & D." *Small Business Economics* 2(1): 25–32.

Loveman, Gary, and Werner Sengenberger. 1991. "The Re-emergence of Small-Scale Production: An International Perspective." *Small Business Economics* 3(1): 1–38.

Lucas, Robert E., Jr. 1978. "On the Size Distribution of Business Firms." *Bell Journal of Economics* 9 (Autumn): 508–523.

MacDonald, James. 1986. "Entry and Exit on the Competitive Fringe." *Southern Economic Journal* 52(3): 640–652.

MacDonald, James. 1985. "Dun & Bradstreet Business Microdata: Research Applications, and the Detection and Correction of Errors." *Journal of Economic and Social Measurement* 13(2): 173–185.

Mahmood, Talat. 1992. "Does the Hazard Rate of New Plants Vary Between High- and Low-Tech Industries?" *Small Business Economics* 4(3): 201–210.

Malerba, F., and L. Orsenigo. 1993. "Technological Regimes and Firm Behavior." *Industrial and Corporate Change* 2(1): 45–72.

Mansfield, Edwin. 1984. "Comment on Using Linked Patent and R & D Data to Measure Interindustry Technology Flows." In Zvi Griliches, ed. *R & D, Patents, and Productivity*. Chicago: University of Chicago Press, pp. 462–464.

Mansfield, Edwin. 1962. "Entry, Gibrat's Law, Innovation, and the Growth of Firms." *American Economic Review* 52(5): 1023–1051.

March, James G. 1982. "Footnotes on Organizational Change." *Administrative Science Quarterly* 26(4): 563–597.

March, James G., and Herbert A. Simon. 1993a. "Organizations Revisited." *Industrial and Corporate Change* 2(3): 299–316.

March, James G., and Herbert A. Simon. 1993b. *Organizations.* 2d ed. Oxford: Basil Blackwell.

Marshall, Alfred. 1923. *Industry and Trade.* London: Macmillan.

Marshall, Alfred. 1920. *Principles of Economics*, 8th ed. London: Macmillan.

Marx, Karl. 1912. *Capital.* Translated by Ernest Untermann. Vol. 1. Chicago: Kerr.

Mata, José. 1994a. "Firm Growth During Infancy." *Small Business Economics* 6(1): 27–40.

Mata, José, and Pedro Portugal. 1994b. "Life Duration of New Firms." *Journal of Industrial Economics* 27(3): 227–246.

Mata, José. 1993a. "Small Firms in Portuguese Manufacturing Industries." In Z. J. Acs and D. B. Audretsch, eds. *Small Firms and Entrepreneurship: An East-West Perspective.* Cambridge: Cambridge University Press, pp. 110–122.

Mata, José. 1993b. "Firm Entry and Firm Growth." *Review of Industrial Organization* 8(5): 567–578.

May-Strobl, Eva. 1981, *Erfolgreiche Existenzgründungen und öffentliche Förderung: Eine vergleichende empirische Analyse geförderter und nichtgeförderter Gründungsunternehmen.* Göttingen: Verlag Otto Schwartz.

McCauley, James. 1981. "A Critical Examination of the Dun & Bradstreet Data Files—A Rebuttal." *Review of Public Data Use* 9: 145–148.

Merton, Robert K., Ailsa P. Gray, Barbara Hockey, and Hanan P. Selvin, eds. 1952. *Reader in Bureaucracy.* Clencoe, IL: Free Press.

Milgrom, Paul. 1988. "Employment Contracts, Influence Activities and Organization Design." *Journal of Political Economy* 96(1): 42–60.

Milgrom, Paul, and John Roberts. 1991. "Bargaining and Influence Costs and the Organization of Economic Activity." In J. Alt and K. Shepsle, eds. *Positive Perspectives on Political Economy.* Cambridge: Cambridge University Press.

Milgrom, Paul, and John Roberts. 1990. "The Economics of Modern Manufacturing: Technology, Strategy, and Organization." *American Economic Review* 80(3): 511–528.

Milgrom, Paul, and John Roberts. 1988. "An Economic Approach to Influence Activities in Organizations." *American Journal of Sociology* 94: 154–179.

Milgrom, Paul, and John Roberts. 1987. "Information Asymmetries, Strategic Behavior, and Industrial Organization." *American Economic Review* 77(2): 184–193.

Mills, David E., and Laurence Schumann. 1985. "Industry Structure with Fluctuating Demand." *American Economic Review* 75(4): 758–767.

Mises, Ludwig. 1951. *Profit and Loss, South Holland*, IL: Consumers—Producers Economic Service.

Moore, John H. 1992. "Measuring Soviet Economic Growth: Old Problems and New Complications." *Journal of Institutional and Theoretical Economics* 148(1): 72–92.

Mueller, Dennis C. 1991. "Entry, Exit, and the Competitive Process." In P. Geroski and J. Schwalbach, eds. *Entry and Market Contestability: An International Comparison*. Oxford: Basil Blackwell, pp. 1–22.

Mueller, Dennic C. 1976. "Information, Mobility, and Profit." *Kyklos* 29(3): 419–448.

Nelson, Richard R. 1992. "U.S. Technological Leadership: Where Did It Come From and Where Did It Go?" In F. M. Scherer and M. Perlman, eds. *Entrepreneurship, Technological Innovation, and Economic Growth: Studies in the Schumpeterian Tradition*. Ann Arbor: University of Michigan Press, pp. 25–50.

Nelson, Richard R. 1984. "Incentives for Entrepreneurship and Supporting Institutions." *Weltwirtschaftliches Archiv* 120(4): 646–661.

Nelson, Richard R., and Sidney G. Winter. 1982. *An Evolutionary Theory of Economic Change*. Cambridge, MA: Harvard University Press.

Nelson, Richard R., and Sidney G. Winter. 1978. "Forces Generating and Limiting Concentration under Schumpeterian Competition." *Bell Journal of Economics* 9 (Autumn): 524–548.

Nelson, Richard R., and Sidney G. Winter. 1974. "Neoclassical vs. Evolutionary Theories of Economic Growth: Critique and Prospectus." *Economic Journal* 84 (December): 886–905.

Neumann, Manfred. 1993. Review of *Entry and Market Contestability: An International Comparison*. P. A. Geroski and J. Schwalbach, eds. *International Journal of Industrial Organization* 11(4): 593–594.

Noren, J. H. 1966. "Soviet Industry Trends in Output, Inputs, and Productivity." In U.S. Congress, Joint Economic Committee, *New Directions in the Soviet Union*, Part II–A. Washington, DC: Government Printing Office, 271–326.

Orr, Dale. 1974. "The Determinants of Entry: A Study of the Canadian Manufacturing Industries." *Review of Economics and Statistics* 56(1): 58–66.

Pakes, Ariel, and R. Ericson. 1987. "Empirical Implications of Alternative Models on Firm Dynamics." Manuscript, Department of Economics, University of Wisconsin-Madison.

Pakes, Ariel, and Zvi Griliches. 1984. "Patents and R & D at the Firm Level: A First Look." In Zvi Griliches (ed.) *R & D, Patents, and Productivity*. Chicago: University of Chicago Press, pp. 55–72.

Pakes, Ariel, and Zvi Griliches. 1980. "Patents and R & D at the Firm Level: A First Report." *Economic Letters* 5: 377–381.

Palfreman, Jon, and Doron Swade. 1991. *The Dream Machine: Exploring the Computer Age*. London: BBC Books.

Pavitt, Keith, M. Robson, and J. Townsend. 1987. "The Size Distribution of Innovating Firms in the U.K.: 1945–1983." *The Journal of Industrial Economics* 55(1): 291–316.

Penrose, Edith T. 1959. *The Theory of the Growth of the Firm*. Oxford: Basil Blackwell.

Perrow, Charles. 1967. "A Framework for the Comparative Analysis of Organizations." *American Sociological Review* 32(1): 194–208.

Perrow, Charles. 1961. "The Analysis of Goals in Complex Organizations." *American Sociological Review* 26(4): 854–866.

Peters, Thomas J., and Robert H. Waterman Jr. 1982. *In Search of Excellence: Lessons from America's Best-Run Companies*. New York: Harper & Row.

Phillips, Almarin. 1994. *Biz Jets: Technology and Market Structure in the Corporate Jet Aircraft Industry*. Boston: Kluwer Academic Publishers.

Phillips, Almarin. 1971. *Technology and Market Structure*. Lexington, MA: D.C. Heath.

Phillips, Bruce D., and Bruce A. Kirchhoff. 1989. "Formation, Growth and Survival: Small Firm Dynamics in the U.S. Economy." *Small Business Economics* 1(1): 65–74.

Piore, Michael J., and Charles F. Sabel. 1984. *The Second Industrial Divide: Possibilities for Prosperity*. New York: Basic Books.

Pratten, C. F. 1971. *Economies of Scale in Manufacturing Industry*. Cambridge: Cambridge University Press.

Reynolds, Stanley S. 1988. "Plant Closings and Exit Behaviour in Declining Industries." *Economica* 55: 493–503.

Riesman, David. 1950. *The Lonely Crowd: A Study of the Changing American Character*, Studies in National Policy No. 3. New Haven: Yale University Press.

Rose, Frank. 1989. *West of Eden: The End of Innocence at Apple Computer*. New York: Viking Press.

Rosenberg, Nathan. 1992. "Economic Experiments." *Industrial and Corporate Change* 1(1): 181–204.

Ross, David R., and Ralph M. Bradburd. 1988. "A General Measure of Multidimensional Inequality." *Oxford Bulletin of Economics and Statistics* 50(4): 429–433.

Sah, R., and J. E. Stiglitz. 1986. "The Architecture of Economic Systems: Hierarchies and Polyarchies. *American Economic Review* 76(4): 716–727.

Santarelli, Enrico, and Alessandro Sterlacchini. 1994. "New Firm Formation in Italian Industry: 1985–89." *Small Business Economics* 6(2): 95–106.

Santarelli, Enrico, and Alessandro Sterlacchini. 1990. "Innovation, Formal vs. Informal R & D, and Firm Size: Some Evidence from Italian Manufacturing Firms." *Small Business Economics* 2(2): 223–228.

Sato, Yoshio. 1989. "Small Business in Japan: A Historical Perspective." *Small Business Economics* 1(2): 121–128.

Saxenian, Anna Lee. 1990. "Regional Networks and the Resurgence of Silicon Valley." *California Management Review* 33(1): 89–112.

Schary, Martha A. 1991. "The Probability of Exit." *Rand Journal of Economics* 22(3): 339–353.

Scheirer, William K. 1991. "Firm Size and Innovation: A Comment." *Small Business Economics* 3(2): 155–156.

Scherer, F. M. 1992. "Schumpeter and Plausible Capitalism." *Journal of Economic Literature* 30(3): 1416–1433.

Scherer, F. M. 1991. "Changing Perspectives on the Firm Size Problem." In Z. J. Acs and D. B. Audretsch, eds. *Innovation and Technological Change. An International Comparison,* Ann Arbor: University of Michigan Press, pp. 24–38.

Scherer, F. M. 1988. Testimony before the Subcommittee on Monopolies and Commercial Law, Committee on the Judiciary, U.S. House of Representatives, February 24.

Scherer, F. M. 1984. *Innovation and Growth: Schumpeterian Perspectives.* Cambridge, MA: MIT Press.

Scherer, F. M. 1983. "The Propensity to Patent." *International Journal of Industrial Organization* 1 (March): 107–128.

Scherer, F. M. 1976. "Industrial Structure, Scale Economies, and Worker Alienation." In Robert T. Masson and P. David Qualls eds. *Essays on Industrial Organization in Honor of Joe S. Bain,* Cambridge, MA: Ballinger, pp. 105–122.

Scherer, F. M. 1973. "The Determinants of Industry Plant Sizes in Six Nations." *Review of Economics and Statistics* 55(2): 135–175.

Scherer, F. M. 1965. "Firm Size, Market Structure, Opportunity, and the Output of Patented Inventions." *American Economic Review* 55 (December): 1097–1125.

Scherer, F. M., Alan Beckenstein, Erich Kaufer, and R. D. Murphy. 1975. *The Economics of Multi-Plant Operation: An International Comparisons Study.* Cambridge, MA: Harvard University Press.

Scherer, F. M., and David Ross. 1990. *Industrial Market Structure and Economic Performance,* 3d ed. Boston: Houghton Mifflin.

Schultz, Theodore W. 1980. "Investment in Entrepreneurial Ability." *Scandinavian Journal of Economics* 82(4): 437–448.

Schultz, Theodore W. 1975. "The Value of the Ability to Deal with Disequilibria." *Journal of Economic Literature* 13 (September): 827–846.

Schumpeter, Joseph A. 1911. *Theorie der wirtschaftlichen Entwicklung, Eine Untersuchung über Unternehmergewinn, Kapital, Kredit, Zins und den Konjunkturzyklus.* Berlin: Duncker und Humblot.

Schumpeter, Joseph A. 1942. *Capitalism, Socialism and Democracy.* New York: Harper and Row.

Schwalbach, Joachim. 1989. "Small Business in German Manufacturing." *Small Business Economics* 1(2): 129–136.

Schwalbach, Joachim. 1987. "Entry by Diversified Firms into German Industries." *International Journal of Industrial Organization* 5 (March): 43–50.

Scott, Richard W. 1987. *Organizations: Rational, Natural, and Open Systems,* 2d ed. Englewood Cliffs, NJ: Prentice Hall.

Servan-Schreiber, J. -J. 1968. *The American Challenge.* London: Hamish Hamilton.

Siegfried, John J., and Laurie B. Evans. 1992. "Entry and Exit in U.S. Manufacturing Industries from 1977 to 1982." In D. B. Audretsch and J. J. Siegfried, eds., *Empirical Studies in*

Industrial Organization: Essays in Honor of Leonard W. Weiss. Ann Arbor: University of Michigan Press, pp. 253–275.

Simon, Herbert A. 1984. "On the Behavioral and Rational Foundations of Economic Dynamics." *Journal of Economic Behavior and Organization* 5(1): 35–36.

Simon, Herbert A. 1957. *Models of Man*. New York: John Wiley.

Simon, Herbert A., and Charles P. Bonini. 1958. "The Size Distribution of Business Firms." *American Economic Review* 48(4): 607–617.

Soete, Luc L. G. 1979. "Firm Size and Inventive Activity: The Evidence Reconsidered." *European Economic Review* 12(4): 319–340.

Stigler, George J. 1961. "The Economics of Information." *Journal of Political Economy* 59(2): 185–193.

Storey, David J., and Steven Johnson. 1987. *Job Generation and Labour Market Changes*. London: Macmillan.

Sylos-Labini, Paolo. 1962. *Oligopoly and Technical Progess*. 2d ed. Cambridge, MA: Harvard University Press.

Thompson, James D. 1967. *Organization in Action*. New York: McGraw-Hill.

Tirole, Jean. 1986. "Hierarchies and Bureaucracies." *Journal of Law, Economics and Organization* 2(3): 181–214.

U.S. Congress. House. 1986. Committee on Banking, Finance and Urban Affairs. Subcommittee on Economic Stabilization, Hearings, *Structuring American Industry for Global Competition*, Washington, DC: Government Printing Office, March.

U.S. Small Business Administration, Office of Advocacy. 1987. *Linked 1976–1984 USEEM User's Guide*, Washington, DC: Government Printing Office, July.

U.S. Small Business Administration. 1986. *The Small Business Data Base: A User's Guide*. Washington, DC: Government Printing Office, July.

Utterback, James M., and Fernando F. Suarez. 1992. "Innovation, Competition, and Industry Structure." *Research Policy* forthcoming.

Vivarelli, Marco. 1991. "The Birth of New Enterprises." *Small Business Economics* 3(3): 215–223.

Wagner, Joachim. 1994. "Small-Firm Entry in Manufacturing Industries." *Small Business Economics* 5(3): 211–214.

Wagner, Joachim. 1992. "Firm Size, Firm Growth, and Persistence of Chance: Testing Gibrat's Law with Establishment Data from Lower Saxony. 1978–1989." *Small Business Economics* 4(2): 125–131.

Weiss, Leonard W. 1991. In David B. Audretsch and Hideki Yamawaki, eds., *Structure, Conduct, and Performance*. New York: New York University Press.

Weiss, Leonard W. ed. 1989 *Concentration and Price*. Cambridge, MA: MIT Press.

Weiss, Leonard W. 1979. "The Structure-Performance Paradigm and Antitrust." *University of Pennsylvania Law Review* 127 (April): 1104–1140.

Weiss, Leonard W. 1976. "Optimal Plant Scale and the Extent of Suboptimal Capacity." In R. T. Masson and P. D. Qualls, eds. *Essays on Industrial Organization in Honor of Joe S. Bain,* Cambridge, MA: Ballinger, pp. 126–134.

Weiss, Leonard W. 1964. "The Survival Technique and the Extent of Suboptimal Capacity." *Journal of Political Economy* 72(3): 246–261.

Weiss, Leonard W. 1963. "Factors in Changing Concentration." *Review of Economics and Statistics* 45(1): 70–77.

White, Lawrence J. 1982. "The Determinants of the Relative Importance of Small Business." *Review of Economics and Statistics* 64(1): 42–49.

Whyte, William H. 1960. *The Organization Man.* Hammondsworth, Middlesex: Penguin.

Williamson, Oliver E. 1985. *The Economic Institutions of Capitalism.* New York: The Free Press.

Williamson, Oliver E. 1975. *Markets and Hierarchies: Antitrust Analysis and Implications.* New York: The Free Press.

Williamson, Oliver E. 1970. *Corporate Control and Business Behavior.* Englewood Cliffs, NJ: Prentice Hall.

Williamson, Oliver E. 1968. "Economies as an Antritrust Defense: The Welfare Tradeoffs." *American Economic Review* 58(1): 18–36.

Winter, Sidney G. 1991. "On Coase, Competence, and the Corporation." In O. E. Williamson and S. G. Winter, eds. *The Nature of the Firm: Origins, Evolution, and Development.* Oxford: Oxford University Press, pp. 179–195.

Winter, Sidney G. 1984. "Schumpeterian Competition in Alternative Technological Regimes." *Journal of Economic Behavior and Organization* 5 (Sept.–Dec.): 287–320.

Yamawaki, Hideki. 1991. "The Effects of Business Conditions on Net Entry: Evidence from Japan." In P. Geroski and J. Schwalbach, eds. *Entry and Market Contestability: An International Comparison.* Oxford: Basil Blackwell, pp. 168–186.

Index